The Atlantic
Slave Trade

PROBLEMS IN WORLD HISTORY SERIES

The Atlantic Slave Trade

Second Edition

*Edited and with an
introduction by*

David Northrup
Boston College

Houghton Mifflin Company   Boston   New York

Editor-in-Chief: Jean L. Woy
Sponsoring Editor: Nancy Blaine
Associate Editor: Julie Dunn
Associate Project Editor: Elisabeth Kehrer
Editorial Assistant: Christine Skeete
Associate Production/Design Coordinator: Christine Gervais
Senior Manufacturing Coordinator: Priscilla Bailey
Senior Marketing Manager: Sandra McGuire

Cover Image: Slaves Below Deck of *Albanez*. Watercolor by Francis
Meynell. National Maritime Museum, London.

Printed in the U.S.A.

Library of Congress Control Number: 2001131536

ISBN: 0-618-11624-9

56789-QW/F-07 06 05 04 03

For Andrew, Sarah, and James

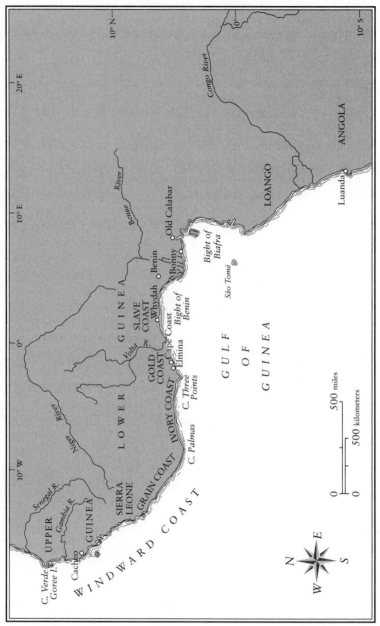

Western Africa, c. 1640–1750 (showing places mentioned in the text).

Contents

Preface

In the few years since the first edition of this anthology appeared, the slave trade from Africa to the Americas has continued to be a subject of lively new research and reinterpretation. Recent studies have explored new issues, proposed new answers to old questions, and provided the basis for a much more precise understanding of this important and sensitive subject. The second edition of *The Atlantic Slave Trade* brings together a representative sample of this new scholarly writing by historians from both sides of the Atlantic, including a dozen readings that are new to this work. It places the modern works in a larger historical context by including some records from contemporary eyewitnesses, both black and white, along with selections from influential older histories of the Atlantic slave trade.

Part I probes the reasons why Africans became the dominant labor force for European settlers in some parts of the Americas. Part II explores the African systems that produced and managed the flow of slaves to the coast, and Part III looks at the European voyages that carried these captives to the Americas. Parts IV and V present a sample of the interpretations that have been offered of the consequences of the slave trade in Africa, in Europe, and in the Americas. Finally, Part VI examines the forces that brought the trade to an end.

As a volume in Houghton Mifflin's Problems in World History series, *The Atlantic Slave Trade* treats a subject whose scope extends beyond the limits of any single continent or nation. During the four centuries of the Atlantic slave trade, Europeans (and European-Americans) transported Africans to the Caribbean, South America, and North America, establishing indelible links among these once separated lands. For this reason this volume can be a useful addition to courses treating either global interactions or the separate histories of the lands the slave trade affected.

I am grateful for the constructive comments of the following historians, who reviewed the table of contents at various stages: Lisa Lindsay, University of North Carolina; DeeAnna Manning, University of Nebraska-Lincoln; G. Ugo Nwokeji, University of Connecticut; David Owusu-Ansah, James Madison University; and Timothy J. Shannon, Gettysburg College.

D. N.

Introduction

Slavery and the slave trade did not begin with the forced migration of enslaved Africans across the Atlantic in the sixteenth century. Harvard sociologist Orlando Patterson opens his great comparative study, *Slavery and Social Death*, with the observation that slavery "has existed from before the dawn of human society . . . in the most primitive societies and in the most civilized. There is no region on earth that has not at some time harbored the institution. Probably there is no group of people whose ancestors were not at one time slaves or slaveholders." Prior to the fifteenth century, most enslaved persons were not Africans. Even the plantation system, so central to the slave experience in the Americas, first appeared in the Mediterranean world.

Yet the Atlantic commerce in African slaves has attracted more attention than any other slave trade because of the magnitude of its historical legacies. First, it brought many millions of Africans to the Americas (four times the number of European immigrants who settled there down to about 1820), leaving a permanent cultural and genetic imprint on many parts of the New World. Second, the creation of slave labor systems in the New World was associated with the first phase of European expansion and the rise of capitalism. Third, the end of the slave trade was the subject of a massive abolitionist campaign that scholars widely have seen as one of the great turning points in Western moral consciousness. Finally, the Atlantic slave trade has been seen not only as affecting Africa during the four centuries of its existence but also as leading to the later European takeover of the continent and causing its present-day underdevelopment.

African slaves played important roles in the conquest and economic development of the Americas from the early days of Spanish colonization. They were also the base upon which Portuguese Brazil became the world's major sugar producer in the early seventeenth century. However, the Atlantic slave trade's greatest importance in the development of the

New World and a vital South Atlantic economy dates from the mid-seventeenth century, when Dutch capitalists transferred the sugar plantation economy from northern Brazil to the West Indies. Wresting Caribbean islands from Spanish control, the English established sugar plantations in Barbados and Jamaica, the French in Saint Domingue (modern Haiti), and other nations elsewhere, significantly increasing the demand for slave labor.

The Atlantic slave trade expanded rapidly because it was put on a firm business footing. Most of the growing number of slaving ships crossing the Atlantic belonged to European trading companies that had established permanent outposts and other contacts along the African coast. Large sums of capital from private investors financed the great trading circuit that ran from Europe to Africa, from Africa to the Americas, and back to Europe. European factories turned out special guns and other goods that were used to buy slaves in Africa, supplemented by cotton textiles brought from India and rum and tobacco from the Americas. European governments protected these profitable commercial empires from outside competition.

The search for slaves opened more and more parts of Africa to the trade. Angola and the adjoining coast north of the Congo River composed the most important trading area overall, whereas the infamous Slave Coast and the Bight of Biafra on the Gulf of Guinea dominated slave trade north of the equator during the century after 1740. From the late eighteenth century, even far distant parts of southeastern Africa were tapped for the Atlantic slave trade. Slaving became a business in Africa, too. In some places networks of slave markets fed victims to the coast, where they were sold by professional African traders and by powerful rulers, who successfully drove up the prices and fees paid by European slave dealers. Yet at its base the trade rested on violence that spread farther and farther inland from the coast. Ultimately, most of those sold into slavery were the victims of war, kidnapping, famine, debt, and social oppression.

By 1700 the West Indies had surpassed Brazil in sugar production, but Portugal's giant South American colony retained its importance as the major destination of the transatlantic slave trade for two more centuries. As Brazil's sugar industry felt the impact of competition, slaves were diverted to almost every sort of job imaginable — they worked as miners, cowboys, stevedores, and factory laborers. In the nineteenth century, investment in new sugar plantations made Cuba a major importer of slaves. The territories that became part of the United States imported a modest share of the slave trade (fewer than the small Caribbean island of Barbados), but on the eve of emancipation, the United States had the largest slave population the Western world ever had seen.

In the eighteenth century, slavery came under mounting attack by philosophical and religious thinkers as well as by slave rebels. Antislavery societies sprang up in many Western countries. Ironically, it was in Great Britain, whose traders dominated the carrying of slaves across the Atlantic, that the largest and most influential abolitionist movement arose. Led by religious idealists—Quakers, Methodists, and evangelical Anglicans—the British abolitionist movement also gained the support of a new industrial middle class, whose members identified slavery with the outmoded political economy of the old colonial system. For both ethical and economic reasons, these people supported the abolition of the slave trade as the first step toward ending slavery.

In 1808 a new law prohibited the participation of British subjects in the Atlantic slave trade. The expiration that same year of a twenty-year ban written into the Constitution permitted the United States Congress to enact similar legislation with regard to American citizens. Other Western nations followed suit: the Netherlands in 1814, France in 1831, Spain (under great pressure from Great Britain) in 1835, Portugal in 1846, and Brazil in 1850. Despite these laws and the enforcement measures spearheaded by the British, the Atlantic slave trade remained vigorous as long as a strong demand for slaves existed. Only after slavery finally was outlawed in the United States, the French and Dutch colonies, and the former Spanish colonies, did the last known slave ships make their crossings in 1867. Brazil and Cuba ended slavery in 1886 and 1888.

For a long time the history of the slave trade was dominated by the writings of the British abolitionists who gathered data on sailings, interviewed sailors and captains in the British slaving ports, and encouraged participants and victims to publish accounts of their experiences. Because their evidence faced close scrutiny from the vested interests in Parliament who defended the slave trade, these abolitionist accounts generally were highly accurate. However, because their intention was not the objective analysis of the operations of the slave trade but a propaganda campaign to move the hearts and minds of members of Parliament and their constituents to end the trade, they concentrated on incidents of such extreme inhumanity that even the most hardhearted would be moved to act.

Understanding of the Atlantic slave trade continues to be shaped by the abolitionist tradition, but two influential works of modern scholarship have directed attention to issues besides the trade's immorality and cruelties. *Capitalism and Slavery,* a brief and readable survey published in 1944 by the young West Indian historian Eric Williams, focused attention on the trade's economic importance. Williams, who later became prime minister of Trinidad and Tobago, argued that the slave trade was of central importance to the rise of commercial capitalism in the seventeenth and eighteenth centuries and that the end of the slave trade was linked intimately with the emergence of the new industrial capitalists, who had good economic reasons for seeking its demise. He also argued that the end of slavery had as much to do with changes in economics as with changes in ideas of morality.

The Atlantic Slave Trade: A Census, published in 1969 by historian Philip D. Curtin, profoundly altered slave trade historiography by examining a different topic. The foremost American-born specialist in the emerging field of African history and later the president of the American Historical Association, Curtin sought the answer to a simple factual question: How many slaves were transported from Africa to the Americas? His estimate, based on published sources then available, was lower than the figure commonly accepted and set off new research and controversy. The careful sifting of archival records by other scholars has improved many of Curtin's original estimates, but his work was crucial in defining areas in need of further study. Scholars at Harvard University's Du Bois Institute have compiled a massive database with information on nearly 28,000 slaving voyages. Such statistical research also permits more precise assessments of the effects of the slave trade in different parts of Africa, of the profits received by different carriers, of the causes of the mortality during the Middle Passage, and of the reasons why slave populations multiplied or failed to multiply in different parts of the Americas.

Interest in the Atlantic slave trade in recent decades has been stimulated not simply by new historical works. In the United States, the successes of the civil rights and black power movements have sparked interest in African American history, including the slave trade and its legacy. The postwar decolonization of Africa has kindled new interest in African history in African, European, and American universities, including a reexamination of the role of the slave trade in African history. Indeed, much recent writing on the Atlantic slave trade is the work of scholars who specialize in African history, and it reflects the scholarly developments in that field. In addition, the end of colonial empires in Asia, Africa, and the West Indies has generated a debate over the persistence of Western economic imperialism and the role of the Atlantic slave trade in the creation of underdevelopment and neocolonialism. Finally, historians' growing focus on the Atlantic as a proper area of study has led to lively debates about the contributions of enslaved Africans to the cultures of the New World and the importance of slavery and the slave trade in the development of Europe and the Americas.

In light of the complexities of the long history of the Atlantic slave trade and of the questions asked by modern constituencies, it is not surprising that many historical controversies remain unresolved. Still, the readings in this volume document recent advances in knowledge about the Atlantic slave trade and show how historical debates can refine our understanding of important issues.

PART

Why Were Africans Enslaved?

Slavery was not born of racism: rather, racism was the consequence of slavery. . . . The origin of Negro slavery was economic, not racial; it had to do not with the color of the laborer, but the cheapness of the labor.

ERIC WILLIAMS

Rather than slavery causing "prejudice," or vice versa, they seem to have generated each other . . . , dynamically joining hands to hustle the Negro down the road to complete degradation.

WINTHROP D. JORDAN

It is simplistic to assume that [negative color] symbolism accounts for growing Muslim and Christian conviction that black Africans were in some way "made" to be slaves. . . . For the Africanization of large parts of the New World was the result not of concerted planning, racial destiny, or immanent historical design but of innumerable local and pragmatic choices.

DAVID BRION DAVIS

1

> *In a profound . . . sense chattel slavery for Africans and Indians in the Americas was . . . a function of the non-slave status that Europeans considered appropriate for themselves.*
>
> DAVID ELTIS

Eric Williams

Economics, Not Racism, as the Root of Slavery

The high level of prejudice against blacks during and after slavery might suggest that the enslavement of Africans began as the result of racism. However, more than a half-century ago, the influential West Indian historian Eric Williams forcefully argued that this was not the case. Slavery caused racism, but economic motives, not racial impulses, caused slavery. The rise of plantation slavery was tied to the development of capitalism; the capitalists' decision to import large numbers of Africans and to hold them in hereditary bondage was based on the fact that enslaved Africans were cheaper than any other available form of labor. In the West Indies and other parts of the Americas, a second cold-blooded financial calculation—that it was cheaper to import a young adult salve than to raise one born in slavery on a plantation—necessitated continuous fresh shipments of enslaved Africans.

Slavery in the Caribbean has been too narrowly identified with the Negro. A racial twist has thereby been given to what is basically an economic phenomenon. Slavery was not born of racism: rather, racism was the consequence of slavery. Unfree labor in the New World was brown, white, black, and yellow; Catholic, Protestant and pagan.

The first instance of slave trading and slave labor developed in the New World involved, racially, not the Negro but the Indian. The Indians rapidly succumbed to the excessive labor demanded of them, the insufficient diet, the white man's diseases, and their inability to adjust themselves to the new way of life. Accustomed to a life of liberty, their constitution and temperament were ill-adapted to the rigors of plantation slavery. As Fernando Ortíz writes: "To subject the Indian to the mines, to their monotonous, insane and severe labor, without tribal sense, without religious ritual, . . . was like taking away from him the meaning of his life. . . . It was to enslave not only his muscles but also his collective spirit." . . .

England and France, in their colonies, followed the Spanish practice of enslavement of the Indians. There was one conspicuous difference — the attempts of the Spanish Crown, however ineffective, to restrict Indian slavery to those who refused to accept Christianity and to the warlike Caribs on the specious plea that they were cannibals. From the standpoint of the British government Indian slavery, unlike later Negro slavery which involved vital imperial interests, was a purely colonial matter. . . . But Indian slavery never was extensive in the British dominions. . . .

The immediate successor of the Indian . . . was not the Negro but the poor white. These white servants included a variety of types. Some were indentured servants, so called because, before departure from the homeland, they had signed a contract, indented by law, binding them to service for a stipulated time in return for their passage. Still others, known as "redemptioners," arranged with the captain of the ship to pay for their passage on arrival or within a specified time thereafter; if they did not, they were sold by the captain to the highest bidder. Others were convicts, sent out by the deliberate policy of the home government, to serve for a specified period. . . .

A regular traffic developed in these indentured servants. Between 1654 and 1685 ten thousand sailed from Bristol alone, chiefly for the West Indies and Virginia. In 1683 white servants represented one-sixth of Virginia's population. Two-thirds of the immigrants to Pennsylvania during the eighteenth century were white servants; in four years 25,000 came to Philadelphia alone. It has been estimated that more than a quarter of a million persons were of this class during the colonial period, and that they probably constituted one-half of all English immigrants, the majority going to the middle colonies.

As commercial speculation entered the picture, abuses crept in. Kidnapping was encouraged to a great degree and became a regular business in such town as London and Bristol. Adults would be plied with liquor, children enticed with sweetmeats. The kidnappers were called "spirits," defined as "one that taketh upp men and women and children and sells them on a shipp to be conveyed beyond the sea." The captain of a ship trading to Jamaica would visit the Clerkenwell House of Correction, ply with drink the girls who had been imprisoned there as disorderly, and "invite" them to go to the West Indies. The temptations held out to the unwary and the credulous were so attractive that, as the mayor of Bristol complained, husbands were induced to forsake their wives, wives their husbands, and apprentices their masters, while wanted criminals found on the transport ships a refuge from the arms of the law. . . .

Convicts provided another steady source of white labor. The harsh feudal laws of England recognized three hundred capital crimes. Typical hanging offences included: picking a pocket for more than a shilling; shoplifting to the value of five shillings; stealing a horse or a sheep; poaching rabbits on a gentleman's estate. Offences for which the punishment prescribed by law was transportation comprised the stealing of cloth, burning stacks of corn, the maiming and killing of cattle, hindering customs officers in the execution of their duty, and corrupt legal practices. Proposals made in 1664 would have banished to the colonies all vagrants, rogues and idlers, petty thieves, gipsies, and loose persons frequenting unlicensed brothels. A piteous petition in 1667 prayed for transportation instead of the death sentence for a wife convicted of stealing goods valued at three shillings and four pence. In 1745 transportation was the penalty for the theft of a silver spoon and a gold watch. One year after the emancipation of the Negro slaves, transportation was the penalty for trade union activity. It is difficult to resist the conclusion that there was some connection between the law and the labor needs of the plantations, and the marvel is that so few people ended up in the colonies overseas. . . .

The political and civil disturbances in England between 1640 and 1740 augmented the supply of white servants. Political and religious nonconformists paid for their unorthodoxy by transportation, mostly to the sugar islands. Such was the fate of many of Cromwell's Irish prisoners, who were sent to the West Indies. So thoroughly was this policy pursued that an active verb was added to the English language — to "barbadoes" a person. Montserrat became largely an Irish colony, and the Irish brogue is still frequently heard today in many parts of the British West Indies. The Irish, however, were poor servants. They hated the English, were always ready to aid England's enemies, and in a revolt in the Leeward Islands in 1689 we can already see signs of that burning indignation which, according to Lecky, gave Washington some of his best soldiers. The vanquished in Cromwell's Scottish campaigns were treated like the Irish before them, and Scotsmen came to be regarded as "the general travaillers and soldiers in most foreign parts." Religious intolerance sent more workers to the plantations. In 1661 Quakers refusing to take the oath for the third time were to be transported; in 1664 transportation, to any plantation except Virginia or New England, or a fine of one hundred pounds was decreed for the third offence for persons over sixteen assembling in groups of five or more under pretence of religion. Many of Monmouth's adherents were sent to Barbados, with orders to be detained as servants for ten years. The prisoners were granted in batches to favorite courtiers, who made handsome profits from the traffic in which, it is alleged, even the Queen shared. A similar policy was resorted to after the Jacobite risings of the eighteenth century. . . .

The institution of white servitude, however, had grave disadvantages. Postlethwayt, a rigid mercantilist, argued that white laborers in colonies would tend to create rivalry with the mother country in manufacturing. Better black slaves on plantations than white servants in industry, which would encourage aspirations to independence. The supply moreover was becoming increasingly difficult, and the need of the plantations outstripped the English convictions. In addition, merchants were involved in many vexatious and costly proceedings arising from people signifying their willingness to emigrate, accepting food and clothes in advance, and then suing for unlawful detention. Indentured servants were not forthcoming in sufficient quantities to replace those who had served their term. On the plantations, escape was easy for the white servant; less easy for the Negro who, if freed, tended, in self-defence, to stay in his locality where he was well known and less likely to be apprehended as a vagrant or runaway slave. The servant expected land at the end of his contract; the Negro, in a strange environment, conspicuous by his color and features, and ignorant of the white man's language and ways, could be kept permanently divorced from the land. Racial differences made it easier to justify and rationalize Negro slavery, to exact the mechanical obedience of a plough-ox or a cart-horse, to demand that resignation and that complete moral and intellectual subjection which alone make slave labor possible. Finally, and this was the decisive factor, the Negro slave was cheaper. The money which procured a white man's services for ten years could buy a Negro for life. As the governor of Barbados stated, the Barbadian planters found by experience that "three blacks work better and cheaper than one white man."

But the experience with white servitude had been invaluable. Kidnaping in Africa encountered no such difficulties as were encountered in England. Captains and ships had the experience of the one trade to guide them in the other. Bristol, the center of the servant trade, became one of the centers of the slave trade. Capital accumulated from the one financed the other. White servitude was the historic base upon which Negro slavery was constructed. The felon-drivers in the plantations became without effort slave-drivers. "In significant numbers," writes Professor Phillips, "the Africans were latecomers fitted into a system already developed."

Here, then, is the origin of Negro slavery. The reason was economic, not racial; it had to do not with the color of the laborer, but the cheapness of the labor. As compared with Indian and white labor, Negro slavery was eminently superior. "In each case," writes Bassett, discussing North Carolina, "it was a survival of the fittest. Both Indian slavery and white servitude were to go down before the black man's superior endurance, docility, and labor capacity." The features of the man, his hair, color and dentifrice, his "subhuman" characteristics so widely pleaded, were only the later rationalizations to justify a simple economic fact: that the colonies needed labor and resorted to Negro labor because it was cheapest and best. This was not a theory, it was a practical conclusion deduced from the personal experience of the planter. He would have gone to the moon, if necessary, for labor. Africa was nearer than the moon, nearer too than the more populous countries of India and China. But their turn was to come. . . .

Negro slavery, thus, had nothing to do with climate. Its origin can be expressed in three words: in the Caribbean, Sugar; on the mainland, Tobacco and Cotton. A change in the economic structure produced a corresponding change in the labor supply. The fundamental fact was "the creation of an inferior social and economic organization of exploiters and exploited." Sugar, tobacco, and cotton required the large plantation and hordes of cheap labor, and the small farm of the ex-indentured white servant could not possibly survive. The tobacco of the small farm in Barbados was displaced by the sugar of the large plantation. The rise of the sugar industry in the Caribbean was the signal for a gigantic dispossession of the small farmer. Barbados in 1645 had 11,200 small white farmers and 5,680 Negro slaves; in 1677 there were 745 large plantation owners and 82,023 slaves. In 1645 the island had 18,300 whites fit to bear arms, in 1667 only 8,300. . . .

Negro slavery therefore was only a solution, in certain historical circumstances, of the Caribbean labor problem. Sugar meant labor—at times that labor has been slave, at other times nominally free; at times black, at other times white or brown or yellow. Slavery in no way implied, in any scientific sense, the inferiority of the Negro. Without it the great development of the Caribbean sugar plantations, between 1650 and 1850, would have been impossible.

Winthrop D. Jordan

The Simultaneous Invention of Slavery and Racism

In his study of colonial Virginia and Maryland, historian Winthrop D. Jordan of the University of Mississippi examines the reasons why the indentured servitude of Europeans and the bondage of Africans, which had existed side by side, gradually developed in opposite directions, with European bondage coming to an end as African slavery increased. While not disagreeing with Williams that slavery had an economic base, Jordan stresses slavery's intellectual and psychological roots. He shows that over time the religious, physical, and cultural differences that distinguished Africans from Europeans came to be perceived primarily in terms of appearance, and specifically of color. He traces the negative associations that "black" had for English persons long before a trade in black Africans came about, and argues that because Africans were not Christians and practiced (or were believed to practice) customs repugnant to the English, the negative associations multiplied. Jordan

From *White Over Black: American Attitudes Toward the Negro, 1550–1812*, by Winthrop D. Jordan, pp. 4–9, 20, 23–26, 28, 80–81, 91–94. Published for the Institute of Early American History and Culture, Williamsburg, Virginia. Copyright © 1968 by the University of North Carolina Press. Used by permission of the publisher.

8 *Winthrop D. Jordan*

stops short of contending that these negative preconceptions caused slavery. Rather, he argues that, at least in Virginia and Maryland, color prejudice and African slavery developed hand in hand.

Englishmen found the natives of Africa very different from themselves. Negroes looked different; their religion was un-Christian; their manner of living was anything but English; they seemed to be a particularly libidinous sort of people. All these clusters of perceptions were related to each other, though they may be spread apart for inspection, and they were related also to circumstances of contact in Africa, to previously accumulated traditions concerning that strange and distant continent, and to certain special qualities of English society on the eve of its expansion into the New World.

The most arresting characteristic of the newly discovered African was his color. Travelers rarely failed to comment upon it; indeed when describing Negroes they frequently began with complexion and then moved on to dress (or rather lack of it) and manners. At Cape Verde, "These people are all blacke, and are called Negros, without any apparel, saving before their privities." . . .

Englishmen actually described Negroes as *black*—an exaggerated term which in itself suggests that the Negro's complexion had powerful impact upon their perceptions. Even the peoples of northern Africa seemed so dark that Englishmen tended to call them "black" and let further refinements go by the board. Blackness became so generally associated with Africa that every African seemed a black man. In Shakespeare's day, the Moors, including Othello, were commonly portrayed as pitchy black and the terms *Moor* and *Negro* used almost interchangeably. With curious inconsistency, however, Englishmen recognized that Africans south of the Sahara were not at all the same people as the much more familiar Moors. Sometimes they referred to Negroes as "black Moors" to distinguish them from the peoples of North Africa. During the seventeenth century the distinction became more firmly established and indeed writers came to stress the difference in color, partly because they delighted in correcting their predecessors and partly because Negroes were being taken up as slaves and Moors, increasingly, were not. In the more detailed and accurate reports about West Africa of the seventeenth century, moreover, Negroes in different regions were described as varying considerably in complexion. In England, however, the initial impression of Negroes was not appreciably modified: the firmest fact about the Negro was that he was "black." . . .

In England perhaps more than in southern Europe, the concept of blackness was loaded with intense meaning. Long before they found that some men were black, Englishmen found in the idea of blackness a way of expressing some of their most ingrained values. No other color except white conveyed so much emotional impact. As described by the *Oxford English Dictionary*, the meaning of *black* before the sixteenth century included, "Deeply stained with dirt; soiled, dirty, foul. . . . Having dark or deadly purposes, malignant; pertaining to or involving death, deadly; baneful, disastrous, sinister. . . . Foul, iniquitous, atrocious, horrible, wicked. . . . Indicating disgrace, censure, liability to punishment, etc." Black was an emotionally partisan color, the handmaid and symbol of baseness and evil, a sign of danger and repulsion.

Embedded in the concept of blackness was its direct opposite— whiteness. . . . White and black connoted purity and filthiness, virginity and sin, virtue and baseness, beauty and ugliness, beneficence and evil, God and the devil.

Whiteness, moreover, carried a special significance for Elizabethan Englishmen: it was, particularly when complemented by red, the color of perfect human beauty, especially *female* beauty. . . .

By contrast, the Negro was ugly, by reason of his color and also his "horrid Curles" and "disfigured" lips and nose. As Shakespeare wrote apologetically of his black mistress,

> My mistress' eyes are nothing like the sun;
> Coral is far more red than her lips' red:
> If snow be white, why then her breasts are dun;
> If hairs be wires, black wires grow on her head.
> I have seen roses damask'd, red and white,
> But no such roses see I in her cheeks.

. . . While distinctive appearance set Africans over into a novel category of men, their religious condition set them apart from Englishmen in a more familiar way. Englishmen and Christians everywhere were sufficiently acquainted with the concept of heathenism that they confronted its living representatives without puzzlement. Certainly the rather sudden discovery that the world was teeming with heathen people made for heightened vividness and urgency in a long-standing problem;

but it was the fact that this problem was already well formulated long before contact with Africa which proved important in shaping English reaction to the Negro's defective religious condition. . . .

Indeed the most important aspect of English reaction to Negro heathenism was that Englishmen evidently did not regard it as separable from the Negro's other attributes. Heathenism was treated not so much as a specifically religious defect but as one manifestation of a general refusal to measure up to proper standards, as a failure to be English or even civilized. There was every reason for Englishmen to fuse the various attributes they found in Africans. During the first century of English contact with Africa, Protestant Christianity was an important element in English patriotism; especially during the struggle against Spain the Elizabethan's special Christianity was interwoven into his conception of his own nationality, and he was therefore inclined to regard the Negroes' lack of true religion as part of theirs. Being a Christian was not merely a matter of subscribing to certain doctrines; it was a quality inherent in oneself and in one's society. It was interconnected with all the other attributes of normal and proper men: as one of the earliest English accounts distinguished Negroes from Englishmen, they were "a people of beastly living, without a God, lawe, religion, or common wealth"—which was to say that Negroes were not Englishmen. Far from isolating African heathenism as a separate characteristic, English travelers sometimes linked it explicitly with barbarity and blackness. . . . In an important sense, then, heathenism was for Englishmen one inherent characteristic of savage men.

The condition of savagery—the failure to be civilized—set Negroes apart from Englishmen in an ill-defined but crucial fashion. Africans were *different* from Englishmen in so many ways: in their clothing, huts, farming, warfare, language, government, morals, and (not least important) in their table manners. Englishmen were fully aware that Negroes living at different parts of the coast were not all alike; it was not merely different reactions in the observers which led one to describe a town as "marvelous artificially builded with mudde walles . . . and kept very cleane as well in their streetes as in their houses" and another to relate how "the doe eate" each other "alive" in some places but dead in others "as we wolde befe or mutton." No matter how great the actual and observed differences among Negroes, though, none of these black men seemed to live like Englishmen. . . .

As with skin color, English reporting of African customs constituted an exercise in self-inspection by means of comparison. The necessity of continuously measuring African practices with an English yardstick of course tended to emphasize the differences between the two groups, but it also made for heightened sensitivity to instances of similarity. Thus the Englishman's ethnocentrism tended to distort his perception of African culture in two opposite directions. While it led him to emphasize differences and to condemn deviations from the English norm, it led him also to seek out similarities (where perhaps none existed) and to applaud every instance of conformity to the appropriate standard. Though African clothing and personal etiquette were regarded as absurd, equivalents to European practices were at times detected in other aspects of African culture. Particularly, Englishmen were inclined to see the structures of African societies as analogous to their own, complete with kings, counselors, gentlemen, and the baser sort. Here especially they found Africans like themselves, partly because they knew no other way to describe a society and partly because there was actually good basis for such a view in the social organization of West African communities. . . .

It would be a mistake, however, to slight the importance of the Negro's savagery, since it fascinated Englishmen from the very first. English observers in West Africa were sometimes so profoundly impressed by the Negro's deviant behavior that they resorted to a powerful metaphor with which to express their own sense of difference from him. They knew perfectly well that Negroes were men, yet they frequently described the Africans as "brutish" or "bestial" or "beastly." The hideous tortures, the cannibalism, the rapacious warfare, the revolting diet (and so forth page after page) seemed somehow to place the Negro among the beasts. The circumstances of the Englishman's confrontation with the Negro served to strengthen this feeling. Slave traders in Africa handled Negroes the same way men in England handled beasts, herding and examining and buying. . . . Africa, moreover, teemed with strange and wonderful animals, and men that killed like tigers, ate like vultures, and grunted like hogs seemed indeed to merit comparison with beasts. In making this instinctive analogy, Englishmen unwittingly demonstrated how powerfully the African's different culture—for Englishmen, his "savagery"—operated to make Negroes seem to Englishmen a radically different kind of men. . . .

From the surviving evidence, it appears that outright enslavement and these other forms of debasement appeared at about the same time in Maryland and Virginia. Indications of perpetual service, the very nub of slavery, coincided with indications that English settlers discriminated against Negro women, withheld arms from Negroes, and—though the timing is far less certain—reacted unfavorably to interracial sexual union. The coincidence suggests a mutual relationship between slavery and unfavorable assessment of Negroes. Rather than slavery causing "prejudice," or vice versa, they seem rather to have generated each other. Both were, after all, twin aspects of a general debasement of the Negro. Slavery and "prejudice" may have been equally cause and effect, continuously reacting upon each other, dynamically joining hands to hustle the Negro down the road to complete degradation. Much more than with the other English colonies, where the enslavement of Negroes was to some extent a borrowed practice, the available evidence for Maryland and Virginia points to less borrowing and to this kind of process: a mutually interactive growth of slavery and unfavorable assessment, with no cause for either which did not cause the other as well. If slavery caused prejudice, then invidious distinctions concerning working in the fields, bearing arms, and sexual union should have appeared *after* slavery's firm establishment. If prejudice caused slavery, then one would expect to find these lesser discriminations preceding the greater discrimination of outright enslavement. Taken as a whole, the evidence reveals a process of debasement of which hereditary lifetime service was an important but not the only part.

White servants did not suffer this debasement. Rather, their position improved, partly for the reason that they were not Negroes. By the early 1660s white men were loudly protesting against being made "slaves" in terms which strongly suggest that they considered slavery not as wrong but as inapplicable to themselves. . . . Free Negro servants were generally increasingly less able to defend themselves against this insidious kind of encroachment. Increasingly, white men were more clearly free because Negroes had become so clearly slave. . . .

In scanning the problem of *why* Negroes were enslaved in America, certain constant elements in a complex situation can be readily, if roughly, identified. It may be taken as given that there would have been no enslavement without economic need, that is, without persistent demand for labor in underpopulated colonies. Of crucial importance, too, was the fact that for cultural reasons Negroes were relatively helpless in the face of European aggressiveness and technology. In themselves, however, these two elements will not explain the enslavement of Indians and Negroes. The pressing exigency in America was labor, and Irish and English servants were available. Most of them would have been helpless to ward off outright enslavement if their masters had thought themselves privileged and able to enslave them. As a group, though, masters did not think themselves so empowered. Only with Indians and Negroes did Englishmen attempt so radical a deprivation of liberty—which brings the matter abruptly to the most difficult and imponderable question of all: what was it about Indians and Negroes which set them apart, which rendered them *different* from Englishmen, which made them special candidates for degradation?

To ask such questions is to inquire into the *content* of English attitudes, and unfortunately there is little evidence with which to build an answer. It may be said, however, that the heathen condition of the Negroes seemed of considerable importance to English settlers in America—more so than to English voyagers upon the coasts of Africa—and that heathenism was associated in some settlers' minds with the condition of slavery. This is not to say that the colonists enslaved Negroes because they were heathens. . . .

. . . For one thing, some of the first Negroes in Virginia had been baptized before arrival. In the early years others were baptized in various colonies and became more than nominally Christian; a Negro woman joined the church in Dorchester, Massachusetts, as a full member in 1641. With some Negroes becoming Christian and others not, there might have developed a caste differentiation along religious lines, yet there is no evidence to suggest that the colonists distinguished consistently between the Negroes they converted and those they did not. It was racial, not religious, slavery which developed in America.

Still, in the early years, the English settlers most frequently contrasted themselves with Negroes by the term *Christian*, though they also sometimes described themselves as *English*; here the explicit religious distinction would seem to have lain at the core of English reaction. Yet the concept embodied by the term *Christian* embraced so much more meaning than was contained in specific doctrinal affirmations that it is scarcely possible to assume on the basis of this linguistic contrast that the colonists set Negroes apart because they were heathen. The historical experience of the English people in the sixteenth century had made for fusion of religion and nationality; the qualities of being English and Christian had become so inseparably blended that it seemed perfectly consistent to the Virginia Assembly in 1670 to declare that "noe negroe or Indian though baptized and enjoyed their owne Freedome shall be capable of any such purchase of Christians, but yet not debarred from buying any of their own nation." . . .

From the first, then, vis-à-vis the Negro the concept embedded in the term *Christian* seems to have conveyed much of the idea and feeling of *we* as against *they*: to be Christian was to be civilized rather than barbarous, English rather than African, white rather than black. The term *Christian* itself proved to have remarkable elasticity, for by the end of the seventeenth century it was being used to define a species of slavery which had altogether lost any connection with explicit religious difference.

David Brion Davis

Sugar and Slavery from the Old to the New World

Yale historian David Davis approaches the roots of slavery from a broader geographical and temporal perspective than either Williams or Jordan, both of whom concentrate on English colonies in the seventeenth and eighteenth centuries. He shows that slaves came in many hues in the medieval Mediterranean and that by a series of historical accidents a sugar plantation system using black African slaves spread from the Mediterranean to islands off the coast of West Africa, across the Atlantic to Brazil, and eventually to the West Indies and North America. In his account, chronology is more important than prejudice.

In some ancient languages the word "slave" simply connoted labor or service. In other languages, however, the word referred at first to the foreign origin of captives, even if it later extended, as in the Third Dynasty of Ur (2345–2308 B.C.), to in-group debt slaves and children who had been sold by their parents. In ancient India the word *dasa* originally referred to the dark-skinned Dravidian people conquered by Aryan invaders. It later came to mean "slave," even though fewer Dravidians seem to have ended up in slavery than in the lowest rungs of the caste system or, worst of all, in the ritually unclean category of untouchables. By the Buddhist period slavery had lost its ethnic connotations and a *dasa* could well be light-skinned.

The origin of the European variants of "slave" presents a somewhat different transition from ethnic reference to a generalized category of "enslavable barbarian." During the late Middle Ages, the Latin *servus* and other ethnically neutral terms gradually gave way to *sclavus*, the root of *schiavo, esclavo, esclave, sclau, Sklave*, and "slave," all meaning a person of "Slavic" origin. According to Charles Verlinden, *sclavus* had as early as the tenth century become legally synonymous with "slave" in the parts of Germany through which pagan Slavic captives were transported to Muslim Spain. But this usage virtually disappeared with the decline of the Umayyad dynasty and the eclipse of the overland trade in slaves to the west. Italian merchants continued to buy large numbers of genuinely Slavic prisoners along the Dalmatian coast, but only in the thirteenth century did they begin to tap one of the most continuously productive sources of slaves in human history—the peoples from Caucasia to the eastern Balkans who were repeatedly subjugated by invaders from Central Asia. Representing a multitude of languages and cultures, these captive Armenians, Circassians, Georgians, Abkhazians, Mingrelians, Russians, Tatars, Albanians, and Bulgarians were no more a distinct people than were the "Negroes" who later ended up as American slaves. By the early thirteenth century, however, these "Slavs," who were highly prized in Egypt, Syria, Cyprus, Sicily, Catalonia, and other Mediterranean markets, had begun to transform the European words for chattel slaves, as distinct from native serfs. Italian notaries applied the label *sclavus* not only to non-Slavic peoples from the Black Sea but also to Muslim captives from such reconquered regions as Majorca and Spain. In 1239 a Corsican notary used *sclava* in recording what Verlinden interprets as the sale of "une négresse captive." The rapid extension of *sclavus* to people of non-Slavic origin suggests a growing assumption that true slavery was appropriate only for pagans and infidels who shared the supposed characteristics of "Slavs," which were almost identical with the later "sambo" stereotype of North American blacks. Since Portugal remained on the periphery of the

Slavic slave trade but became increasingly involved in religious warfare with Muslim North Africa, the word *escravo* had to compete with such terms as *mouro, guineu,* and *negro.* Later on, the French *noir* and English "black" became virtual synonyms for "slave." Much earlier, the Arabic word for slave, *'abd,* had come to mean only a black slave and, in some regions, to refer to any black whether slave or free.

In antiquity, however, bondage had nothing to do with physiognomy or skin color. It is true that various Greek writers insisted that slavery should be reserved for "barbarians," but they considered Ethiopians no more barbarous than the fair Scythians of the north. Skin color and other somatic traits they attributed to the effects of climate and environment. . . .

But the association of blackness with death, danger, evil, and grief has been common to many cultures, and it is simplistic to assume that such symbolism accounts for the growing Muslim and Christian conviction that black Africans were in some way "made" to be slaves. The first objection, as we have already seen, is that "Slavs" and other light-skinned peoples were said to have all the slavish characteristics later attributed to black Africans. The second objection is that color symbolism is usually abstract, ambiguous, and reversible. The black devils and demons of early Christian iconography were usually pure fantasies, as devoid of ethnic traits as the medieval Black Madonnas; yet in medieval Europe, which Islam had largely sealed off from Africa, specifically "Negroid" blacks were depicted among the resurrected saints on the Day of Judgment and as camel drivers or attendants in scenes of the Adoration. By the early fifteenth century one of the Magi or Kings had become an ethnically recognizable "Negro," a transformation extended in the thirteenth century to Saint Maurice, protector of the Holy Roman Empire. . . .

With such cautionary points in mind, it still seems likely that the derogatory meanings of blackness were intensified by religious cosmologies that envisioned spiritual progress as the triumph of the children of light over the pagan or infidel children of darkness. Color symbolism, like the garbled interpretations of the biblical curse of Canaan, provided additional justification for new patterns of enslavement shaped by the Islamization of the trans-Saharan caravan trade. For devout Muslims the crucial and troublesome question was who could legally be enslaved. Apart from Christian enemies who might be ransomed by their brethren, the answer increasingly focused on pagan Africans or on blacks of presumably pagan origin. . . .

By the eighth and ninth centuries, Arabic literature was already merging blackness of skin with a variety of derogatory physical and characterological traits. . . . [F]or medieval Arabs, as for later Europeans, the blackness of Africans suggested sin, damnation, and the devil. Although Arab and Iranian writers usually followed classical authorities in attributing the blacks' physical traits to climatic and other environmental forces, including the astrological effects of the planet Saturn, they increasingly invoked the biblical curse of Canaan to explain why the "sons of Ham" had been blackened and degraded to the status of natural slaves as punishment for their ancestor's sin. The precise origins of this argument, which was later taken up by European Christians and expounded as unshakable dogma in the nineteenth-century American South, are still obscure. . . .

From the accursed "sons of Ham" to the image of carefree blacks dancing an Arabic equivalent of "the long-tailed blue," one encounters in the Middle Ages the same stereotypes used to justify North American slavery to an age increasingly attuned to spurious connections between race and human progress. Or almost the same, since nineteenth-century Americans, unlike medieval Muslims, tried to deny recognition of the blacks' military and sexual capabilities. . . .

If one takes the New World as a whole, one finds that the importation of African slaves far surpassed the flow of European immigrants during the first three and one-third centuries of settlement. From Brazil and the Caribbean to Chesapeake Bay, the richest and most coveted colonies—in terms of large-scale capital investment, output, and value of exports and imports—ultimately became dependent on black slave labor. Yet the enslavement of whites persisted and at times even flourished on both Christian and Muslim shores of the Mediterranean and the Black seas, in eastern Europe and Russia, and even in western Europe, where lifelong sentences to the galleys became an acceptable and utilitarian substitute for capital punishment. And as David W. Galenson reminds us, "the use of bound white laborers preceded the use of black slaves in every British American colony, and it was only after an initial reliance on indentured servants for the bulk of their labor needs that the planters of the West Indies and the southern mainland colonies turned to slaves." Despite the gains of recent scholarship, a full explanation of the transition from white and Amerindian servitude to Afro-American slavery must await more detailed studies of every colony, of transatlantic transport, and of the changing labor markets in the Americas, Europe, and especially Africa. For the Africanization of large parts of the New World was the result not of concerted planning, racial destiny, or immanent historical design but of innumerable local and pragmatic choices made in four continents. The following discussion can do no more than trace some important continuities between such choices and point to the often bitterly ironic connections between the extension of black slavery and white concepts of progress.

The story begins, . . . with the revival of the ancient Mediterranean slave trade that accompanied the early expansion of western Europe. . . .

Slavery had always been pervasive and deeply entrenched in southern Italy, Sicily, Crete, Cyprus, Majorca, and Mediterranean Spain. These regions had all been subject to Muslim conquest and Christian reconquest; they remained frontier outposts, vulnerable to raids but also the closest beneficiaries of centuries of Christian-Muslim terrorism and trade. Sicily and the other Mediterranean islands were coveted prizes in the chesslike contests involving Normans, Germans, Aragonese, the Italian city-states, Byzantines, and the papacy. With respect to the history of "progress," these slaveholding and extraordinarily cosmopolitan societies were at the forefront of Western commercial, agricultural, and technological innovation, despite the ravages of war and political instability. . . .

The critical factor appears to have been the supply of labor available from regions that were ravaged by warfare or that lacked the political power and stability to protect their subjects. The plantation-oriented economies of the Mediterranean eagerly absorbed Moorish, Greek, and Caucasian slaves as long as they could be obtained at a tolerable price, though the price multiplied many times as a result of the demographic crisis and escalating labor costs of the fourteenth century. When Ottoman conquests later closed off the traditional sources of foreign labor, the Christian slaveholding regions turned to blacks from sub-Saharan Africa until that flow of labor was increasingly diverted to more profitable markets to the west. . . .

But apart from the temporary Iberian and Mediterranean demand for black slave labor, it was clearly sugar and the small Atlantic islands that gave a distinctive shape to New World slavery. Today it is difficult to appreciate the importance of the rugged, volcanic Atlantic islands as crucibles of New World institutions. The pattern of trade winds and ocean currents made all the islands crossroads of navigation, landmarks

Canoe ferrying slaves to a Portuguese slaver anchored in the Bonny River, 1837. (Peabody Essex Museum)

and stopovers for the ships of every maritime nation engaged legally or illegally in trade with West Africa, Asia, the West Indies, and Brazil. The Portuguese government understood the strategic value of permanent settlements along the vital sea lanes from the Azores to São Tomé, in the Gulf of Guinea close to the equator. The Cape Verdes and São Tomé were also ideal bases for trading ventures along the disease-ridden African coast. But in fifteenth-century Portugal, in contrast to England of the late sixteenth and early seventeenth centuries, there was no "excess" population of unemployed and dangerous laborers. Sidney M. Greenfield persuasively suggests that the only migrants who could be induced to settle Madeira were a few artisans and other workers who aspired to escape manual labor and achieve landholding and "noble" status. The colonists probably relied on captives from the Canary Islands to construct a system of irrigation canals from treacherous mountain ravines to the fertile but arid lands below. By the 1440s black slaves had begun to supplement or replace the Guanches. For some decades the colonists cultivated mainly cereals, but by the mid-fifteenth century there was sufficient sugar production to warrant the use of a hydraulic mill, or *engenho*, in place of hand presses. . . . By the 1490s Madeira had become a wealthy sugar colony wholly dependent on the labor of African slaves. As the first true colony committed to sugar monoculture and black slave labor, it was the transitional prototype for later mercantilist ideals of empire. Madeiran sugar, outstripping the production of the entire Mediterranean, was being shipped or reexported by the late 1490s to England, France, Italy, and even the eastern Mediterranean. Columbus, who lived for over a decade in Madeira, had the foresight to take sugar plants from the Canary Islands on his voyages to the "Indies."

. . . Even before English privateers saw Spanish sugar plantations in the Caribbean or began capturing cargoes of Brazilian sugar in the sea warfare of the late sixteenth century, northern Europeans had been directly involved in the Madeiran sugar boom. São Tomé occupied an equally strategic site, roughly one hundred miles west of Cape Gabon at the junction of wind systems that powered both northbound and southbound Atlantic traffic. After a long period of experiment and disappointment, Madeiran planters aided by the ubiquitous Genoese finally took advantage of São Tomé's fertile and well-watered soil. As early as 1495 Antwerp had begun receiving sugar from São Tomé, which during the first half of the sixteenth century imported more African slaves than Europe, the Americas, or the other Atlantic islands. The spectacular success of São Tomé and neighboring Príncipe made it clear that sugar and slaves could become the keys to imperial wealth and power.

. . . Black slavery took root in the Americas in a slow, spasmodic, and seemingly haphazard way, but even the last three-quarters of the sixteenth century gave ample and cumulative evidence that the fortunes of the New World depended on Africa. . . .

There can be no doubt that both the Spanish and Portuguese turned to African labor as a more reliable and durable substitute for captive aborigines, who seemed in the sixteenth century to be on the path to extinction. Philip D. Curtin notes that in the tropical lowlands such African diseases as malaria and yellow fever not only increased the mortality of Amerindians but also long prevented the formation of a self-sustaining population of European immigrants. "Slavery," he adds, "became the dominant form of labor organization wherever the impact of disease was most critical. . . . Non-European immigrants from Africa [became] epidemiologically preferable to Europeans." Peter H. Wood has also suggested that the English settlers in South Carolina found Africans particularly desirable for rice cultivation because of their relative immunity to malaria and yellow fever as well as their native experience in cultivating rice.

Without disputing the importance of epidemiology, one must be wary of a "medical" explanation of the New World's transition to black slavery. During the first centuries of colonization whites, blacks, and Amerindians all suffered extraordinary mortality rates, but certain peoples were always considered more expendable than others; much ultimately depended on the supply and cost of alternative forms of labor. For example, young British indentured workers flocked to Barbados during the colony's initial tobacco era of the late 1620s and 1630s. In 1640, just before Barbadian landowners began switching from tobacco to sugar, the island contained fewer than one thousand blacks and approximately nine thousand whites, mostly bound laborers; even this recently reduced estimate slightly exceeded the contemporary white population of Virginia, which had been settled twenty years earlier than Barbados and was populated mainly by the same kind of aspiring young indentured servants. Although mortality was generally much higher in the West Indies than on the North American mainland, Barbados was fairly salubrious by seventeenth-century standards. Early colonists were relatively isolated from bubonic plague, smallpox, influenza, and other European killers; malaria did not appear in the seventeenth century, and yellow fever, possibly introduced by slave ships, did not strike until 1647. There was also an abundance of food. Even in the sugar-boom decade of 1650–60, the net white migration to Barbados rose to 16,970, only 553 below the combined net white migration to Virginia and Maryland in the same decade. But in Barbados white workers were increasingly displaced by black slaves. White workers began to avoid the West Indies, and freed servants began an exodus to the North American mainland, only after the islands were becoming wholly transformed by sugar and black slaves.

The historical epidemiologists also tend to overlook the fact that long before Virginia became committed to black slavery, the colony had been a "death trap," as Edmund S. Morgan puts it, for Englishmen foolhardy enough to settle there. From 1625 to 1640 it probably took fifteen thousand English immigrants to add fewer than seven thousand to the cumulative white population. Yet a plantation economy developed and flourished with white indentured labor; planters continued to favor importing white servants when an alternative supply of black slaves was available and after white mortality had been significantly reduced. By the time Virginia turned decisively to African labor, in the 1680s, the colony had already overcome most of the "seasoning" hazards for blacks as well as for whites.

The most telling point, however, is the mortality of African slaves themselves in every colony south of the Chesapeake. While Africans were not as vulnerable as Amerindians to Old World diseases, the Amerindians were not subjected to thousands of miles of land and sea travel under the most oppressive conditions. The assumption that Africans were somehow "hardier" necessarily omits the unrecorded death tolls from place of capture or initial sale even to the African coast. Planters could disregard such losses unless the cumulative costs inflated the price of slaves to a prohibitive level. But from about 1680 to 1780, despite a fourfold rise in real prices offered for slaves on the African coast, the tropical colonies affirmed that it was cheaper to import a productive slave from Africa than to raise a child to working age. Philip Curtin suggests that since African captors and middlemen could sell trade slaves for much less than the cost of reproduction, the appropriate economic "model" is burglary, and highly sophisticated burglary at that. Moreover, in the period 1640–1700 British planters in Barbados, Jamaica, and the Leeward Islands apparently accepted a loss of 164,000 slaves in order to increase their holdings by a bare 100,000. According to Richard S. Dunn, who works from Curtin's estimates, "between 1708 and 1735 the Barbadians imported 85,000 new slaves in order to lift the black population on this island from 42,000 to 46,000." While various factors accounted for the failure of slave populations to reproduce themselves, similar conditions prevailed throughout the Caribbean and Brazil. One can hardly conclude, therefore, that colonists chose African labor in order to minimize the loss of life.

In parts of the Old World, as we have seen, black slavery was an established institution by the beginning of the sixteenth century. There was nothing inevitable, however, about the transfer of the same institution to the various colonies of the New World. In view of the Iberians' extraordinary and unprecedented attempts to halt the enslavement of Amerindians, it was not inconceivable that African captives would eventually be accorded a protected status above chattel slavery. No one could have predicted that black chattel slavery would flourish in Mexico and Peru until the mid-seventeenth century and then gradually give way to other and more subtle forms of coerced labor; or that the institution would languish in Cuba until the sugar boom of the early nineteenth century. . . .

It was Brazil rather than Hispanic America that provided the model. Of the nearly ten million Africans who survived the voyage to the New World, well over one-third landed in Brazil and between 60 and 70 percent ended up in the sugar colonies. As early as the 1520s sugar cane was being cultivated in the Pernambuco region of Brazil, but despite the aid of experienced planters from Madeira and São Tomé, the industry developed very slowly. It took time for the Portuguese to clear the coast of French Huguenot settlers, to subdue hostile Amerindians, and to experiment with Amerindian slaves sold by the Paulista *bandeirantes* until an adequate supply of Africans became available. Sugar production, as we have noted, required a concentrated force of productive and dependable workers who had little opportunity to flee and join fellow tribesmen in the interior, as Amerindians were often able to do. It was only in the 1570s, after the growth of Portuguese influence in the Kongo Kingdom and the founding of Portuguese Luanda in Angola, that northeastern Brazil began to receive massive numbers of African slaves (some of whom managed to escape to *mocambos*, or organized settlements of fugitives). In 1570 Brazil was still producing less sugar than Madeira; thirty years later production had increased almost sevenfold, and Brazil had become one of the wealthiest colonies in human history.

David Eltis

The Cultural Roots of African Slavery

Williams and Jordan mention in passing that Europeans did not enslave other Europeans. Canadian historian David Eltis, a specialist in Atlantic migration at Queens University, makes that issue the center of his analysis. He argues that Africans were not enslaved simply for economic reasons, for it would have been more convenient and probably cheaper to bring enslaved Europeans to the New World. He also suggests it was not prejudice

From David Eltis, *The Rise of African Slavery in the Americas*, 2000, pp. 64–72, 78–80, 83–84. Reprinted with the permission of Cambridge University Press.

against blacks that produced the African slave trade, but the unconscious exemption from enslavement Europeans gave themselves. Thus, Eltis endorses a cultural explanation for slavery.

If we wish to understand the origins of African slavery in the New World or indeed in the pre-Columbian Old World, we must first explore the labor options of early modern Europeans—both those that were tried and those that were not. Second, we need to assess how close Europeans came to imposing slavery or slavelike conditions on other Europeans and finally what for them set slavery apart as a status for others. These steps will help clarify the cultural and ideological parameters that at once shaped the evolution of African New World slavery and kept Europeans as non-slaves. . . .

Although there is no evidence that Europeans ever considered instituting full chattel slavery of Europeans in their overseas settlements, the striking paradox is that no sound economic reasons spoke against it. By the seventeenth century, the most cursory examination of relative costs suggests that European slaves should have been preferred to either European indentured labor or African slaves. And while native Americans were cheap to enslave, their life expectancy and productivity in post-Columbian plantation conditions hardly compared with that of pre-industrial or, indeed, post-industrial Europeans. . . .

Moreover, . . . there were elements in the master-servant relationship in all European states in the late medieval period that could, and in several cases did, provide the basis for a revival of serfdom. And, if serfdom, why not slavery? Serfdom had disappeared in Sweden, Scotland, and the Low Countries no later than the early fourteenth century. But the institution not so much reappeared as appeared for the first time in Eastern Europe after these dates—and on a large scale. As already noted, marginal elements of European societies—convicts and vagrants—might have been candidates for forced labor in the Americas, but not only these. As late as the immediate antebellum period, there were ideologues in the southern United States who advocated slavery for poor whites as well as blacks.

From the strictly economic standpoint there were strong arguments in support of using European rather than African slave labor. The crux of the matter was shipping costs, which comprised by far the greater part of the price of imported bonded labor in the Americas. First, although the wind system of the Atlantic reduced the differential somewhat, it was normally quicker to sail directly to the Americas from Europe than to sail via Africa. In addition mortality and morbidity among both crews and passengers (or slaves) were lower in the north Atlantic than in the south. If we take into account the time spent collecting a slave cargo on the African coast as well, then the case for sailing directly from Europe with a cargo of Europeans appears stronger again. In the 1680s the Royal African Company (RAC) would often hire ships to carry slaves on its behalf. The hire rate was typically between £5 and £6 per slave landed alive in the Americas—a price that was understood to cover the full cost of sailing to Africa, acquiring slaves, and carrying them to the RAC's agents in the West Indies. The return cargo from the Americas was a separate speculation. The cost of shipping convicts to Barbados and the Leeward Islands at this time was similar. As noted later, however, ships carrying convicts, indentured servants, and fare-paying passengers always carried far fewer people per ton than did slave ships. There is little doubt that if ships carrying Europeans had been as closely packed as those carrying Africans, costs per person would have been much lower for Europeans than for Africans.

A further reason for using European rather than African slave labor derives from relative prices of African slaves and convict English labor—the nearest the English came to using Europeans as chattel slaves. Unskilled male convicts from England and Ireland sold for £16 each in Maryland in the years 1767–75 at a time when newly arrived African male slaves in the prime age group were selling for about triple this amount in Virginia and Maryland. The British males worked for ten years or less, the Africans for life. If convicts and their descendants had been sold into a lifetime of service, it is reasonable to suppose that planters would have been ready to pay a higher price for them. At this higher price, the British government and merchants might have found ways to provide more convicts. Shipping costs alone would not have interfered with the process. From this standpoint, convicts could have been sold into lifelong servitude for a price little more than that for seven or ten years of labor. Thus in the absence of an improbably rapid decline in slave prices as buyers switched from Africans to Europeans, we might suppose that there were no shipping cost barriers to European slaves forming the basis of the plantation labor forces of the Americas. . . .

Indeed enslavement in Europe might have been less costly than its African counterpart. First, transportation costs, which loomed so large within Africa, were bound to be lower in a subcontinent where major population centers were located near navigable waters. . . . Second, population growth in western Europe in general, and England in particular, was considerable during the era of the slave trade. Despite a net migration of 2.7 million from the mid-sixteenth to mid-nineteenth century, England's population rose sevenfold. Scholars debate the impact on the African population of the loss of twelve million people to the Americas. It is certain that this number of additional emigrants from a more heavily populated Europe over the same period would have had a negligible effect.

Arguments that Africans could stand up to the epidemiology of the Caribbean are irrelevant here. Whatever the European-African mortality differentials, a hostile disease environment was never enough to prevent European indentured servants from working in the Caribbean sugar sector. Medical evidence would be pertinent only if Europeans had never labored in the Caribbean under any labor regime or if European slavery had been tried and found wanting because of excess mortality. In fact, peoples of Europe and Africa died prematurely for different reasons in the Caribbean, but life expectancies for the two groups were not very different. . . .

In fact, nearly one thousand convicts a year left Britain in the half-century after 1718. This may not seem like many compared to an African slave trade drawing twenty-five thousand a year from Africa in the last third of the seventeenth century and rising to an average of fifty thousand a year in the half century after 1700. Yet consider that the population of England was only 7 percent that of Europe in 1680, and, if the rest of Europe had followed the English practice in proportion, fourteen thousand convicts would have been available. A traffic in degredados from Portuguese possessions to Brazil and Angola existed from the sixteenth to the nineteenth century, and the massive fortifications at Havana and San Juan, as well as Spanish outposts in North Africa, were built in part with Iberian convicts. Germanic states that lacked maritime facilities sold convicts to Italian city states for galley service. In France about a thousand convicts a year arrived at Marseille in the later seventeenth and early eighteenth centuries, but these were all male and mostly between twenty and thirty-five years of age. The potential for a large, more demographically representative traffic in French convicts is clear.

Possible sources other than convicts were numerous. Prisoners from wars, as in Africa, could have provided many additional plantation laborers. The English were well aware of the cheap labor possibilities of the latter. Just when sugar production in Barbados was expanding most rapidly and within a year or two of their acquisition of Jamaica, the English used Scottish prisoners taken at the Battle of Dunbar and Dutch prisoners (taken from Dutch naval vessels) to help drain the fens. Indeed, when in rebellion, the Irish and Scots alone could have filled the labor needs of the English colonies. Nor does this speculation fully incorporate vagrants and the poor. A properly exploited system drawing on convicts, prisoners, and vagrants from all countries of Europe could easily have provided fifty thousand forced migrants a year without serious disruption to either international peace or existing social institutions that generated and supervised these potential European victims. If such an outflow had been directed to the plantation colonies, it is also unlikely that mercantilist statesmen would have questioned either the scale or the direction of the flow.

More specifically, British convicts could have replaced African slaves in the Chesapeake, the destination of most transport ships. The first recorded shipment of convicts dates to 1615. Until 1770 the number of convict arrivals was at least two-thirds that of slaves in total, although in the 1730s and 1740s slave arrivals were between two and four times larger. If all whites and their subsequent progeny sent against their will to the colonies had been accorded the slave status of African immigrants, there is no reason why the number of white slaves in Maryland and Virginia would not have been at least as large as the actual black slave population at the end of the colonial period. . . .

Given these transportation and production cost advantages European slave labor would have been no more expensive and probably substantially cheaper. Slavery in the Americas (white slavery) would have been extensive in the sixteenth and seventeenth centuries before African slaves arrived in large numbers. Plantations would have developed more quickly and European consumers would have enjoyed an accelerated flow of sugar and tobacco. The fact that African slavery in the Americas took longer to evolve than any European counterpart would have done—at least in North America—is accounted for by the greater costs of moving people from Africa as opposed to Europe.

It was, of course, inconceivable that any of the labor pools mentioned earlier (convicts, prisoners of war, or vagrants) could have been converted into chattel slaves. The barrier to European slaves in the Americas lay not only beyond shipping and enslavement costs but also beyond any strictly economic sphere. The English Vagrancy Act of 1547 prescribing slavery was never enforced. The seventy-two English political prisoners who were taken at Salisbury in 1654 and sent to Barbados the next year claimed to be "[f]ree-born People of this Nation, now in Slavery" and were able to petition Parliament in 1659; they occasioned an extensive discussion there not extended to Africans for another 130 years. There were serfs in Scotland as we have seen but there were no slaves. Across the English Channel a 1716 law was necessary to deny slaves brought privately to France their enfranchisement when they arrived in the country. In Spain, Portugal, and all Mediterranean countries by the sixteenth century, Moors and Africans could be slaves. Christians, which meant in practice Europeans, because non-Europeans who became Christian remained slaves, could not. Even Jews were less likely to be enslaved in Spain by the later Middle Ages. In 1492, they were expelled, not enslaved. . . .

. . . Throughout Europe the state could take the lives of individuals in Europe, but enslavement was no longer an alternative to death; rather it had become a fate worse than death and as such was reserved for non-Europeans. Europeans would accept lawbreakers and prisoners as slaves only if they were not fellow Europeans. Conceptions of insider had expanded to include the European subcontinent whereas for Africans and American Indians a less than continent-wide definition of insider still pertained. In a profound but scarcely novel sense chattel slavery for Africans and Indians in the Americas was thus a function of the non-slave status that Europeans considered appropriate for themselves—a situation with historical parallels in many slave societies. . . .

States, merchants, and consumers of plantation produce all stood to gain from shipping convicts, prisoners, and indeed indentured servants in slavelike conditions. The fact that they did not do so says something about the views that European merchants and ultimately European societies held on the status of different migrant groups. Few societies in history have enslaved people they consider to be their own. . . . The relevant issue was who was to be considered "their own." In some African societies shared ethnicity and language might even mean an increased likelihood of enslavement—at least for women and children—given the focus on kin groups and their expansion through absorption of outsiders. In the Americas, slave raids of one Iroquois nation on another were not uncommon. But in western Europe, even the most degraded member of European society was spared enslavement. Only in the rather limited case of Amerindians in the Spanish Americas was such treatment extended to non-Europeans. This barrier was akin to the Muslim bar against the enslavement of non-Muslims, not in the sense that the basis of enslavement was religious, but rather that in both Muslim and Christian societies slavery came to be mainly African despite the fact that in both, slaves often converted to the faith of their owners. . . .

Explanations for these attitudes are more difficult to establish than the fact that such attitudes existed. . . . From one side of the ideological divide such reluctance might appear as a function of shared community values; from the other, it points to the resistance that would have inevitably followed or else manipulation on the part of the elite. The most serious strike in the preindustrial northeastern coal industry occurred in 1765 when mine owners attempted to follow their Scottish counterparts down a road that led to serfdom for workers. But what seems incontestable is that in regard to slavery the sense of the appropriate was shared across social divisions and cannot easily be explained by ideological differences or power relationships among classes. Outrage at the treatment of Africans was rarely expressed at any level of society before the late eighteenth century. The moral economy of the English crowd, like the various Christian churches, was preoccupied with other issues. When the immorality of coerced labor was recognised, the recognition appeared across all social groups at about the same time. Attempts to account for the failure of Europeans to enslave their own in terms of solidarity among the potential slaves do not seem promising. If the elite could kill Irish, Huguenots, Jews, prisoners of war, convicts, and many other marginalised groups, why could they not enslave them? The English considered those from the Celtic fringe different from themselves but, after the eleventh century at least, not different enough to enslave. For elite and non-elite alike enslavement remained a fate for which only non-Europeans were qualified.

PART

II The Slave Trade Within Africa

VARIETY OF OPINION

[A] great body of the Negro inhabitants of Africa have continued [in a state of slavery] from the most early period of their history. . . . There are regular markets, where slaves . . . are bought and sold.

MUNGO PARK

Few of the [179] informants had spent much time as slaves. . . . [T]hey were enslaved in their home district and immediately taken down to the coast.

P. E. H. HAIR

Of 100 people seized in Africa, 75 would have reached the market-places in the interior; . . . 64 . . . would have arrived at the coast; . . . 57 would have boarded the ships; . . . and 48 or 49 would have lived to behold their first master in the New World.

JOSEPH C. MILLER

The strong preference of the slave sellers for guns . . . reinforces the slave-gun cycle theory according to which . . . slave gatherers bought more firearms to capture more slaves to buy more firearms.

JOSEPH E. INIKORI

[T]he more we know about African warfare and resulting enslavement, the less clear and direct the connections between war and the export of slaves becomes.

JOHN THORNTON

Mungo Park

West Africa in the 1790s

Until the last decades of the Atlantic trade there is very little direct evidence of the mechanisms that delivered slaves to Europeans at the coast. The Scotsman Mungo Park was one of the first Europeans to travel into inland regions of Africa and to observe how people became slaves. He found that most were prisoners taken in warfare and raids, but that others lost their free status as the result of famine, debt, or crimes. Captives were either kept as slaves in Africa or sold abroad.

The slaves in Africa, I suppose, are nearly in the proportion of three to one to the freemen. They claim no reward for their services, except food and cloathing; and are treated with kindness or severity, according to the good or bad disposition of their masters. Custom, however, has established certain rules with regard to the treatment of slaves, which it is thought dishonourable to violate. Thus, the domestic slaves, or such as are born in a man's own house, are treated with more lenity than those which are purchased with money. The authority of the master over the domestic slave, as I have elsewhere observed, extends only to

From Mungo Park, *Travels in the Interior Districts of Africa: Performed in the Years 1795, 1796, and 1797* (London: John Murray, 1816).

reasonable correction: for the master cannot sell his domestic, without having first brought him to a public trial, before the chief men of the place. But these restrictions on the power of the master extend not to the case of prisoners taken in war, nor to that of slaves purchased with money. All these unfortunate beings are considered as strangers and foreigners, who have no right to the protection of the law, and may be treated with severity, or sold to a stranger, according to the pleasure of their owners. There are, indeed, regular markets, where slaves of this description are bought and sold; and the value of a slave in the eye of an African purchaser, increases in proportion to his distance from his native kingdom; for when slaves are only a few days' journey from the place of their nativity, they frequently effect their escape: but when one or more kingdoms intervene, escape being more difficult, they are more readily reconciled to their situation. On this account, the unhappy slave is frequently transferred from one dealer to another, until he has lost all hopes of returning to his native kingdom. The slaves which are purchased by the Europeans on the Coast, are chiefly of this description; a few of them are collected in the petty wars, hereafter to be described, which take place near the Coast; but by far the greater number are brought down in large caravans from the inland countries, of which many are unknown, even by name, to the Europeans. The slaves which are thus brought from the interior, may be divided into two distinct classes: *first*, such as were slaves from their birth, having been born of enslaved mothers; *secondly*, such as were born free, but who afterwards, by whatever means, became slaves. Those of the first description are by far the most numerous; for prisoners taken in war (at least such as are taken in open and declared war, when one kingdom avows hostilities against another) are generally of this description. The comparatively small proportion of free people, to the enslaved, throughout Africa, has already been noticed; and it must be observed, that men of free condition, have many advantages over the slaves, even in war time. They are in general better armed, and well mounted; and can either fight or escape with some hopes of success; but the slaves, who have only their spears and bows, and of whom great numbers are loaded with baggage, become an easy prey. Thus, when Mansong, King of Bambarra, made war upon Kaarta . . . , he took in one day nine hundred prisoners, of which number not more than seventy were free men. This account I received from Daman Jumma, who had thirty slaves at Kemmoo, all of whom were made prisoners by Mansong. Again, when a freeman is taken prisoner, his friends will sometimes ransom him by giving two slaves in exchange; but when a slave is taken, he has no hopes of such redemption. . . .

Slaves of the second description, generally become such by one or other of the following causes, 1. *Captivity*. 2. *Famine*. 3. *Insolvency*. 4. *Crimes*. A freeman may, by the established customs of Africa, become a slave by being taken in war. War is, of all others, the most productive source, and was probably the origin of slavery; for when one nation had taken from another, a greater number of captives than could be exchanged on equal terms, it is natural to suppose that the conquerors, finding it inconvenient to maintain their prisoners, would compel them to labour; at first, perhaps, only for their own support; but afterwards to support their masters. Be this as it may, it is a known fact, that prisoners of war in Africa, are the slaves of the conquerors; and when the weak or unsuccessful warrior, begs for mercy beneath the uplifted spear of his opponent, he gives up at the same time his claim to liberty; and purchases his life at the expence of his freedom. . . .

The wars of Africa are of two kinds, which are distinguished by different appellations: that species which bears the greatest resemblance to our European contests, is denominated *killi*, a word signifying "to call out," because such wars are openly avowed, and previously declared. Wars of this description in Africa, commonly terminate, however, in the course of a single campaign. A battle is fought, the vanquished seldom think of rallying again; the whole inhabitants become panic struck; and the conquerors have only to bind the slaves, and carry off their plunder and their victims. Such of the prisoners as, through age or infirmity, are unable to endure fatigue, or are found unfit for sale, are considered as useless; and I have no doubt are frequently put to death. The same fate commonly awaits a chief, or any other person who has taken a very distinguished part in the war. And here it may be observed that, notwithstanding this exterminating system, it is surprising to behold how soon an African town is rebuilt and repeopled. The circumstance arises probably from this; that their pitched battles are few; the weakest know their own situation, and seek safety in flight. When their country has been desolated, and their ruined towns and villages deserted by the enemy, such of the inhabitants as have escaped the *sword*, and the *chain*, generally return, though with cautious steps, to the place of their nativity; for it seems to be the universal wish of mankind, to spend the evening of their days where they passed their infancy. . . .

The other species of African warfare is distinguished by the appellation of *tegria*, "plundering or stealing." It arises from a sort of hereditary feud which the inhabitants of one nation or district bear towards another. No immediate cause of hostility is assigned, or notice of attack given; but the inhabitants of each watch every opportunity to plunder and distress the objects of their animosity by predatory excursions. These are very common, particularly about the beginning of the dry season, when the labour of the harvest is over and provisions are plentiful. Schemes of vengeance are then meditated. The chief man surveys the number and activity of his vassals, as they brandish their spears at festivals; and elated with his own importance, turns his whole thoughts towards revenging some depredation or insult, which either he or his ancestors may have received from a neighbouring state.

Wars of this description are generally conducted with great secrecy. A few resolute individuals, headed by some person of enterprise and courage, march quietly through the woods, surprise in the night some unprotected village, and carry off the inhabitants and their effects, before their neighbours can come to their assistance. One morning, during my stay at Kamalia, we were all much alarmed by a party of this kind. The king of Fooladoo's son, with five hundred horsemen, passed secretly through the woods, a little to the southward of Kamalia, and on the morning following plundered three towns belonging to Madigai, a powerful chief in Jallonkadoo.

The success of this expedition encouraged the governor of Bangassi, a town of Fooladoo, to make a second inroad upon another part of the same country. Having assembled about two hundred of his people, he passed the river Kokoro in the night, and carried off a great number of prisoners. Several of the inhabitants who had escaped these attacks, were afterwards seized by the Mandingoes, as they wandered about in the woods or concealed themselves in the glens and strong places of the mountains.

These plundering excursions always produce speedy retaliation; and when large parties cannot be collected for this purpose, a few friends will combine together, and advance into the enemy's country, with a view to plunder, or carry off the inhabitants. A single individual has been known to take his bow and quiver, and proceed in like manner. Such an attempt is doubtless in him an act of rashness; but when it is considered that in one of these predatory wars, he has probably been deprived of his child, or his nearest relation, his situation will rather call for pity than censure. The poor sufferer, urged on by the feelings of domestic or paternal attachment, and the ardour of revenge, conceals himself among the bushes, until some young or unarmed person passes by. He then, tiger-like, springs upon his prey; drags his victim into the thicket, and in the night carries him off as a slave.

When a Negro has, by means like these, once fallen into the hands of his enemies, he is either retained as the slave of his conqueror, or bartered into a distant kingdom; for an African, when he has once subdued his enemy, will seldom give him an opportunity of lifting up his hand against him at a future period. A conqueror commonly disposes of his captives according to the rank which they held in their native kingdom. Such of the domestic slaves as appear to be of a mild disposition, and particularly the young women, are retained as his own slaves. Others that display marks of discontent, are disposed of in a distant country; and such of the freemen or slaves, as have taken an active part in the war, are either sold to the Slatees, or put to death. War, therefore, is certainly the most general, and most productive source of slavery; and the desolations of war often (but not always) produce the second cause of slavery, *famine*; in which case a freeman becomes a slave to avoid a greater calamity.

Perhaps, by a philosophic and reflecting mind, death itself would scarcely be considered as a greater calamity than slavery; but the poor Negro, when fainting with hunger, thinks like ESAU of old; *"behold I am at the point to die, and what profit shall this birthright do to me?"* There are many instances of free men voluntarily surrendering up their liberty to save their lives. During a great scarcity which lasted for three years, in the countries of the Gambia, great numbers of people became slaves in this manner. . . . Large families are very often exposed to absolute want: and as the parents have almost unlimited authority over their children, it frequently happens, in all parts of Africa, that some of the latter are sold to purchase provisions for the rest of the family. When I was at Jarra, Daman Jumma pointed out to me three young slaves which he had purchased in this manner. I have already related another instance which I saw at Wonda: and I was informed that in Fooladoo, at that time, it was a very common practice.

The third cause of slavery, is *insolvency*. Of all the offences (if insolvency may be so called) to which the laws of Africa have affixed the punishment of slavery, this is the most common. A Negro trader commonly contracts debts on some mercantile speculation, either from his neighbours, to purchase such articles as will sell to advantage in a distant market, or from the European traders on the Coast; payment to be made in a given time. In both cases, the situation of the adventurer is exactly the same. If he succeeds, he may secure an independency. If he is unsuccessful, his person and services are at the disposal of another; for, in Africa, not only the effects of the insolvent, but even the insolvent himself, are sold to satisfy the lawful demands of his creditors.

The fourth cause above enumerated, is *the commission of crimes, on which the laws of the country affix slavery as a punishment*. In Africa, the only offences of this class are murder, adultery, and witchcraft; and I am happy to say, that they did not appear to me to be common. In cases of murder, I was informed, that the nearest relation of the deceased had it in his power, after conviction, either to kill the offender with his own hand, or sell him into slavery. When adultery occurs, it is generally left to the option of the person injured, either to sell the culprit, or accept such a ransom for him as he may think equivalent to the injury he has sustained. By witchcraft, is meant pretended magic, by which the lives or healths of persons are affected: in other words, it is the administering of poison. No trial for this offence, however, came under my observation while I was in Africa; and I therefore suppose that the crime, and its punishment, occur but very seldom.

When a freeman has become a slave by any one of the causes before mentioned, he generally continues so for life, and his children (if they are born of an enslaved mother) are brought up in the same state of servitude. There are, however, a few instances of slaves obtaining their freedom, and sometimes even with the consent of their masters; as by performing some singular piece of service, or by going to battle, and bringing home two slaves as a ransom; but the common way of regaining freedom is by escape; and when slaves have once set their minds on running away, they often succeed. Some of them will wait for years before an opportunity presents itself, and during that period shew no signs of discontent. In general, it may be remarked that slaves who come from a hilly country, and have been much accustomed to hunting and travel, are more apt to attempt their escape, than such as are born in a flat country, and have been employed in cultivating the land.

Such are the general outlines of that system of slavery which prevails in Africa; and it is evident from its nature and extent, that it is a system of no modern date. It probably had its origin in the remote ages of antiquity, before the Mahomedans explored a path across the Desert.

How far it is maintained and supported by the slave traffic, which, for two hundred years, the nations of Europe have carried on with the natives of the Coast, it is neither within my province, nor in my power, to explain. If my sentiments should be required concerning the effect which a discontinuance of that commerce would produce on the manners of the natives, I should have no hesitation in observing, that, in the present unenlightened state of their minds, my opinion is, the effect would neither be so extensive or beneficial, as many wise and worthy persons fondly expect.

P. E. H. Hair

African Narratives of Enslavement

In this selection, Professor Paul Hair of the University of Liverpool (U.K.) analyzes the many tales of enslavement collected by a German missionary in Sierra Leone from Africans rescued from slave ships by British patrols in the first part of the nineteenth century. He enhances the value of these rare accounts by actual slaves by identifying where they came from and grouping them by the causes of their enslavement. His results are very close to Park's impressions, except for a much lower incidence of people born to slavery.

S. W. Koelle in his *Polyglotta Africana* of 1854 . . . supplied notes on 210 informants, but only 179 were definitely stated to be ex-slaves. . . . Of the ex-slaves, 177 were men and 2 women. Koelle chose these informants, out of the 40,000 or so ex-slaves in the Freetown district in 1850, because each individual (occasionally, two individuals) represented a different African language. Hence . . . the informants were

Excerpted from "The Enslavement of Koelle's Informants," *Journal of African History* 6.2, 1965, pp. 193–201. Reprinted with the permission of Cambridge University Press.

drawn from a very large number of language groups, covering a large part of West and West Central Africa and a few outlying districts in East Africa. Though the societies involved were so various and so scattered, the accounts of the informants' enslavement, analysed below, suggest a general pattern of reaction to the economic and social opportunities — and intrusions — of the slave trade. . . .[Because] we have available here only 179 biographical records of a process involving many millions of unrecorded life-histories . . . , we take care to indicate the provenance — by language — of each informant discussed in any detail. (The first name given is always Koelle's name for the language: while the name in capitals is either the modern name for the language, or the name of a better known grouping which includes the language. . . .)

. . . [A]lmost all were enslaved before they were forty; three-quarters were enslaved before they were thirty; one-half were enslaved during their twenties. . . . The earliest enslavement date was 1795, the latest 1847. Three-quarters of the informants had been enslaved — that is, in almost all cases, had left their homeland — more than ten years before the date of interview; and nearly half had been enslaved more than twenty years before. The oldest man interviewed was probably nearly eighty, the youngest was in his early twenties. . . .

Few of the informants had spent much time as slaves. Five of them had spent periods of years in America (and had come to Freetown after emancipation), and twenty-nine had spent periods of years in Africa, mainly as slaves to Africans. The remainder had reached Sierra Leone shortly after enslavement (though an exact period of months or years was seldom stated); that is, they were enslaved in their home district and immediately taken down to the coast (a journey which occasionally took many months, however), and were shortly afterwards captured aboard a slave ship and brought straightway to Freetown. . . .

Manner of Enslavement: (a) War

Forty-eight of the informants (34% of those detailing their manner of enslavement) had been "taken in war." Twenty-five of these, and two who had been "kidnapped," were taken by the Fula during their razzias. These extended from the Futa Jalon (modern Guinea) to Adamawa (Cameroons). Thus, two Soso/SUSU were captured by the Fula *c.* 1820 and *c.* 1830, while about a dozen men from tribes of Adamawa and the North Cameroons provided evidence of Fula raids from 1820 onwards.

> *About his twenty-fourth year [c. 1825], a people came from a far and unknown country, who were called Beliyi or Bedeyi, and burnt all their towns, the capital not excepted, so that all who could run, escaped into the woods. There he [an Afudu/TANGALE] was caught by them. . . .*

> *Two years before Nyamsi, or Andrew Wilhelm of Freetown, [a Param/BAMILEKE] was kidnapped [c. 1825], the Tebale had invaded his country and committed the most ferocious atrocities: e.g., they took children by their legs and dashed their brains out against trees: ripped up the pregnant women: caught four hundred children of the King's family and the families of other great men, made a large fire, and burnt them alive. . . .*

> *. . . the Tebale who had come from afar on horses and had conquered many countries, spreading terror before them on account of their poisoned weapons, by a mere touch of which they killed their enemies . . . [c. 1835, a Bagba/?NKOM].*

> *. . . the Fula and Nupes invaded and conquered Jumu, destroying all its towns. In this war he was taken captive . . . [a Jumu/YORUBA].*

> *Lamaji, or John Smith of Campbell Town [a Gbali/GBARI], born at Gugu where he lived to see three grandchildren when he was kidnapped by some Fulani . . . [c. 1847].*

Here he may also be mentioned the JAR man who, as a boy of twelve was sent to the Fula emir of Bauchi, as part of the annual tribute of slaves. But the Fula biter was sometimes bit:

> *Adamu, or Edward Klein of Freetown [a Fulbe/FULA] brought up in Kano, had been five years married to his two wives when he had to join the annual war-expedition [in 1845] against the Maladis, an independent Hausa tribe, on which occasion they had to flee from the Maladis and he was caught in the flight by night. This enabled the Maladis who had caught him to carry him to another country by stealth, and to sell him there: for there is a law among the Maladis that all Fulbe taken in war are to be killed forthwith.*

> *Samba, [a Pulo/FULA] born in the town of Ganyeg, where he also resided till his eldest child was twelve years old, when he was taken prisoner on a plundering expedition against the Mandengas . . . [c. 1810].*

Manner of Enslavement: (b) Kidnapping

Forty-three of Koelle's informants (30%) stated that they had been 'kidnapped' into slavery. Many gave no further details and appear to have been kidnapped by fellow-tribesmen. . . . Travel outside the homelands was dangerous.

> *Sem, or Peter Kondo of Gloucester, [a Kaure/TEM] born in the village Wuram, where he was brought up and was probably upwards of thirty years old when he was kidnapped in the Basare country, where he had gone to buy corn.*

> *Yapanda, or William Seck of Wellington, [a Tiwi/TIV], born in the village of Torowo, where he lived till his twenty-fourth year, when he was kidnapped on a trading-tour to Hausa.*

William Harding, an Ondo/YORUBA, was kidnapped on a trading journey by the Ijesha/YORUBA. An Abaja/IBO and an Oworo/YORUBA were each kidnapped by "a treacherous friend." The treacherous friend of a Muntu/YAO enticed him on board a Portuguese ship and then took money for him. A Bagbalang/GRUSI was kidnapped at the instigation of his brother-in-law.

Manner of Enslavement: (c) Sold by Relatives or Superiors

Ten of the informants who did not claim they were kidnapped (7%) stated that they were sold by relatives or tribal superiors. Of those who gave details, it is clear that in some cases the victim considered he had been treated badly.

> *Fije, of John Campbell, [a Mahi/EWE] born in the town of Igbege, where he grew up, married two wives, and on his father's death, inherited twenty-two more . . . when he was sold by his uncle because he had not presented him with a female slave and cows on his father's death.*

> *Runago, or Thomas Nicol of Kissy, [a Bidjogo/BIDYOGO] had a child who was just beginning to walk when he was sold by his elder brother to the Portuguese because they could not agree.*

> *Dosu, of John Carew of Freetown, [a Mahi/EWE] . . . had a child about six years old when he was sold by his elder brother on account of*

> *a quarrel respecting the property of their father who had been killed in
> a war against the Dahomeyans.*

> *Aboyade, or James Cole, hawker at Freetown, [a YORUBA] born in
> the town Ogbomosho, where he lived till his first child was about three
> years old, when he was sold by a war-chief, because he refused to give
> him his wife.*

A Diwala/DUALA boy of sixteen was sold to the Portuguese by his
guardian, his parents being dead: a Mbofon/NDE was sold by his relatives for a gun and powder: a Bumbete/MBETE from the Congo was
sold because his mother had run away from his father, presumably by
his father's family. The case of a Cameroons man may be included
under this heading.

> *Edia, or Thomas Renner of Bathurst, [a Nhalemoe/MBO] born in the
> village of Baningar, where he also grew up, had seven wives and a child
> of about ten years of age, when he was sold by his countrymen out of
> jealousy of his ability and influence. . . .*

Manner of Enslavement: (d) Debt

Ten informants (7%) stated that they had been sold to pay debts, in most
cases not of their own contracting. A KAMUKU was sold because of a
debt incurred by his father, a butcher: a Baseke/KOTA and a Nki/BOKI
were also sold because of paternal debts. Responsibility for debts was
considered to extend further than the family circle.

> *Nyamse, or James Hardy of Freetown, [a Bamom/BAMILEKE] . . . lived
> in Tiapon, a town five days' journey from the capital, to his twenty-fourth
> year, when he was seized on a trading tour to the Bakoan country, for the
> debt of another Tiapon man.*

> *Tete, or Frederick Gibbon of Freetown, [an Adampe/EWE] born in the
> town of Gbotue, where he was married and had a child five years of age,
> when he was seized by the Gaja people, because another Gbotue man,
> with whom he was in no wise connected, owed them a debt.*

Possibly some of those who were "sold by relatives" were sold to pay
debts. In rare cases the obligation for the debt was fully accepted by the
victim, and one such case is reported by Koelle. The account is moving
and deserves to be repeated in full.

Oga, or John Tailor of Freetown, [a Yala/IYALA] born in the town of Gbeku, where he also grew up, married five wives and had thirteen children, eleven of whom died and the eldest of the two remaining was about twenty years of age when a friend sent him to buy a slave, returning with whom they were attacked by a wild cow which killed the slave. The friend then wanted to sell the messenger [i.e., the son] as a restitution for the loss of his slave: but Oga, rather than have his son lose his liberty, offered himself as a slave and was accordingly sold. He was afterwards captured and brought to Sierra Leone, where he has now been twenty years and is the only representative of his tribe. He is now a very old grey-headed man.

Manner of Enslavement: (e) Judicial Process

Persons who were condemned by judicial process in African societies were often enslaved. Sixteen of Koelle's informants (11%) admitted that they had been condemned, and it is likely that some of those who only stated that they had been "sold by relatives" were also, by the laws of their own society, "criminals."

Eleven men . . . had been sold "on account of adultery," a charge which they did not challenge. Two related cases were these:

Asu, or Thomas Harry of Hastings [a Konguang/ANYANG] . . . married two wives, the unfaithfulness of one of whom led him to slay a man, on which account he was sold by the king.

Nanga, or John Smart of Freetown [a Lubalo/KIMBUNDU] born in the town of Mulukala, where he lived to about his twenty-fourth year, when he was given in pawn by his mother for a brother of hers, who had been sold on account of adultery: but before he could be redeemed by his mother, he was placed in the hands of the Portuguese in Loando, who at once shipped him.

Another man, a Melong/MBO was enslaved for murder; an Ihewe/BINI was "sold on a charge of theft"; and a Kanyika/LUBA "had one child which could not walk when he was sold on account of bad conduct." Two men from the Congo coast had been enslaved because of witchcraft accusations.

Kumbu, or Thomas Parker of Wilberforce [a Nyombe/KONGO] . . . had a child about five years old, when he was sold because his sister had been accused of witchcraft.

> *Bembi, or William Davis of Freetown [a Pangela/UMBUNDU] . . . was sold in about his twenty-eighth year because his family had been accused of having occasioned the king's death by means of witchcraft.*

Conclusion

Some of the brief life-histories recorded by Koelle describe odd facets of individual behaviour. Nineteenth-century Africans, while exhibiting the normal tendency to conformity of behaviour, were also capable of a wide range of individual reaction to intrusive events.

> *Tando, or John James of Gloucester [a Mbe/BAMILEKE] . . . has been in Sierra Leone ten years with five countrymen, all of whom appear to be very stupid; thus, e.g., one of them who had eight wives and five children in his country could not even count up to five: and when I expressed my astonishment at this, he said, "Please, Sir, I was a gentleman's son in my country, and they do nothing but eat, sleep and make war."*

> *Muhammodu [a Pulo/FULA] . . . born in the town of Wurokone . . . was taken to Jamaica more than forty years ago, and after nine years' stay there to Sierra Leone, where he has now been a discharged soldier for twenty years. I give his specimen chiefly in order to furnish an opportunity for judging the great strength of a Fula's memory; for beside his long absence from home, Muhammodu is a drunkard, resides in Sierra Leone quite by himself, and holds no intercourse with other Fulbe.*

> *Musewo, or Toki Petro of Freetown [a SONGO] born in the town Bopunt, where he was kidnapped in about his fifteenth year and carried to Loanda. He remained there twenty-one years, during most of which time he was employed by the Portuguese Henrique Consale to buy Songo slaves, with whom he had always to speak Songo. At his master's death, he became free and went to the Brasils, where he was employed by a Portuguese in the African slave-trade for six years, during which period he made the passage seven times; but in the eighth the ship was captured by the cruisers and brought to Freetown.*

. . . [T]he 179 life-histories here analysed may be claimed to present a miniature of the slave trade within Western tropical Africa in the early nineteenth century, which, though limited in scope and perhaps largely confirmatory of accepted accounts, is well-nigh unique in that it is based solely on information supplied by individual Africans.

Joseph C. Miller

West Central Africa

In his acclaimed account of the Angolan slave trade, Professor Joseph C. Miller of the University of Virginia reconstructs Africans' long, painful, and deadly treks from the deep interior of the continent to the ships awaiting them in the coastal ports. Miller's calculation of the deaths during each stage of the trade is a chilling reminder of the callous losses of human life, although it may be that losses on the way to the coast were lower in other parts of Africa.

. . . The background hunger and epidemics that sometimes forced patrons to give up clients and compelled parents to part with children set a tone of physical weakness and vulnerability behind slaving in the interior. Where warfare and violence stimulated the initial capture, the victims would have begun their odysseys in exhausted, shaken, and perhaps wounded physical condition. Though the buyers preferred strong adult males, the people actually captured in warfare, even in pitched battles between formal armies, included disproportionately high numbers of less fit women and children, since the men could take flight and leave the less mobile retinue of young and female dependents to the pursuers. People sold for food, the last resort in time of famine, also started out physically ill-prepared for the rigors of the journey to come. In the commercialized areas, lords, creditors, and patrons, employing less dramatic methods to seize and sell the dependents who paid for imports or covered their debts, would have selected the least promising among their followings—young boys, older women, the sick, the indebted, the troublesome, and the lame. Populations raided consistently by stronger neighbors, harassed and driven from their homes and fields, and refugee populations hiding on infertile mountaintops could not have been as well-nourished as stronger groups who yielded fewer of their members to the slave trade.

The mixture of people swept off by thousands of isolated decisions and haphazard actions separated into two distinguishable drifts of people. One was a slow, favored one composed principally of the stronger and healthier women and younger children that dissipated into the communities of western central Africa, to remain there as wives and slaves for months or years, or perhaps for life. The debilitated residue became the faster-flowing and sharply defined main channel of people destined for immediate sale and export, victims of drought and raids at the source, joined by small feeder streams of older youths ejected from local communities along its banks as it flowed westward, along with a few women and older folk, and a variety of outcasts and criminals.

The flow headed for the Atlantic coast thus carried weakened individuals relatively vulnerable to disease and death, even by the low health standards of their time. These slaves were not necessarily constitutionally weaker than those left behind or kept but, rather, individuals taken at defenseless and enfeebled moments in their lives. Their temporarily reduced ability to withstand the stresses of enslavement, dislocation, and forced travel could not have failed to produce higher incidences of sickness and death among them than among the population of western central Africa as a whole, even without adding the physical traumas of violent seizure or the psychological shocks of nonviolent enslavement. . . .

These slaves advanced from the hands of their captors, sometimes with periods of rest and partial recuperation in villages along the way, into the market centers where African sellers met European and Luso-African slave-buyers in the interior. People raised in small, dispersed settlements would have encountered the much more volatile disease environments among populations concentrated along the trails, at the staging posts, and finally in the marketplaces themselves. Those from more densely inhabited areas, and even captives who had lived along the roads, encountered new disease environments as they moved into terrain unlike that of their native lands and came into direct contact with foreigners. They would have suffered accordingly from pathogens against which they had no immunities.

The slaves' diets also deteriorated. Whatever plantains, sorghum, or millet they might have eaten at home, supplemented by a healthy variety of game, other crops, and wild plants, as they moved westward they depended increasingly on manioc—the dietary staple that was cheapest to grow, easiest to transport, and most resistant to spoilage—prepared poorly in one form or another. Fresh fruits and vegetables and meat virtually disappeared from their diet. Much of what they were given rotted or became vermin-infested. They were unlikely to have received foods of any sort in quantities sufficient to sustain them, particularly in their weakened conditions, and with vicious circularity they grew too weak to carry what little they were given as they moved. Those who stumbled from weakness were driven onward to keep the remainder moving, all bound together. They drank from inadequate water supplies along the way, sometimes streams, but often not, owing to the tendency of the trails to follow the elevated ridges along the watersheds and the caravan drivers' preference for travel in the dry months. Pools dug out at stopping places were often contaminated from the concentrations of slave caravans that built up around them.

Under such conditions, the slaves developed both dietary imbalances and sheer nutritional insufficiencies. Scurvy, so common among slaves who lived to cross the southern Atlantic that it was known as the *mal de Loanda* (or "Luanda sickness"), was the primary recognized form of undernourishment. The symptoms appeared on slave ships at sea long before they could have developed from shortages of rations on board except among slaves already debilitated by weeks or months of a diet restricted to low vitamin, low acetic acid starches like manioc. With innocent destructiveness some physicians prescribed more manioc as an anti-escorbutic. The slaves who died along the path must have suffered malnutrition to a degree approaching sheer starvation. Racialist Portuguese theories of tropical medicine at the time misdiagnosed the condition, holding that blacks needed to eat less than whites, since they could thrive for days at a time on nothing more than a few millet heads and a kola nut.

The alterations in diet and the amoeba in contaminated water supplies must also have caused the early spread of dysenteries and other intestinal disorders, the infamous "flux" that the British lamented among the slaves they carried across the Atlantic, known as *câmaras* among the Portuguese. Infected excreta left everywhere about water sources, in camp sites, and in the slave pens of the marketplaces assured that few individuals escaped debilitating and dehydrating epidemics of bloody bacillary dysenteries.

Exposure to the dry-season chill in the high elevations and to damp nights spent sitting in open pathside camps, utter lack of clothing and shelter, and increasingly weakened constitutions all contributed to the appearance of respiratory ailments vaguely described as *constipações*. As slaves neared the marketplaces and the main routes running from them down to the coast, they grew weaker and more susceptible to parasites and other diseases that swept in epidemic form through the coffles. The slave trade must have been a veritable incubator for typhus, typhoid, and other fevers or *carneiradas*, particularly smallpox, and other diseases that broke out in times of drought and famine from their usual confinement in the streams of slaves into the general rural population. The normal concentration of these diseases along the commercial routes may have contributed to the impression of overwhelming deadliness that Portuguese held of most of the central African interior, since every European who ventured there necessarily walked within these reservoirs of slave-borne infection on the pathways leading to the interior.

The inferable lethal consequences of malnutrition, disease, and other hardships along the path were death rates that rose at an increasing tempo as slaves flowed into the central channels of the slave trade, perhaps to catastrophic levels in the range of 400–600 per 1,000 per annum by the time slaves reached the coast. One experienced Luanda merchant reported that slavers toward the second half of the eighteenth century expected to lose about 40 percent of their captives to flight and death between the time they purchased them in the interior and the time they put them aboard the ships in Luanda. If the westward march averaged about six months from the central highlands or the Kwango valley, where most agents of the town merchants bought slaves at that time, and deaths in the seaport ran about 15 percent, that estimate would mean 25 percent of the slaves died en route to the coast. Such a figure would imply a mean death rate between time of purchase and time of arrival in the towns of 500 per 1,000 per year. In practice, lower death rates at the outset of the trek would have risen at an increasing rate to peak somewhere above that level at the coast, but averaging out to that overall percentage loss. A certain proportion of the losses would have been attributable to flight and to theft, leaving a bit less than the reported total owing to mortality.

Flight from the slave coffles heading toward the coast, though impossible to estimate precisely in terms of frequency, was not uncommon. Despite the nutritional and epidemiological odds against the slaves, some individuals somehow found the strength to flee their captors. Slaves fled from the marketplaces of the interior, taking refuge among the very people who had just sold them to the Europeans. As they neared the coast, they found willing, though often calculatingly self-interested, asylum among the independent Africans living on either side of Luanda, south of the Kwanza in Kisama, and north of the Dande among the southern Kongo of Musulu. Some fugitives established maroon colonies of their own within Portuguese territory, and there are hints that a major colony of renegades existed throughout the century virtually on the outskirts of Luanda. Some of these colonies had extensive fields and fortifications, including up to forty houses and populations of about 200 people, and lived by raiding Portuguese slave-run plantations in the river valleys. . . .

The slave population entering Luanda was heavily weighted toward younger males by the eighteenth century, reflecting the strain on western central African populations by that time and the widespread resort to debt as means of creating slaves. Older men (*barbados*) also passed through Luanda in significant numbers. Predominant among the women were young females, with a scattering of prime (nubile) women, mothers with infants, and girls, precisely the category of slave that African lords must have been least willing to give up and therefore a further indication of demographic and commercial pressures then bearing on the slave supply zones. . . .

All slaves trembled in terror at meeting the white cannibals of the cities, the first Europeans whom many of the slaves would have seen. They feared the whites' intention of converting Africans' brains into cheese or rendering the fat of African bodies into cooking oil, as well as burning their bones into gunpowder. They clearly regarded the towns as places of certain death, as indeed they became for many, if not for the reasons slaves feared. . . .

The great majority of the slaves went directly to the slave pens of the city's large expatriate merchants. These barracoons—known as *quintais* (singular *quintal*), a word also applied to farmyards for keeping animals— were usually barren enclosures located immediately behind the large two-story residences in the lower town, but traders also constructed them around the edges of the city and on the beach. Large numbers of slaves accumulated within these pens, living for days and weeks surrounded by walls too high for a person to scale, squatting helplessly, naked, on the dirt and entirely exposed to the skies except for a few adjoining cells where they could be locked at night. They lived in a "wormy morass" (*ascarozissimo charco*) and slept in their own excrement, without even a bonfire for warmth. One observer described "two hundred, sometimes three and four hundred slaves in each *quintal*, and there they stayed, ate, slept, and satisfied every human necessity, and from there they infected the houses and the city with the most putrid miasmas; and because dried fish is their usual and preferred food, it was on the walls of these *quintais* and on the roofs of the straw dwellings that such preparation was done, with manifest damage to the public health." To the smell of rotting fish were added the foul odors of the slaves' dysenteries and the putrid fragrance of the bodies of those who died. The stench emanating from these squalid prisons overpowered visitors to the town.

At Benguela the slave pens were about 17 meters square, with walls 3 meters or more in height, and they sometimes contained as many as 150 to 200 slaves, intermixed with pigs and goats also kept in them. That left about two square meters per individual, or barely enough to lie down and to move about a bit. In some instances, at least, the walls had openings cut in them, through which guards outside could thrust musket barrels to fire on slaves within who grew unruly. . . .

The slaves' wait in the barracoons, filthy and unhealthful as it was, leaves the impression of food and water adequate to begin the long process of recuperation from the greater hardships of enslavement and the westward trail. Daily visits to the bay to bathe afforded some slaves an opportunity for limited personal hygiene even amidst the squalor of the slave pens, though they received little that would require cash expenditures by their managers: no clothing, and food barely adequate to sustain them until they would be sold or handed on to the care of the ships' captains waiting to transport them to Brazil. Living conditions for slaves at Benguela would have been worse, owing to the greater shortages of food and water there than in Luanda. But in both ports the sheer opportunity for rest after the rigors of the march from the interior and the availability of salt, iodine, and protein from fish probably allowed the strongest of the young male slaves to recover some of the strength drained from them on their way to the coast. The most penurious merchant could have honestly prided himself on restoring the captives he received toward health, in conformity with his responsibilities to their owners. There may even have been some modest substance to merchants' exaggerated claims that they were doing so. . . .

. . . A general estimate on the order of 10 to 15 percent ought not to be far out of line for mid- to late-eighteenth-century mortality among the slaves held at Angolan ports. It is probable, though undocumented, that rates had been higher in the past and declined through the 1700s, except in periods of drought and famine. The damages wrought by famine in the town, too, were lessened after the 1760s by the operation of the *terreiro público* public granary. . . .

The annualized mortality rate for the slaves' stay on the coast . . . would have averaged twice the mean for the preceding months on the trails of the interior, mostly as an extension of the highest rates attained toward the end of their march to the sea into their first few days or weeks in the city. Slaves from higher elevations in the interior would have succumbed to unfamiliar diseases endemic along the coast soon after their arrival. Death rates probably declined perceptibly thereafter, and many slaves boarded the ships in physical condition marginally stronger than the near-delirium in which they had stumbled into the city.

When the day of the slaves' departure finally dawned, they and their owners and managers set out along yet another tortuous course leading from the slave pens through the long chain of government officials charged with enforcing the maze of rules intended to protect the slaves' bodies and souls and the revenues of the king, though in fact often to the enhancement of none of these. The procedures had been relatively simple earlier in the eighteenth century, but later efforts to curtail tight-packing and smuggling and to improve supplies of food and water aboard the slave ships gradually lengthened the gantlet through which they passed. . . .

. . . Of 100 people seized in Africa, 75 would have reached the marketplaces in the interior; 85 percent of them, or about 64 of the original 100, would have arrived at the coast; after losses of 11 percent in the barracoons, 57 or so would have boarded the ships; of those 57, 51 would have stepped onto Brazilian soil, and 48 or 49 would have lived to behold their first master in the New World. The full "seasoning" period of 3–4 years would leave only 28 or 30 of the original 100 alive and working. A total "wastage" factor of about two-thirds may thus be estimated for the late-eighteenth-century Angolan trade, higher earlier in the trade, probably a bit lower by the 1820s, with slaves from the wetter equatorial latitudes always showing a lower mortality rate than those from Luanda and Benguela. As such, even at that late date it was a number amply large to rivet the fatalistic attention of the slavers in the Angolan trade and the merchants supporting them, to force all involved to stress speed, and to prompt the wealthy and powerful to organize its financial structures so as to avoid, where they could, the risks and costs resulting from mortality they could not control. It was literally, and sadly, true that "if few die the profit is certain, but if many are lost so also is their owner."

Joseph E. Inikori

Guns for Slaves

Nigerian-born Joseph Inikori, a historian at the University of Rochester, examines the flow of firearms into Africa in exchange for slaves. While stressing that African demand largely determined the quantity and quality of weaponry imported, he also argues that firearm imports stimulated warfare to obtain the slaves that paid for the guns.

The very high demand for guns which prevailed in West Africa in the eighteenth century is reflected in the fact that £1 sterling of guns had a much greater purchasing power in West Africa than £1 sterling of other goods. . . . The general pressure on gun manufacturers whenever the volume of English trade to West Africa was on the increase is a further proof of the great demand for guns in the trade. . . . It was not for nothing, therefore, that while the bill to abolish the slave trade was being debated in the British parliament, the gun manufacturers in and around Birmingham petitioned the House of Commons that the abolition of the slave trade would be extremely detrimental to them, because "by such abolition the greatest, and perhaps only, efficient nursery for artificers in the art of manufacturing of arms, would be destroyed."

But, important as firearms and ammunition were in West African trade at this time, we have no estimates of the quantities annually imported over particular periods. . . . Very fortunately, the account prepared for the British House of Commons in 1806 by William Irving, the Inspector General of Imports and Exports of Great Britain, shows the official and real values of ordnance and small arms exported from England to the coast of Africa for ten years, 1796–1805. Private records of English merchants trading to the coast of Africa show the prices of various types of guns (6,530 in all) exported to the African coast over the same period. From this the average price of guns exported from England to West Africa during this period has been calculated. . . . This average price has

"The Import of Firearms into West Africa, 1750–1807: A Quantitative Analysis," *Journal of African History*. 18.3, 1977, pp. 340–341, 343, 345–346, 348–351, 361–362. Reprinted with the permission of Cambridge University Press.

been used . . . to compute the number of guns annually exported from England to the coast of Africa. . . .

This calculation shows that between 1796 and 1805 a total of 1,615,309 guns were imported into West Africa from England, giving an annual average of 161,531. This may be compared with the statement made in 1765 by Lord Shelburne, that Birmingham alone had been sending more than 150,000 guns yearly to the African coast during the preceding twenty or twenty-five years. Taking into account quantities made in other parts of England (in particular Liverpool, Bristol and London) and sent to the African coast, Shelburne's statement could be interpreted to mean that about 200,000 guns were exported annually from England to the coast of Africa from the 1740s to 1765. . . .

The available evidence points to the fact that the other European countries who traded to the West Coast of Africa expended, at least, as many guns per unit of payment for goods purchased as the English. Therefore, the figures of imports from England can be used to estimate total imports from all parts, based on England's share of the total trade. . . . While some margin of error should be expected, the share of the total trade held by English merchants suggested by these figures, about 45 percent, may not be far from the mark, either way. Using this share with the import figures from England gives something between 444,000 and 333,000 as the total number of guns annually imported into the West Coast of Africa in the second half of the eighteenth century. . . .

The use to which the firearms imported were put seems to be the most controversial issue relating to firearms in Africa. At one time it was suggested that the firearms were "ostensibly for decorating the habitation of some Negro chieftain." This was refuted in 1790 by Alexander Falconbridge. Asked by a committee of enquiry whether he had "ever observed in the houses of any of the chiefs or great men, guns in a considerable number, as if kept for the purpose of show or ornament," he replied that "I have seen a great number in their houses with different kinds of goods, which I always understood were for trade," speaking particularly of Bonny where he had been more on shore than any other place.

More recently, it has been suggested that the most important use to which firearms were put in Africa was the protection of crops, the introduction of Indian corn being related to firearms. Other writers argue that the introduction of firearms into Africa represented an important technical innovation in slave gathering, the imported firearms being used primarily for raids and wars directed to the acquisition of captives for sale. . . .

The strong preference of the slave sellers for guns indicates very strongly the connexion between firearms and the acquisition of slaves. It reinforces the slave-gun cycle theory according to which the states and individual or groups of individual slave gatherers bought more firearms to capture more slaves to buy more firearms. . . . For some states the necessity may have been imposed by defence requirements. But for the professional slave gatherers the firearms represented important inputs.

This is not to say, however, that the guns acquired through the sale of slaves were employed solely for the gathering of slaves. The private slave gatherer who purchased firearms for that purpose may have at the same time used his private materials in time of need to fight the wars of the state, the clan, the village, etc.—wars of aggression, retaliation or defence, unconnected or only indirectly connected with slaving. Where slave gathering was a state affair, the slave-gathering state may not only have waged offensive wars calculated for the capture of slaves. Its slave-gathering activities would of necessity provoke attack by its neighbours and so be forced to defend itself. On the other hand, the "non-slaving" states that acquired large quantities of firearms through the sale of slaves did so in order to be able to defend themselves effectively against the onslaught of slave-gathering states and others. Because slave-gathering by its very nature provoked inter-territorial wars in different ways, in addition to inter-territorial conflicts arising from other causes, firearms acquired for slave-gathering or for defence against slave-gatherers may have been employed in a host of operations not directly connected with slave-gathering. And, for that matter, firearms purchased for slave-gathering and/or military purposes may also have been put to peaceful uses at the same time by the possessors, particularly for hunting and firing during ceremonial occasions. . . .

. . . The implication of all this is that the firearms imported into West Africa in the second half of the eighteenth century were used mainly for slave-gathering and the wars largely stimulated by the latter. This is why the most important slave exporting areas of the time, in particular, the Bonny trading area, were also the largest firearms importers in West Africa during this period. Not only did the Bonny trading area import more guns absolutely than other parts of West Africa, but also, it imported far more guns for every slave exported. Whereas the observations of contemporaries on the low quality of the firearms imported into West Africa are generally supported by the evidence, they contain a great deal of exaggeration. A large proportion of the firearms were very much better than the contemporary observers would want us to believe. What is important, however, is that the firearms seem largely to have served the purpose for which the African buyers purchased them. If this were not the case, firearms which were more efficient in meeting slave sellers' needs would have been brought to the coast in the face of the keen competition for slaves by the European merchants in the second half of the eighteenth century. It is remarkable, indeed, that the most important slave exporting area of this period, Bonny, tended to import more of the cheaper and low quality types of guns. Finally, it seems likely that the use to which firearms imported were put in West Africa changed over time. It is most likely that hunting became the most important employment of firearms after 1900.

John Thornton

Warfare and Slavery

In his widely read and influential study of Africans in the Atlantic world, John Thornton rejects the notion that a guns-for-slaves cycle drove the movement of slaves to the coast. Basing his argument on the nature of African warfare and the size of African states, Thornton relies heavily on the existence of large slave populations *within* African societies. Thus, his argument resembles that of Mungo Park two centuries earlier.

We have established so far that Africans were not under any direct commercial or economic pressure to deal in slaves. Furthermore, we have seen not only that Africans accepted the institution of slavery in their own societies, but that the special place of slaves as private productive property made slavery widespread. At the beginning, at least, Europeans were only tapping existing slave markets. Nevertheless, one need not accept that these factors alone can explain the slave trade. There are scholars who contend that although Europeans did not invade the continent and take slaves themselves, they did nevertheless promote the slave trade through indirect military pressure created by European control of important military technology, such as horses and guns. In this scenario—the "gun–slave cycle" or "horse–slave cycle"—Africans were compelled to trade in slaves, because without this commerce they could not obtain the necessary military technology (guns or horses) to defend themselves from any enemy. Furthermore, possession of the technology made them more capable of obtaining slaves, because successful war guaranteed large supplies of slaves.

Hence, through the operation of their control over the "means of destruction," . . . Europeans were able to influence Africans indirectly. They could direct commerce in ways that helped them and also compel Africans to wage wars that might otherwise not have been waged. This would cause Africans to seek more slaves than they needed for their own political and economic ends and depopulate the country against their wishes. The quantitative increase would exceed Africans' own judgment of a proper level of exports. In the end, this not only might increase economic dependence but could result in large-scale destruction of goods, tools, and ultimately development potential. Hence, in the end, Africans would be helpless, exploited junior partners in a commerce directed by Europe.

However, this argument will ultimately not be any more sustainable than the earlier commercial and economic ones. Certainly in the period before 1680, European technology was not essential for warfare, even if Africans did accept some of it. Likewise, it is much easier to assert than to demonstrate that Africans went to war against their will or solely to service the slave trade. Indeed the more we know about African warfare and resulting enslavement, the less clear and direct the connections between war and the export slave trade become.

The contemporary evidence strongly supports the idea that there was a direct connection between wars and slavery, both for domestic work and for export. . . .

Thus the fact that military enslavement was by far the most significant method is important, for it means that rulers were not, for the most part, selling their own subjects but people whom they, at least, regarded as aliens. The fact that many exported slaves were recent captives means that they were drawn from those captured in the course of warfare who had not yet been given an alternative employment within Africa. In these cases, rulers were deciding to forgo the potential future use of these slaves. Some of the exports were slaves whom local masters wished to dispose of for one reason or another and those who had been captured locally by brigands or judicially enslaved. . . .

The causes and motivations behind these wars are crucial for understanding the slave trade. Philip Curtin has examined the Senegambian slave trade of the eighteenth century and has proposed a schema for viewing African warfare that resulted in slave captures that can be fruitfully applied to the earlier period as well. He proposes that wars be classified as tending toward either an economic or a political model. In the economic model the wars were fought for the express purpose of acquiring slaves and perhaps to meet demands from European merchants; in the political model wars were fought for mostly political reasons, and slaves were simply a by-product that might yield a profit. Both models are seen as "ideal types," and individual wars might contain a mixture of motives, of course. On the whole, however, Curtin believes that the eighteenth-century Senegambian data support a political, rather than the economic, model.

Actually, discerning between an economic and a political model is not easy in practice. . . . This issue goes to the heart of the unusual nature of African politics and one of the matters that makes it different from Eurasian politics. Just as slavery took the place of landed property in Africa, so slave raids were equivalent to wars of conquest. For this reason, one must apply a different logic to African wars than the equations of political motives equals war of conquest and economic motives equals slave raid. This analysis changes our understanding of the objectives of war and must ultimately change our assessment of African warfare.

[Paul] Lovejoy, for example, has proposed that warfare was endemic in Africa as a result of political fragmentation. In other words, the very fact that Africa had few large-scale political units meant that wars would be more frequent, and thus enslavement increased. As fragmentation increased (a situation that he believes took place during the period of the slave trade), war naturally increased. Underlying this is the assumption that a political situation of small states would naturally lead to a movement to consolidate them into larger, Eurasian-style polities. Thus, although African politics actually determined the course of warfare, the intrinsic structure of those politics created more wars. Furthermore, one need not consider most wars as being explained by the economic model but by the political model, in which wars were an attempt to remedy the fragmentation by consolidating power. The failure to consolidate was thus the fuel that fired the slave trade.

Lovejoy's solution would be more helpful if it were true that there is a correlation between political centralization and peace, but unfortunately this does not seem to have been the case. . . .

In all, only perhaps 30 percent of Atlantic Africa's area was occupied by states with surface areas larger than 50,000 square kilometers, and at least half of that area was occupied by states in the medium-sized (50,000–150,000 square kilometers) range. The rest of Atlantic Africa was occupied by small, even tiny, states. . . . [B]roken down by population, a portion considerably greater than half of all the people in Atlantic Africa lived in the ministates, because these states were found in the most densely populated parts of the region.

Thus, one can say with confidence that political fragmentation was the norm in Atlantic Africa. By this account, the "typical" Atlantic African probably lived in a state that had absolute sovereignty but controlled a territory not exceeding 1,500 square kilometers (smaller than many American counties, perhaps the area occupied by a larger city). Populations might vary considerably; in the sparsely inhabited areas of central Africa, such a state might have 3,000–5,000 inhabitants, but on the densely inhabited Slave and Gold coasts it could control as many as 20,000–30,000 people. Virtually all the land from the Gambia River along the coast to the Niger delta was in states of this size, and much of the land stretching into the interior. In areas like Angola, ministates like these occupied the mountainous land between Kongo and Ndongo and the area of the Kwanza River between Ndongo and the larger states of the central highlands.

In short, enlargement of scale does not seem to have been a priority for leaders. Historians, anxious to assert that Africans did build large states, have to some extent focused too much attention on the empires and the medium-sized states, and thus the point is often overlooked. But the reasons for Africa's small states were probably not the result of some sort of backwardness that prevented them from seeing the advantages of larger units.

One reason for the smallness of scale (not necessarily the only one) may derive from the legal system, which did not make land private property, and may also explain why the Americas, the other world area without landed property, was also the home of small and even tiny states (outside its own few dramatic empires). In Eurasia, control over large areas of land was essential, because it was through grants of land that one rewarded followers, and this land was normally worked by tenants of one kind or another. Eurasians were relatively less interested in controlling people, for without land, the people's labor could not be assigned or its reward collected by landowners. African states were not concerned with land — for as long as there was no population pressure on the land, more people could always be accommodated. Hence, African wars that aimed at acquiring slaves were in fact the exact equivalent of Eurasian wars aimed at acquiring land. The state and its citizens could increase their wealth by acquiring slaves and did not need to acquire land, unless they were short of land at home (which was not the case, as far as we can tell).

The acquisition of slaves instead of land in wars had other advantages. Whereas conquest of land necessarily required administration of larger areas and expansion of military resources, the acquisition of slaves only required a short campaign that need not create any new administrative conditions. Moreover, conquest of land and its subsequent government usually required sharing the proceeds of land with existing landlords, state officials, and other wealthy members of the defeated state, who might be defeated but usually still had to be co-opted. Slaves, on the other hand, were unable to bargain as wealthy landlords might have and could be integrated individually or in small groups into existing structures. . . . Many Africans retained females from the raids and sold off males, because the Atlantic trade often demanded more males than females. . . .

Increasing wealth through warfare and enslavement was of course a cheap way of increasing power. Slaves could be captured in wars and in raids and carried back to the home territory by the victors and put to work, without the attacking armies having to conquer and occupy territory. For small states with small armies, this was a logical way to become richer. But of course, in the medium-sized states and empires, territorial expansion also took place. . . . [E]nslavement of the conquered population allowed the rulers of the expanding state to increase their personal wealth and also to build armies and administrative corps of direct dependents, just as the revenues from the conquered territories provided continuous new income. Thus, external expansion could also increase wealth, and the slaves that were a by-product of the wars of expansion could increase centralization at home.

All these factors resulted in an enormous slave population in Africa at the time of the arrival of the first Europeans and during the whole era of the slave trade. They meant that the necessary legal institutions and material resources were available to support a large slave market, one that anyone could participate in, including Europeans and other foreigners. Those who held slaves and did not intend to use them immediately could also sell them, and indeed, this is why the number of African merchants who dealt in slaves was large. . . .

This interpretation of African politics has reemphasized the importance of domestic slavery in Africa. Obviously, slaves were sufficiently important that one could find many in African societies. Likewise, as we have suggested, exports tended to be drawn from those slaves who were recently captured and had not yet found a place in the society of their enslavers. This aspect of slavery obviously places emphasis on the African decisions concerning which slaves to sell to Europeans and when. These decisions were in turn a product of the specific situation in each country, including price and availability of slaves. In large measure, the decision to participate in the Atlantic trade required that specific conditions be met, and countries often entered and left the trade. . . .

Although I have shown that African wars led to enslavement on a large scale and that African politics can explain even slaves raids that seem to have no political motive, the hypothesis that Europeans influenced African behavior through control over military resources must still be addressed. Given the significance of warfare for expansion of wealth in Africa, the military case must be carefully examined.

Certainly, Europeans did participate, wherever possible, in African politics, often as "military experts" or advisors, occasionally as armed mercenaries. They did this both officially through government-sponsored assistance programs, such as the aid that Portugal gave to Kongo in 1491, 1509, 1512, and 1570, or unofficially and without authorization, as in the support for Ndongo in the 1520s, the help that gunners gave to the Mane in the 1550s, and perhaps the assistance to Benin in the 1510s and 1520s. Other foreigners of European origin also provided assistance—Hawkins's help in Sierra Leone and Ulsheimer's in Benin are two more sixteenth- and early seventeenth-century examples. Acceptance of this assistance might simply be seen as the desire of centralizers to make use of foreign, rather than local, officials and dependents as a means of keeping local political debts to a minimum and of creating a dependent bureaucracy. But it is also clear that Europeans provided new military techniques and technology as well, perhaps at the price of demanding more vigorous participation in the slave trade than their patrons wished.

However, the kind of military assistance that Europeans in the sixteenth and seventeenth centuries could render in Africa was not as decisive as much of the writing on the "gun–slave" and "horse–slave" cycles implies. . . . European firearms and crossbows, the missile weapons that differed most from those in use in Africa, were designed to counteract armored cavalry or for naval warfare in Europe. Although they had great range and penetrating power (capabilities that developed out of a long-standing projectile-versus-armor contest), they had a very slow rate of fire. For Africans, who generally eschewed armor, the advantages of range (penetrating power being relatively unimportant) were more than offset by the disadvantages of the slow rate of fire, except in special circumstances. . . .

In summary, we can say that although European arms may have assisted African rulers in war in some cases, they were not decisive. It is unlikely that any European technology or assistance increased the Africans' chances of waging successful war (as the Portuguese in Angola could surely have attested) or that it made the attackers suffer fewer losses. Therefore, Europeans did not bring about some sort of military revolution that forced participation in the Atlantic trade as a price for survival.

It is possible to conclude that European influence over the slave trade may not have been significant in the first century and a half of the trade simply by acknowledging that Africans had slaves and a slave trade already, and that early forms of European military technology and organization were not critical to the success of African armies. But it might still be possible to argue that ultimately Europeans forced Africans to exceed their capacity to deliver slaves at a later period when high demands for slaves and improved military technology played a more important role. . . .

African exports of slaves expanded dramatically beginning in the mid-seventeenth century, to the point where the number of exported slaves grew from being a relatively small number relative to the total population of the African regions from which they were taken to having a major demographic impact. Virtually all the work on the volume of the slave trade shows that the total number of slaves exported increased relative to the total areas or to the (estimated) African populations involved. The negative demographic impacts, although somewhat apparent in the beginning of the period in some areas (such as central Africa), intensified and spread to virtually the whole of Atlantic Africa. In the late eighteenth century much of Africa reached demographic exhaustion. . . .

There are several possible explanations for the growth of the slave trade in these areas. Both Curtin and Lovejoy have suggested that increases in the price of slaves, which can be documented for the period, might have enticed more slaves from their owners. It may have encouraged more "economic model" wars, and it may have persuaded owners that it would be better to forgo domestic use in exchange for the higher price available from the Atlantic trade. Also, owners of slaves living far from the coast might be willing to bear the transport costs of moving slaves to the coast if a higher price were offered. This explanation does give European merchants a role in the growth of enslavement in Africa, but it clearly places the economic decisions in the hands of Africans.

Other explanations focus simply on the increase in wars caused by African political dynamics, discounting the role of trade. The connection between African trade, control over the trade, and politics is a complex and controversial one, but for our purposes, such an explanation still rules out European coercion.

Finally, of course, there is the idea that European coercion, either direct or indirect, is responsible for the increase in warfare, which resulted in more slaves for the Atlantic. In the late seventeenth century the musket was developed into a more effective weapon. Moreover, very large numbers of such weapons were produced as European armies re-armed into bodies in which every infantryman carried a musket. Naturally enough, larger quantities of the improved weapons were also available to ship to Africa, where, it is argued, they may have revolutionized warfare. Thus, by directing weapons selectively to those willing to supply slaves, European merchants may have been able to effect the gun–slave cycle. . . .

African rulers continued to engage in wars, not unlike those of previous centuries, and naturally, as the new weapons figured more prominently in warfare, acquiring supplies of the weapons became important. Thus, in the late seventeenth century and into the eighteenth century, civil wars troubled the Senegambian states, and often pretenders sought and acquired weapons in order to make their claims. But it would be incorrect to say that somehow Europeans had persuaded the potential candidates to seek power in order to get slaves, even if they did delight in the prospect of increased slaves as a result. Senegalese state leaders built up substantial armies of slave soldiers, and often these armies engaged in local raiding (frequently without royal permission), which proved quite disruptive, but neither the origin of these armed forces nor their kings' lack of ability or desire to control them was the result of European policies or pressures.

In conclusion, then, we must accept that African participation in the slave trade was voluntary and under the control of African decision makers. This was not just at the surface level of daily exchange but even at deeper levels. Europeans possessed no means, either economic or military, to compel African leaders to sell slaves.

The willingness of Africa's commercial and political elite to supply slaves should be sought in their own internal dynamics and history. Institutional factors predisposed African societies to hold slaves, and the development of Africa's domestic economy encouraged large-scale trading and possession of slaves long before Europeans visited African shores. The increase in warfare and political instability in some regions may well have contributed to the growth of the slave trade from those regions, but one cannot easily assign the demand for slaves as the cause of the instability, especially as our knowledge of African politics provides many more internal causes. Given the commercial interests of African states and the existing slave market in private hands in Africa, it is not surprising that Africans were able to respond to European demands for slaves, as long as the prices attracted them.

PART

 **III** The Middle
Passage

—————— VARIETY OF OPINION ——————

*I was now persuaded that I had got into a world of bad spirits, and that
they were going to kill me.*

OLAUDAH EQUIANO

*Here we have nearly one-third given apparently for the average loss on
the passage, and this estimated by the slave-dealers themselves on the
American side of the Atlantic.*

THOMAS FOWELL BUXTON

*One conclusion that might be drawn is that, in reducing the estimated
total export of slaves from about twenty million to about ten million, the
harm done to African societies is also reduced by half. This is obvious
nonsense.*

PHILIP D. CURTIN

*Thousands of ship crossings have now been statistically analyzed, and
none show a correlation of any significance between either tonnage or
space available and mortality.*

HERBERT S. KLEIN

[I]t appears that over the three and a half centuries of the transatlantic slave trade, perhaps 15 per cent (or over 1.5 million) of those who embarked at the African coast died during the Atlantic crossing.

DAVID ELTIS AND DAVID RICHARDSON

Olaudah Equiano

An African's Ordeal

Few Africans who crossed the Atlantic on a slave ship had both the opportunity and the desire to write of their experiences. One who did was Olaudah Equiano (who also used the name Gustavus Vassa). Modern scholarship has questioned whether the vivid details he recounts of a passage in the 1750s from his home among the Igbo people of modern Nigeria to the West Indies are really personal reminiscences. Even if he enhanced his account with the recollections of others, it captures the horrors and suffering of the infamous Middle Passage of the three-sided trade linking Europe, Africa, and the Americas.

One day, when all our people were gone out to their works as usual, and only I and my dear sister were left to mind the house, two men and a woman got over our walls, and in a moment seized us both and, without giving us time to cry out, or to make resistance, they stopped our mouths, and ran off with us into the nearest wood. Here they tied our hands, and continued to carry us as far as they could, till night came on, when we reached a small house, where the robbers halted for refreshment, and spent the night. We were then unbound, but were not able to take any food; and, being quite overpowered by fatigue and grief, our only relief was some sleep, which allayed our misfortune for a short time. The next morning we left the house, and continued travelling all the day. For a long time we had kept to the woods, but at last we came to a road which I believed I knew. I now had some hopes of being

From *The Interesting Narrative of the Life of Olaudah Equiano, or Gustavus Vassa, the African*, 6th ed. (London, 1793), pp. 31–33, 45–49, 51–53.

Olaudah Equiano. (Royal Albert Memorial Museum, Exeter, Devon, UK/Bridgeman Art Library International Ltd., London-New York)

delivered; for we had advanced but a little way before I discovered some people at a distance, on which I began to cry out for their assistance; but my cries had no other effect than to make them tie me faster and stop my mouth, and then put me in a large sack. They also stopped my sister's mouth, and tied her hands, and in this manner we proceeded till we were out of the sight of these people. When we went to rest the following night they offered us some victuals; but we refused them; and the only comfort we had was in being in one another's arms all that night, and bathing each other with our tears. But alas! We were soon deprived of even the smallest comfort of weeping together. The next day proved a day of greater sorrow than I had yet experienced; for my sister and I were separated, while we lay clasped in each other's arms: it was in vain that we besought them not to part us: she was torn from me, and immediately carried away, while I was in such a state of distraction not to be described. I cried and grieved continually; and for several days did not eat any thing but what they forced into my mouth. At length, after many days travelling, during which I had often changed masters, I got into the hands of a chieftain, in a very pleasant country. . . .

. . . I continued to travel, sometimes by land, sometimes by water, through several different countries, and various nations, till, at the end of six months after I had been kidnapped, I arrived at the sea coast. . . .

The first object which saluted my eyes when I arrived on the coast was the sea, and a slave ship, which was then riding at anchor, and waiting for its cargo. These filled me with astonishment, which was soon converted into terror, which I am yet at a loss to describe nor the then feelings of my mind. When I was carried on board I was immediately handled, and tossed up, to see if I were sound by some of the crew; and I was now persuaded that I had got into a world of bad spirits, and that they were going to kill me. Their complexions too differing so much from ours, their long hair, and the language they spoke, which was very different from any I had ever heard, united to confirm me in this belief. Indeed, such were the horrors of my views and fears at the moment, that, if ten thousand worlds had been my own, I would have parted with them all to have exchanged my condition with that of the meanest slave in my own country. When I looked around the ship too, and saw a large furnace or copper boiling, and a multitude of black people of every description chained together, every one of their countenances expressing dejection and sorrow, I no longer doubted of my fate; and, quite overpowered with horror and anguish, I fell motionless on the deck and fainted. When I recovered a little, I found some black people about me, who, I believed were some of those who brought me on board, and had been receiving their pay; they talked to me in order to cheer me, but all in vain. I asked them if we were not to be eaten by those white men with horrible looks, red faces, and long hair? They told me I was not; and one of the crew brought me a small portion of spirituous liquor in a wine glass; but, being afraid of him, I would not take it out of his hand. One of the blacks therefore took it from him, and gave it to me, and I took a little down my palate, which, instead of reviving me, as they thought it would, threw me into the greatest consternation at the strange feeling it produced, having never tasted any such liquor before. Soon after this, the blacks who brought me on board went off, and left me abandoned to despair. I now saw myself deprived of any chance of returning to my native country, or even the least glimpse of hope of gaining the shore, which I now considered as friendly; and I even wished for my former slavery, in preference to my present situation, which was filled with horrors of every kind, still heightened by my ignorance of what I was to undergo. I was not long suffered to indulge my grief; I was soon put down under the decks, and there I received such a salutation in my nostrils as I had never experienced in my life; so that, with the loath-someness of the stench, and crying together, I became so sick and low that I was not able to eat, nor had I the least desire to taste any thing. I now wished for the last friend, Death, to relieve me; but soon, to my grief, two of the white men offered me eatables; and, on my refusing to eat, one of them held me fast by the hands, and laid me across, I think, the wind-lass, and tied my feet, while the other flogged me severely. I had never ex-perienced any thing of this kind before; and, although not used to the water, I naturally feared that element the first time I saw it, yet, neverthe-less, could I have got over the nettings, I would have jumped over the side, but I could not; and, besides, the crew used to watch us very closely who were not chained down to the decks, lest we should leap into the water: and I have seen some of these poor African prisoners severely cut for attempting to do so, and hourly whipped for not eating. This indeed was often the case with myself. In a little time after, amongst the poor chained men I found some of my own nation, which in a small degree gave ease to my mind. I inquired of them what was to be done with us? They gave me to understand we were to be carried to these white people's country to work for them. I was then a little revived, and thought if it were no worse than working, my situation was not so desperate: but still I feared I should be put to death, the white people looked and acted, as I thought, in so savage a manner; for I had never seen among any people such in-stances of brutal cruelty; and this not only shewn toward us blacks, but also to some of the whites themselves. One white man in particular I saw, when we were permited [*sic*] to be on deck, flogged so unmercifully that he died in consequence of it; and they tossed him over the side as they would have done to a brute. This made me fear these people the more; and I expected nothing less than to be treated in the same manner. . . .

The stench of the hold while we were on the coast was so intolerably loathsome, that it was dangerous to remain there for any time, and some of us had been permitted to stay on the deck for the fresh air; but now that the whole ship's cargo were confined together, it became absolutely pesti-lential. The closeness of the place, and the heat of the climate, added to the number in the ship, which was so crowded that each had scarcely room to turn himself, almost suffocated us. This produced copious per-spirations, so that the air became unfit for respiration, from a variety of loathsome smells, and brought on a sickness amongst the slaves, of which many died, thus falling victims to the improvident avarice, as I may call it, of their purchasers. This wretched situation was again aggravated by the galling of the chains, now become insupportable; and the filth of the necessary tubs, into which the children often fell, and were almost suffocated. The shrieks of the women and the groans of the dying, rendered the whole a scene of horror almost inconceivable. Happily perhaps for myself I was soon reduced so low here that it was thought necessary to keep me almost always on deck; and from my extreme youth I was not put in fetters. In this situation I expected every hour to share the fate of my companions, some of whom were almost daily brought on deck at the point of death, which I began to hope would soon put an end to my miseries. Often did I think many of the inhabitants of the deep much more happy than myself; I envied them the freedom they enjoyed, and as often wished I could change my condition for theirs. Every circumstance I met with served only to render my state more painful, and heightened my apprehensions and my opinion of the cruelty of the whites. One day they had taken a number of fishes, and when they had killed and satisfied themselves with as many as they thought fit, to our astonishment who were on the deck, rather than give any of them to us to eat, as we expected, they tossed the remaining fish into the sea again, although we begged and prayed for some as well as we could, but in vain; some of my countrymen, being possessed by hunger, took an opportunity, when they thought no one saw them of trying to get a little privately, but they were discovered, and the attempt procured them some very severe floggings.

One day, when we had a smooth sea, and moderate wind, two of my wearied countrymen, who were chained together (I was near them at the time), preferring death to such a life of misery, somehow made through the nettings, and jumped into the sea; immediately another quite dejected fellow, who, on account of his illness was suffered to be out of irons, also followed their example; and I believe many more would very soon have done the same, if they had not been prevented by the ship's crew who were instantly alarmed. Those of us that were the most active were in a minute put down under the deck; and there was such a noise and confusion amongst the people of the ship as I have never heard before, to stop her, and get the boat out to go after the slaves. However, two of the wretches were drowned, but they got the other, and afterwards flogged him unmercifully, for thus attempting to prefer death to slavery. In this manner we continued to undergo more hardships than I can now relate; hardships which are inseparable from this accursed trade.

Thomas Fowell Buxton

An Abolitionist's Evidence

Sir Thomas Fowell Buxton was a member of the British Parliament who turned his attention from domestic prison reform to the abolition of the slave trade. His major work, the *African Slave Trade*, was published in 1839, long after Britain had ceased carrying slaves but before other nations had done so. The grisly details of the slave trade Buxton gleaned from eyewitnesses and official sources were meant to keep up pressure on governments to end the trade. Note his mention of the abolitionist work of Olaudah Equiano (Gustavus Vassa) as an adult.

It was well observed by Mr. Fox, in a debate on the Slave Trade, that

> *True humanity consists not in a squeamish ear; it consists not in starting or shrinking at such tales as these, but in a disposition of heart to relieve misery. True humanity appertains rather to the mind than to the nerves, and prompts men to use real and active endeavours to execute the actions which it suggests.*

In the spirit of this observation, I now go on to remark, that the first feature of this deadly passage, which attracts our attention, is the evident insufficiency, in point of tonnage, of the vessels employed, for the cargoes of human beings which they are made to contain. . . .

We have a faithful description of the miseries of the middle passage, from the pen of an eye-witness, Mr. Falconbridge. His account refers to a period antecedent to 1790. He tells us that

> *The men Negroes, on being brought aboard ship, are immediately fastened together two and two, by handcuffs on their wrists, and by irons riveted on their legs. . . . They are frequently stowed so close as to admit of no other posture than lying on their sides. Neither will the height between decks, unless directly under the grating, permit them the indulgence of an erect posture, especially where there are platforms, which is generally the case. These platforms are a kind of shelf, about eight or nine feet in breadth, extending from the side of the ship towards the*

From Thomas Fowell Buxton, *The Atlantic Slave Trade and Its Remedy* (London, 1840), pp. 122, 124–133, 135–139, 172–175.

center. They are placed nearly midway between the decks, at the distance of two or three feet from each deck. Upon these the Negroes are stowed in the same manner as they are on the deck underneath.

After mentioning some other arrangements, he goes on to say,

It often happens that those who are placed at a distance from the buckets, in endeavouring to get to them, tumble over their companions, in consequence of their being shackled. These accidents, although unavoidable, are productive of continual quarrels, in which some of them are always bruised. In this distressed situation they desist from the attempt, and . . . this becomes a fresh source of broils and disturbances, and tends to render the situation of the poor captive wretches still more uncomfortable.

In favourable weather they are fed upon deck, but in bad weather their food is given to them below. Numberless quarrels take place among them during their meals; more especially when they are put upon short allowance, which frequently happens. In that case, the weak are obliged to be content with a very scanty portion. Their allowance of water is about half a pint each, at every meal.

Upon the negroes refusing to take sustenance, I have seen coals of fire, glowing hot, put on a shovel, and placed so near their lips as to scorch and burn them, and this has been accompanied with threats of forcing them to swallow the coals, if they any longer persisted in refusing to eat. These means have generally the desired effect. I have also been credibly informed that a certain captain in the Slave Trade poured melted lead on such of the negroes as obstinately refused their food.

Falconbridge then tells us that the negroes are sometimes compelled to dance and to sing, and that, if any reluctance is exhibited, the cat-o'-nine-tails is employed to enforce obedience. He goes on to mention the unbounded licence given to the officers and crew of the slavers, as regards the women; and, speaking of the officers, he says, they

are sometimes guilty of such brutal excesses as disgrace human nature. . . . But, . . . the hardships and inconveniences suffered by the negroes during the passage are scarcely to be enumerated or conceived. They are far more violently affected by the sea-sickness than the Europeans. It frequently terminates in death, especially among the women. The exclusion of the fresh air is among the most intolerable. Most ships have air-ports; but, whenever the sea is rough and the rain heavy, it becomes necessary to shut these and every other conveyance by which air is admitted. The fresh air being thus excluded, the negroes' rooms very soon grow intolerably hot. The confined air, rendered noxious by the effluvia exhaled from

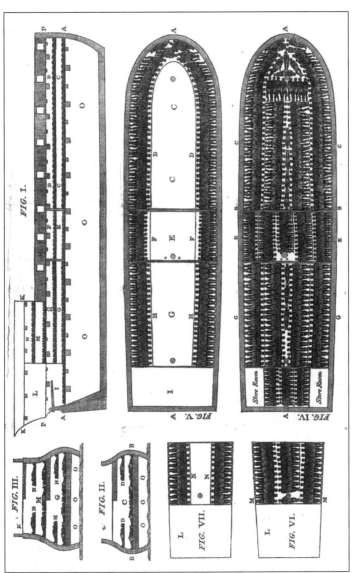

Plan for the distribution of slaves in the British slave ship *Brookes*. (Peabody Essex Museum)

their bodies, and by being repeatedly breathed, soon produces fevers and fluxes, which generally carry off great numbers of them. During the voyages I made, I was frequently a witness to the fatal effects of this exclusion of the fresh air. I will give one instance, as it serves to convey some idea, though a very faint one, of the state of these unhappy beings. Some wet and blowing weather having occasioned the portholes to be shut, and the gratings to be covered, fluxes and fevers among the negroes ensued. My profession requiring it, I frequently went down among them, till at length their apartments became so extremely hot as to be only sufferable for a very short time. But the excessive heat was not the only thing that rendered their situation intolerable. The deck, that is, the floor of their rooms, was so covered with the blood and mucus which had proceeded from them in consequence of the flux, that it resembled a slaughter-house. It is not in the power of human imagination to picture to itself a situation more dreadful or more disgusting. . . .

He proceeds to notice the case of a Liverpool vessel which took on board at the Bonny River nearly 700 slaves (more than three to each ton!); and Falconbridge says,

By purchasing so great a number, the slaves were so crowded, that they were even obliged to lie one upon another. This occasioned such a mortality among them, that, without meeting with unusual bad weather, or having a longer voyage than common, nearly one-half of them died before the ship arrived in the West Indies.

He then describes the treatment of the sick as follows:

The place allotted for the sick negroes is under the half-deck, where they lie on the bare plank. By this means, those who are emaciated frequently have their skin, and even their flesh, entirely rubbed off, by the motion of the ship, from the prominent parts of the shoulders, elbows, and hips, so as to render the bones in those parts quite bare. The excruciating pain which the poor sufferers feel from being obliged to continue in so dreadful a situation, frequently for several weeks, in case they happen to live so long, is not to be conceived or described. Few indeed are ever able to withstand the fatal effects of it. The surgeon, upon going between decks in the morning, frequently finds several of the slaves dead, and, among the men, sometimes a dead and a living negro fastened by their irons together.

He then states that surgeons are driven to engage in the "Guinea Trade" by the confined state of their finances; and that, at most, the only way in which a surgeon can render himself useful, is by seeing that the food is properly cooked and distributed to the slaves:

When once the fever and dysentery get to any height at sea, a cure is scarcely ever effected.

One-half, sometimes two-thirds, and even beyond that, have been known to perish. Before we left Bonny River no less than fifteen died of fevers, and dysenteries, occasioned by their confinement.

Falconbridge also told the Committee of 1790, that,

in stowing the slaves, they wedge them in, so that they had not as much room as a man in his coffin: that, when going from one side of their rooms to the other, he always took off his shoes, but could not avoid pinching them; and that he had the marks on his feet where they bit and scratched him. Their confinement in this situation was so injurious, that he has known them to go down apparently in good health at night, and be found dead in the morning.

Any comment on the statement of Falconbridge must be superfluous: he had been a surgeon in slave-ships, he was a respectable witness before the Committee of Inquiry in 1790, and gave the substance of this statement in evidence. And it ought to be borne in mind that he was an eye-witness of the scenes which he has described. His evidence is the more valuable, when it is considered that we have long been debarred from testimony equally credible and direct: as, since 1807, Britain has taken no part in the slave-traffic; and it has been the policy of the foreign nations who have continued the trade to conceal, as far as they could, the horrors and miseries which are its attendants.

Mr. Granville Sharpe (the zealous advocate of the negro) brought forward a case which aroused public attention to the horrors of this passage. In his Memoirs we have the following account taken from his private memoranda:

March 19, 1783. Gustavus Vas[s]a called on me with an account of 132 negroes being thrown alive into the sea, from on board an English slave-ship.

The circumstances of this case could not fail to excite a deep interest. The master of a slave-ship trading from Africa to Jamaica, and having 440 slaves on board, had thought fit, on a pretext that he might be distressed on his voyage for want of water, to lessen the consumption of it in the vessel, by throwing overboard 132 of the most sickly among the slaves. On his return to England, the owners of the ship claimed from the insurers the full value of those drowned slaves, on the ground that there was an absolute necessity for throwing them into the sea, in order to save the remaining crew, and the ship itself. The underwriters contested the existence of the alleged necessity; or, if it had existed, attributed it to the ignorance and improper conduct of the master of the vessel. This contest of pecuniary interest brought to light a scene of horrid brutality which had been acted during the execution of a detestable plot. From the trial it appeared that the ship Zong, *Luke Collingwood master, sailed from the island of St. Thomas, on the coast of Africa, September 6, 1781, with 440 slaves and fourteen whites on board, for Jamaica, and that in the November following she fell in with that island; but, instead of proceeding to some port, the master, mistaking, as he alleges, Jamaica for Hispaniola, ran her to leeward. Sickness and mortality had by this time taken place on board the crowded vessel: so that, between the time of leaving the coast of Africa and the 29th of November, sixty slaves and seven white people had died; and a great number of the surviving slaves were then sick and not likely to live. On that day the master of the ship called together a few of the officers, and stated to them that, if the sick slaves died a natural death, the loss would fall on the owners of the ship; but, if they were thrown alive into the sea, on any sufficient pretext of necessity for the safety of the ship, it would be the loss of the underwriters, alleging, at the same time, that it would be less cruel to throw sick wretches into the sea, than to suffer them to linger out a few days under the disorder with which they were afflicted.*

To this inhuman proposal the mate, James Kelsal, at first objected; but Collingwood at length prevailed on the crew to listen to it. He then chose out from the cargo 132 slaves, and brought them on deck, all or most of whom were sickly, and not likely to recover, and he ordered the crew by turns to throw them into the sea. "A parcel" of them were accordingly thrown overboard, and, on counting over the remainder the next morning, it appeared that the number so drowned had been fifty-four. He then ordered another parcel to be thrown over, which, on a second counting on the succeeding day, was proved to have amounted to forty-two.

On the third day the remaining thirty-six were brought on deck, and, as these now resisted the cruel purpose of their masters, the arms of twenty-six were fettered with irons, and the savage crew proceeded with the diabolical work, casting them down to join their comrades of the former days. Outraged misery could endure no longer; the ten last victims sprang disdainfully from the grasp of their tyrants, defied their power, and, leaping into the sea, felt a momentary triumph in the embrace of death. . . .

Such were some of the cruelties of the middle passage towards the end of the last century; and it might have been expected that, since that time, some improvement should have taken place; but it is not so: the treatment of slaves by the British, subsequent to the Slave Regulation Act, and down to 1808, was mildness itself, when compared with the miseries consequent on the trade, and the system which has been pursued in the vain attempt to put it down, since that period to the present time. . . .

Since 1808 the English Government has, with various success, been indefatigably engaged in endeavouring to procure the co-operation of foreign powers for the suppression of the Slave Trade. In virtue of the treaties which have been entered into, many vessels engaged in the traffic have been captured; and much information has been obtained, which has been regularly laid before Parliament. A few of the cases which have been detailed will now be noticed, for the purpose of ascertaining whether the miseries which have been narrated have ceased to exist; or whether they do not *now* exist in a more intense degree than at any former period.

The first case I notice is that of the Spanish brig *Carlos,* captured in 1814. In this vessel of 200 tons, 512 negroes had been put on board (nearly 180 *more* than the complement allowed on the proportion of five slaves to three tons). The captor reported that

> *they were so miserably fed, clothed, &c., that any idea of the horrors of the Slave Trade would fall short of what I saw. Eighty were thrown overboard before we captured her. In many instances I saw the bones coming through the skin from starvation.*

In the same year (1814) the schooner *Aglae,* of 40 tons, was captured with a cargo of 152 negroes (nearly four to each ton).

> *The only care seemed to have been to pack them as close as possible, and tarpaulin was placed over tarpaulin, in order to give the vessel the appearance of being laden with a well-stowed cargo of cotton and rice.*

In 1815 a lieutenant of the navy thus describes the state of a Portuguese slaver, the *St. Joaquim:* he says,

> *That within twenty-two days after the vessel had left Mozambique thirteen of the slaves had died: that between the capture and their arrival at Simon's Bay, the survivors of them were all sickly and weak, and ninety-two of them afflicted with the flux; that the slaves were all stowed together, perfectly naked, and nothing but rough, unplaned planks to crouch down upon, in a hold situated over their water and provisions, the place being little more than two feet in height, and the space allowed for each slave so small, that it was impossible for them to avoid touching and pressing upon those immediately surrounding. The greater part of them were fastened, some three together, by one leg, each in heavy iron shackles, a very large proportion of them having the flux. Thus they were compelled,*

&c. (here a scene of disgusting wretchedness is described.)

> *The pilot being asked by Captain Baker how many he supposed would have reached their destination, replied, "About half the number that were embarked."*

We have next the case of the *Rodeur*, as stated in a periodical work, devoted to medical subjects, and published at Paris. This vessel, it appears, was of 200 tons burden. She took on board a cargo of 160 negroes, and after having been fifteen days on her voyage, it was remarked that the slaves had contracted a considerable redness of the eyes, which spread with singular rapidity. At this time they were limited to eight ounces of water a-day for each person, which quantity was afterwards reduced to the half of a wine-glass. By the advice of the surgeon, the slaves who were in the hold were brought upon deck for the advantage of fresh air; but it became necessary to abandon this expedient, as many of them who were affected with nostalgia threw themselves into the sea, locked in each other's arms. The ophthalmia, which had spread so rapidly and frightfully among the Africans, soon began to infect all on board, and to create alarm for the crew. The danger of infection, and perhaps the cause which produced the disease, were increased by a violent dysentery, attributed to the use of rain-water. The number of the blind augmented every day. The vessel reached Guadaloupe on June 21, 1819, her crew being in a most deplorable condition. Three days after her arrival, the only man who during the voyage had withstood the influence of the contagion, and whom Providence appeared to have preserved as a guide to his unfortunate companions, was seized with the same malady. Of the negroes, thirty-nine had become perfectly blind, twelve had lost one eye, and fourteen were affected with blemishes more or less considerable.

This case excited great interest, and several additional circumstances connected with it were given to the public. It was stated that the captain caused several of the negroes who were prevented in the attempt to throw themselves overboard, to be shot and hung, in the hope that the example might deter the rest from a similar conduct. It is further stated, that upwards of thirty of the slaves who became blind were thrown into the sea and drowned; upon the principle that had they been landed at Guadaloupe, no one would have bought them, while by throwing them overboard the expense of maintaining them was avoided, and a ground was laid for a claim on the underwriters by whom the cargo had been insured, who are said to have allowed the claim, and made good the value of the slaves thus destroyed.

What more need be said in illustration of the extremity of suffering induced by the middle passage, as demonstrated by the case of the *Rodeur?* But the supplement must not be omitted. At the time when only one man could see to steer that vessel, a large ship approached,

> which appeared to be totally at the mercy of the wind and the waves. The crew of this vessel, hearing the voices of the crew of the Rodeur, *cried out most vehemently for help. They told the melancholy tale as they passed along,—that their ship was a Spanish slave-ship, the* St. Leon; *and that a contagion had seized the eyes of all on board, so that there was not one individual sailor or slave who could see. But alas! this pitiable narrative was in vain; for no help could be given. The* St. Leon *passed on, and was never more heard of! . . .*

I will endeavour to give a summary of the extent of the mortality incident to the middle passage. Newton states, that in his time it amounted to one-fourth, on the average, of the number embarked.

From papers presented to the House of Lords, in 1799, it appears that, in the year 1791, (three years after the passing of the Slave Carrying Regulation Act,) of 15,754 negroes embarked for the West Indies, &c., 1378 died during the passage, the average length of which was fifty-one days, showing a mortality of 8¾ per cent.

The amount of the mortality in 1792 was still greater. Of 31,554 slaves carried from Africa, no fewer than 5,413 died on the passage, making somewhat more than 17 per cent. in fifty-one days.

Captain Owen, in a communication to the Admiralty, on the Slave Trade with the eastern coast of Africa, in 1823, states

> That the ships which use this traffic consider they make an excellent voyage if they save one-third of the number embarked: some vessels are so fortunate as to save one-half of their cargo alive.

Captain Cook says, in the communication to which I have before alluded, as to the East coast traffic,

> If they meet with bad weather, in rounding the Cape, their sufferings are beyond description; and in some instances one-half of the lives on board are sacrificed. In the case of the Napoleon, *from Quilimane, the loss amounted to two-thirds. It was stated to me by Captains and Super-cargoes of other slavers, that they made a profitable voyage if they lost fifty per cent.; and that this was not uncommon.*

Caldcleugh says, "Scarcely two-thirds live to be landed."

Governor Maclean, of Cape Coast, who has had many opportunities of acquiring information on the subject, has stated to me, that he considers the average of deaths on the passage to amount to one-third.

Captain Ramsay, R.N., who was a long time on service with the Preventive Squadron, also stated to me, that the mortality on the passage across the Atlantic must be greater than the loss on the passage to Sierra Leone, from the greater liberty allowed after capture, and from the removal of the shackles. He believes the average loss to be one-third.

Rear-Admiral Sir Graham Eden Hamond, Commander-in-Chief on the South American station, in 1834, thus writes to the British Consul at Monte Video:

> A *slave-brig of 202 tons was brought into this port with 521 slaves on board. The vessel is said to have cleared from Monte Video in August last, under a licence to import 650 African colonists.*
>
> *The licence to proceed to the coast of Africa is accompanied by a curious document, purporting to be an application from two Spaniards at Monte Video, named Villaca and Barquez, for permission to import 650 colonists, and 250 more*—to cover the deaths on the voyage.

Here we have nearly one-third given apparently for the average loss on the passage, and this estimated by the slave-dealers themselves on the American side of the Atlantic.

Philip D. Curtin

A Historian's Recount

The horrors that abolitionists such as Equiano and Buxton catalogued remain central to our understanding of the Middle Passage, but many modern historians have worked hard to define what was typical of a slaving voyage. Philip Curtin's immensely important 1969 study did much to start this trend by showing that the once accepted estimates of the size and destinations of the slave trade were of dubious accuracy. In the last part of this excerpt, this

Curtin, Philip D. *The Atlantic Slave Trade.* © 1969. Reprinted by permission of the University of Wisconsin Press.

historian of Africa and the Atlantic summarizes his recalculation of the origins, destinations, and overall size of the slave trade.

This book . . . seeks to explore old knowledge, not to present new information. Its central aim is to bring together bits and pieces of incommensurate information already published, and to do this for only one aspect of the trade—the measurable number of people brought across the Atlantic. How many? When? From what parts of Africa? To what destinations in the New World? . . .

This book is . . . written with an implicit set of rules that are neither those of monographic research, nor yet those of a survey. Historical standards for monographic research require the author to examine every existing authority on the problem at hand, and every archival collection where part of the answer may be found. This has not been done. The rulebook followed here sets another standard. I have surveyed the literature on the slave trade, but not exhaustively. Where the authorities on some regional aspect of the trade have arrived at a consensus, and that consensus appears to be reasonable in the light of other evidence, I have let it stand. Where no consensus exists, or a gap occurs in a series of estimates, I have tried to construct new estimates. But these stop short of true research standards. I have not tried to go beyond the printed sources, nor into the relevant archives, even when they are known to contain important additional data. The task is conceived as that of building with the bricks that exist, not in making new ones. This often requires the manipulation of existing data in search of commensurates. In doing this, I have tried to show the steps that lead from existing data to the new synthesis. Not everyone will agree with all the assumptions that go into the process, nor with all the forms of calculation that have been used. But this book is not intended to be a definitive study, only a point of departure that will be modified in time as new research produces new data, and harder data worthy of more sophisticated forms of calculation. It will have served its purpose if it challenges others to correct and complete its findings.

This point is of the greatest importance in interpreting any of the data that follow. One danger in stating numbers is to find them quoted later on with a degree of certitude that was never intended. This is particularly true when percentages are carried to tenths of 1 per cent, whereas in fact the hoped-for range of accuracy may be plus or minus 20 per cent of actuality. Let it be said at the outset, then, that most of the quantities that follow are wrong. They are not intended to be precise as given, only approximations where a result falling within 20 per cent of actuality is a "right" answer—that is, a successful result, given the quality of the underlying data. It should also be understood that some estimates will not even reach that standard of accuracy. They are given only as the most probable figures at the present state of knowledge. These considerations have made it convenient to round out most quantities to the nearest one hundred, including data taken from other authors.

All of this may seem to imply estimates of limited value on account of their limited accuracy. For many historical purposes, greater accuracy is not required, and some of the most significant implications of this quantitative study would follow from figures still less accurate than these. Their principal value is not, in any case, the absolute number, an abstraction nearly meaningless in isolation. It is, instead, the comparative values, making it possible to measure one branch of the slave trade against another.

Some readers may miss the sense of moral outrage traditional in histories of the trade. This book will have very little to say about the evils of the slave trade, still less in trying to assign retrospective blame to the individuals or groups who were responsible. This omission in no way implies that the slave trade was morally neutral; it clearly was not. The evils of the trade, however, can be taken for granted as a point long since proven beyond dispute. . . .

The principal secondary authorities and the principal textbooks are, indeed, in remarkable agreement on the general magnitude of the [Atlantic slave] trade. Most begin with the statement that little is known about the subject, pass on to the suggestion that it may be impossible to make an accurate numerical estimate, and then make an estimate. The style is exemplified by Basil Davidson's *Black Mother*, the best recent general history of the slave trade.

> *First of all, what were the round numbers involved in this forced emigration to which the African-European trade gave rise, beginning in the fifteenth century and ending in the nineteenth? The short answer is that nobody knows or ever will know: either the necessary records are missing or they were never made. The best one can do is to construct an estimate from confused and incomplete data.*
>
> *. . . For the grand total of slaves landed alive in the lands across the Atlantic an eminent student of population statistics, Kuczynski, came*

to the conclusion that fifteen millions might be "rather a conservative figure." Other writers have accepted this figure, though as a minimum: some have believed it was much higher than this.

Roland Oliver and J. D. Fage in their *Short History of Africa*, the most widely-read history of Africa to appear so far, are less concerned to express their uncertainty, and they too come to a total estimate in the vicinity of fifteen million slaves landed. They go a step farther, however, and subdivide the total by centuries. . . .

The total is again given as a minimum, and it is clearly derived from R. R. Kuczynski. Indeed, Professor Fage gave the same breakdown in his *Introduction to the History of West Africa* and in his *Ghana*, where the citation of Kuczynski is explicit. The estimate is repeated by so many other recent authorities that it can be taken as the dominant statement of present-day historiography. Some writers cite Kuczynski directly. Others, like Robert Rotberg in his *Political History of Tropical Africa*, strengthen the case by citing both Kuczynski and a second author who derived his data from Kuczynski. Rotberg, however, improved on his authorities by raising the total to "at least twenty-five million slaves," an increase of two-thirds, apparently based on the general assurance that the fifteen-million figure was likely to be on the low side. Another alternative, chosen by D. B. Davis for his Pulitzer-Prize-winning *Problem of Slavery in Western Culture*, is not to bother with Kuczynski (who wrote, after all, more than thirty years ago), but to go directly to a recent authority—in this case to the words of Basil Davidson quoted above.

Since Kuczynski is at the center of this web of citations, quotations, and amplifications, it is important to see just how he went about calculating his now-famous estimates. The crucial passage in *Population Movements* does indeed present a general estimate of fifteen million or more slaves landed in the Americas, and it includes the distribution by centuries. . . . But Kuczynski himself shows no evidence of having made any calculation on his own. He merely found these estimates to be the most acceptable of those made by earlier authorities, and the particular authority he cited is none other than W. E. B. Du Bois.

Du Bois was, indeed, an eminent authority on Negro history, but Kuczynski's citation does *not* lead back to one of his works based on historical research. It leads instead to a paper on "The Negro Race in the United States of America," delivered to a semi-scholarly congress in London in 1911—a curious place to publish something as important as an original, overall estimate of the Atlantic slave trade—and in fact the paper contains no such thing. Du Bois's only mention of the subject in the place cited was these two sentences:

> *The exact number of slaves imported is not known. Dunbar estimates that nearly 900,000 came to America in the sixteenth century, 2,750,000 in the seventeenth, 7,000,000 in the eighteenth, and over 4,000,000 in the nineteenth, perhaps 15,000,000 in all.*

The real authority, then, is neither Kuczynski nor Du Bois, but Dunbar. Though Du Bois's offhand statement was not supported by footnotes or bibliography, the author in question was Edward E. Dunbar, an American publicist of the 1860s. During the early part of 1861, he was responsible for a serial called *The Mexican Papers*, devoted to furthering the cause of President Juárez of Mexico and of the Liberal Party in that country. The Liberals had just won the War of the Reform against their domestic opponents, but they were hard pressed by European creditors and threatened with possible military intervention—a threat that shortly materialized in the Maximilian affair. Dunbar's principal task was to enlist American sympathy, and if possible American diplomatic intervention, in support of Juárez' cause. But Dunbar was a liberal, by implication an anti-slavery man in American politics, and he published *The Mexican Papers* during the last months of America's drift into civil war. It was therefore natural that he should write an article called "History of the Rise and Decline of Commercial Slavery in America, with Reference to the Future of Mexico," and it was there that he published a set of estimates of the slave trade through time. . . . He remarked that these were only his own estimates, and he made the further reservation (so often repeated by his successors) that they were probably on the low side. . . .

The sequence is an impressive tower of authority, though it also suggests that even the best historians may be unduly credulous when they see a footnote to an illustrious predecessor. Basil Davidson should have identified the original author as "an obscure American publicist," rather than "an eminent student of population statistics," but the *ad hominem* fallacy is present in either case. Dunbar's obscurity is no evidence that he was wrong; nor does Kuczynski's use of Dunbar's estimates make them correct. The estimates were guesses, but they were guesses educated by a knowledge of the historical literature. They earned the approval of later generations who were in a position to be still better informed. Even though no one along the way made a careful effort to calculate the size of the trade from empirical evidence, the Dunbar estimates nevertheless represent a kind of consensus. . . .

It is now possible to look at the long-term movement of the Atlantic slave trade over a period of more than four centuries. [Figure 1] sums up the pattern of imports for each century, while [Figure 2] shows the same data [by destination]. Together, these data make it abundantly clear that the eighteenth century was a kind of plateau in the history of the trade—the period when the trade reached its height, but also a period of slackening growth and beginning decline. The period 1741–1810 marks the summit of the plateau, when the long-term annual average rates of delivery hung just above 60,000 a year. The edge of the plateau was reached, however, just after the Peace of Utrecht in 1713, when the annual deliveries began regularly to exceed 40,000 a year, and the permanent drop below 40,000 a year did not come again until after the 1840s. Thus about 60 per cent of all slaves delivered to the New World were transported during the century 1721–1820. Eighty per cent of the total were landed during the century and a half, 1710–1850.

The higher rates of growth, however, came at earlier phases of the trade. The highest of all may have been an apparent growth at the rate of 3.3 per cent per year between the last quarter of the fifteenth century and the first quarter of the sixteenth, but the data for this early period are too uncertain for confidence in this figure. In the smoothed-out long-term annual averages of the graph, the growth of the trade was remarkably constant at a remarkably uniform rate over more than two centuries. Two periods of stability or possible decline occur, one between the first and second quarters of the sixteenth century and again between 1601–25 and 1626–50. Aside from these periods, the growth rate was an overall 2.2 per cent per year in the last half of the sixteenth century and the first quarter of the seventeenth, and at about the same rate during the equivalent period a century later. But during the first four decades of the eighteenth century, the growth rate was 0.7 per cent.

These trends are not surprising. They run parallel to the growth of the South Atlantic System traced in the literature on qualitative evidence. The nineteenth-century portion of the curve is less predictable from the present literature, but hardly surprising. The slave trade began to decline in the 1790s—not after 1808 with the legal abolition of the British trade. . . . One of the common older views of the slave trade holds that a last burst of imports took place between about 1802 and

FIGURE 1. Major trends of the Atlantic slave trade, in annual average number of slaves imported.

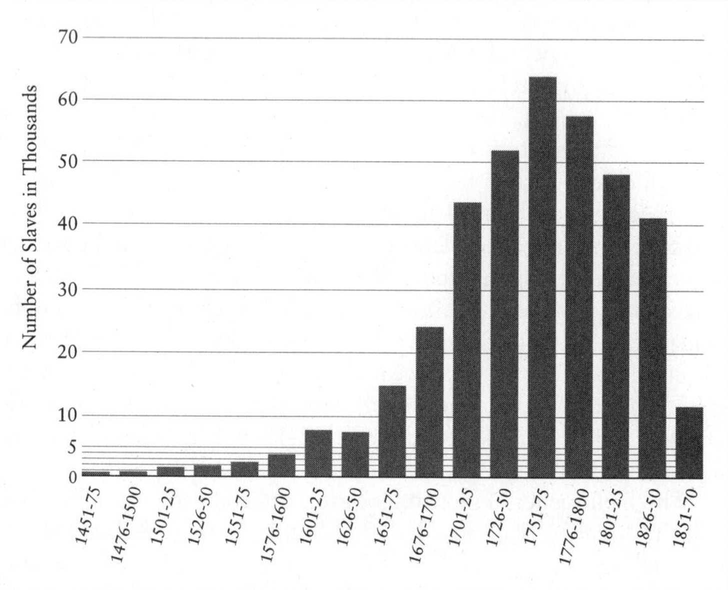

Source: Philip D. Curtin, *The Atlantic Slave Trade,* Figure 26. Data from Tables 33, 34, 65, 67.

1807, as planters sought to fill out their slave gangs before the trade became illegal. This pattern may be true of imports into the Anglo-Saxon territories, but not for the slave trade as a whole. Instead, the general trend shows a drop to the 1810's, then a rise in the 1820's. At first glance, the removal of British shipping from the trade in 1808 made no difference at all in the totals transported.

But this interpretation is probably mistaken. In the eighteenth century, warfare was the really important influence on the short-run rise and fall of the slave trade. There is no reason to expect this pattern to have changed at the end of the century. The drop of the 1790's seems to be accountable to the Napoleonic Wars, and it continued into the decade of the 1800's. After the wars, and especially after such a long period of warfare, an enormous backlog of demand would be expected, and the trade might well have shot up to meet that demand—had it not

FIGURE 2. Destinations of the Atlantic slave trade by importing regions, 1451–1870.

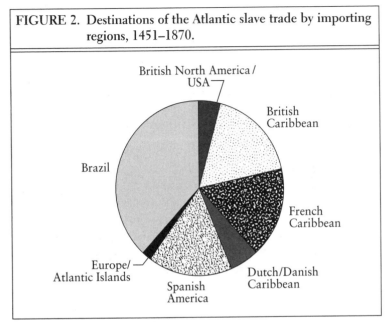

Source: Philip D. Curtin, *The Atlantic Slave Trade*, Table 77.

been for British abolition and the early work of the anti-slave-trade patrols at sea. The trade recovered somewhat in the 1820's, but the recovery was drastically dampened by the anti-slavery movement and by the shifts to new carriers (like Spain) and new sources (like Mozambique). In short, the quantitative impact of British abolition on the trade as a whole is obscured by other influences, but not completely missing.

The present projections also suggest a solution to some of the nineteenth-century controversies that still influence historical literature. Fig. [1] . . . shows a high and sustained level of annual average import from the 1810's through the 1840's—not a sharp drop as a result of abolition, nor yet a boom carrying the slave trade to new heights in the 1830's. Although an annual average export in excess of 135,000 a year is still mentioned by some authorities, it is clearly based on the Foreign Office estimate of 1848, apparently made without sufficient evidence and with a clear political interest in trying to show Parliament that the anti-slavery blockade had been effective. If the estimates here are correct, it *was* effective in diverting about 8 per cent of the trade, perhaps in keeping the trade from going even higher; but the trade nevertheless continued, at a level about a third less than its eighteenth-century peak. It was sustained first by the postwar boom of the 1820's, then by the sugar boom in Cuba and the coffee boom in Brazil. Really significant decline came only with the 1850's, when Brazil, the largest single importer, dropped from the trade. Steep as the final decline of the 1850's and 1860's appears to have been, the rate of import in the 1860's, the last important decade of the trade, nevertheless exceeded the rate for any period before the seventeenth century.

It would be premature to generalize about the impact of the slave trade on African societies over these four centuries. On the other hand, historians have already begun to do so. The range of opinion runs the gamut from the view that the slave trade was responsible for virtually every unfavorable development in Africa over these centuries, to the opposite position that even the slave trade was better than no trade, that it was therefore a positive benefit to the African societies that participated. Since the results of this survey could be brought into the argument on either side, it is appropriate to enter a few caveats.

One conclusion that might be drawn is that, in reducing the estimated total export of slaves from about twenty million to about ten million, the harm done to African societies is also reduced by half. This is obvious nonsense. The demographic consequences of moving any number of people from any society can have meaning only in relation to the size of the society, the time-period concerned, the age and sex composition of the emigrants and of the society from which they depart. Until we know at least the size of the African population that supplied the slaves, the demographic implications of the ten-million estimate are just as indeterminate as those of the twenty-million estimate. As for the social or political consequences of the slave trade to African societies, these would not necessarily vary directly with the number exported. . . .

At best, the export data of the slave trade can be suggestive. If the dominant African pattern at the height of the slave trade was that of the militarized, slave-catching society, systematically preying on its neighbors, the export projections should show a relatively large and continuous supply of slaves from these hunter societies; and the slaves themselves should have been mainly from the less organized neighbors. This pattern does not emerge clearly from the slave-export data of eighteenth-century Africa. Some ports, notably the city-states of the Bight of Biafra, did produce a continuous supply that may imply slave-catching as an economic enterprise. Elsewhere, the rapid shift in sources of supply from one region to another suggests that by-product enslavement was the dominant feature, or that, if systematic slave-hunting were tried, it could not be maintained.

These weaknesses of quantitative evidence are important to keep in mind, if only because of a popular tendency to regard numbers as more "scientific" and reliable than other kinds of data. A great deal more could nevertheless be profitably done with the quantitative study of the slave trade. More and better samples of slave origins and better data on the numbers carried by the trade at particular times should make it possible to project the annual flow of slaves from particular societies, to take only one example. Even if the dimensions of the slave trade outlined here were as accurate as limited sources will ever allow—and they are not—still other dimensions of far greater significance for African and Atlantic history remain to be explored.

Herbert S. Klein

Profits and Losses

A professor of Latin American history at Columbia University, Herbert Klein summarizes a generation of research by scholars inspired by Curtin's statistical approach. Klein finds that the financial profits and the losses of human life associated with the slave trade, although substantial, were much smaller than the rough guesses of earlier historians. Like Curtin, he finds careful measurement a more useful tool than moral outrage in discovering the trade's secrets.

In recent decades there has been a fundamental change in the study of the Atlantic slave trade. From almost total neglect, the trade has become an area of major concern to economists and historians who have dedicated themselves to analyzing the African experience in America.

From Herbert S. Klein, "Economic Aspects of the Eighteenth-Century Atlantic Slave Trade," in *The Rise of the Merchant Empires*, edited by James D. Tracy, 1990, pp. 287, 299, 303–308. Reprinted with the permission of Cambridge University Press.

Especially since the publication by Philip Curtin of his masterly synthesis *The Atlantic Slave Trade: A Census* in 1969, a massive amount of archival research has resulted in publications both of collections of documents from all the major archives of Europe, America, and Africa and of major works of synthesis on the demography, politics, and economics of the slave trade. . . .

From the work of the European economic historians, it is now evident that slave trade profits were not extraordinary by European standards. The average 10 percent rate obtained in studies of the eighteenth-century French and English slave traders was considered a good profit rate at the time but not out of the range of other contemporary investments. From a recent detailed study of the nineteenth century, it would seem that profits doubled in the next century largely as a result of rising slave prices in America, which in turn were due to the increasing suppression of the trade by the British navy. On average (except for some extraordinary voyages to Cuba in the 1850s), the rate of profit for nineteenth-century slavers was just under 20 percent. Thus, while profits in the special period of suppression in the nineteenth century were quite high, even these profits were not astronomic. . . .

The conceptions prevalent in the popular literature about the relative costs of African slaves have their corollary hypotheses about the economics of their transportation. It was assumed that the low cost of the slaves made it profitable to pack in as many as the ship could hold without sinking and then accept high rates of mortality during the Atlantic crossing. If any slaves delivered alive were pure profit, then even the loss of several hundred would have made economic sense. But if the slaves were not a costless or cheap item to purchase, then the corresponding argument about "tight packing" also makes little sense. In fact, high losses on the crossing resulted in financial loss on the trip, as many ship accounts aptly prove.

Even more convincing than these theoretical arguments against reckless destruction of life is the fact that no study has yet shown a systematic correlation of any significance between the numbers of slaves carried and mortality at sea. Thousands of ship crossings have now been statistically analyzed, and none show a correlation of any significance between either tonnage or space available and mortality.

This does not mean that slaves were traveling in luxury. In fact, they had less room than did contemporary troops or convicts being transported. It simply means that after much experience and the exigencies of the trade, slavers only took on as many slaves as they could expect to cross the Atlantic safely. From scattered references in the pre-1700 period it seems that provisioning and carrying arrangements were initially deficient. But all post-1700 trade studies show that slavers carried water and provisions for double their expected voyage times and that in most trades they usually carried slightly fewer slaves than their legally permitted limits.

This increasing sophistication in the carrying of slaves was reflected in declining rates of mortality. In the pre-1700 trade, mean mortality rates over many voyages tended to hover around 20 percent. In turn this mean rate reflected quite wide variations, with many ships coming in with very low rates and an equally large number experiencing rates of double or more than double the mean figure. But in the post-1700 period the mean rates dropped, and the variation around the mean declined. By mid-century the mean stood at about 10 percent, and by the last quarter of the century all trades were averaging a rate of about 5 percent. Moreover the dispersion around these mean rates had declined, and two-thirds of the ships were experiencing no more than 5 percent variation above or below the mean rate.

These declines in mortality were due to the standardization increasingly adopted in the trade. First of all there developed a specialized and specifically constructed vessel used in the slave trade of most nations. By the second half of the eighteenth century slave ships were averaging two hundred tons among all European traders, a tonnage that seemed best to fit the successful carrying potential of the trade. Slave traders were also the first of the commercial traders to adopt copper sheathing for their ships, which was a costly new method to prolong the life of the vessels and guarantee greater speed. It should be stressed that these slave trade vessels were much smaller ships than Europeans used in either the West Indian or East Indian trades. This in turn goes a long way to explaining why the famous model of a triangular trade, long the staple of western textbooks, is largely a myth. This myth was based on the idea that the slave ships performed the multiple tasks of taking European goods to Africa, transporting slaves to America, and then bringing back the sugar or other slave-produced American staple for Europe all on the same voyage. In fact, the majority of American crops reached European markets in much larger and specially constructed West Indian vessels designed primarily for this shuttle trade; the majority of slavers returned to Europe with small cargoes or none at all; and in the largest slave trade of them all—that of Brazil—no slavers either departed from or returned to Europe.

All traders carried about two and a half slaves per ton, and although there was some variation in crew size and ratios, all slave trade ships carried at least twice the number of seamen needed to man the vessel, and thus double or more than that of any other long-distance oceanic trade. This very high ratio of sailors to tonnage was due to the security needs of controlling the slave prisoners. All the European slave traders were also using the same provisioning, health, and transportation procedures. They built temporary decks to house the slaves and divided them by age and sex. Almost all Europeans adopted smallpox vaccinations at about the same time, all carried large quantities of African provisions to feed the slaves, and all used the same methods for daily hygiene, care of the sick, and so on. This standardization explains the common experience of mortality decline, and it also goes a long way to rejecting contemporaneous assertions that any particular European trader was "better" or more efficient than any other.

Although these firmly grounded statistics on mortality certainly destroy many of the older beliefs about "astronomic" mortality and tight packing, there does remain the question of whether a 5 percent mortality rate for a thirty- to fifty-day voyage for a healthy young adult is high or low. If such a mortality rate had occurred among young adult peasants in eighteenth-century France, it would be considered an epidemic rate. Thus, although Europeans succeeded in reducing the rate to seemingly low percentages, these rates still represented extraordinary high death rate figures for such a specially selected population. Equally, although troop, immigrant, and convict mortality rates in the eighteenth century approached the slave death numbers, in the nineteenth century they consistently fell to below 1 percent for transatlantic voyages. For slaves, however, these rates never fell below 5 percent for any large group of vessels surveyed. There thus seems to have been a minimum death rate caused by the close quarters during transport, which the Europeans could never reduce.

Death in the crossing was due to a variety of causes. The biggest killers were gastrointestinal disorders, which were often related to the quality of food and water available on the trip, and fevers. Bouts of dysentery were common and the "bloody flux" as it was called could break out in epidemic proportions. The increasing exposure of the slaves to dysentery increased both the rates of contamination of supplies and the incidence of death. It was dysentery that accounted for the majority of deaths and was the most common disease experienced on all voyages. The astronomic rates of mortality reached on occasional voyages were due to outbreaks of smallpox, measles, or other highly communicable diseases that were not related to time at sea or the conditions of food and water supply, hygiene, and sanitation practices. It was this randomness of epidemic diseases that prevented even experienced and efficient captains from eliminating very high mortality rates on any given voyage.

Although time at sea was not usually correlated with mortality, there were some routes in which time was a factor. Simply because they were a third longer than any other routes, the East African slave trades that developed in the late eighteenth and nineteenth centuries were noted for overall higher mortality than the West African routes, even though mortality per day at sea was the same or lower than on the shorter routes. Also, just the transporting together of slaves from different epidemiological zones in Africa guaranteed the transmission of a host of local endemic diseases to all those who were aboard. In turn, this guaranteed the spread of all major African diseases to America.

Along with the impact of African diseases on the American populations, the biases in the age and sex of the migrating Africans also had a direct impact on the growth and decline of the American slave populations. The low ratio of women in each arriving ship, the fact that most of these slave women were mature adults who had already spent several of their fecund years in Africa, and the fact that few children were carried to America were of fundamental importance in the subsequent history of population growth. It meant that the African slaves who arrived in America could not reproduce themselves. The African women who did come to America had lost some potential reproductive years and were even less able to reproduce the total numbers of males and females in the original immigrant cohort, let alone create a generation greater than the total number who arrived from Africa. Even those American regions that experienced a heavy and constant stream of African slaves still had to rely on importation of more slaves to maintain their slave populations, let alone increase their size. Once that African migration stopped, however, it was possible for the slave populations to begin to increase through natural growth, so long as there was no heavy out-migration through emancipation.

It was this consistent negative growth of the first generation of African slaves which explains the growing intensity of the slave trade to

America in the eighteenth and early nineteenth centuries. As the demand for American products grew in European markets because of the increasingly popular consumption of tobacco, cotton, coffee, and above all sugar, the need for workers increased and this could be met only by bringing in more Africans. It was only in the case of the United States that the growth of plantation crop exports to Europe did not lead to an increasing importation of African slaves. This was largely due to the very early North American experience of the local slave population achieving a positive growth rate and thus supplying its increasing labor needs from the positive growth of its native-born slave population. Although most demographic historians have shown that the Creole slave populations had positive growth rates from the beginning and that it was the distortions of the African-born cohorts that explain overall decline, more traditional historians have tried to explain the increasing demand for slaves as due to the low life expectancy of the Afro-American slave population. Much cited is the contemporary belief found in the planter literature of most colonies that the Afro-American slave experienced an average working life of "seven years." This myth of a short-lived labor force was related to the observed reality of slave population decline under the impact of heavy immigration of African slaves. Observers did not recognize the age and sexual imbalance of these Africans as a causal factor for the negative population growth of the slave labor force. Rather, they saw this decline as related to a very high mortality and low life expectancy. Yet all recent studies suggest both a positive rate of population growth among native-born slaves and a life expectancy well beyond the so-called average seven working years in all American societies.

The average life expectancy of slave males was in the upper twenties in Brazil, for example, and in the midthirties for the United States, which might suggest an average working life of at least twenty years in Brazil and twenty-five years in the United States. But this average figure, of course, takes into account the very high infant mortality rates. For those slaves who survived the first five years of life—and these are the only ones we are concerned with here—the comparable life expectancies was [*sic*] in the midthirties for the Brazilians and lower forties for the U.S. slaves. This suggests that the average working life was, at a minimum, twenty-five years for Brazilian slaves and thirty years for the U.S. ones—both figures far from the supposed seven-year average postulated in most histories.

David Eltis and David Richardson

The Achievements of the "Numbers Game"

Massive new research set off by Curtin's recalculations culminated in the publication on CD-ROM of a vast database of nearly 30,000 slaving voyages. In the next reading, two of the database's international team of researchers, David Eltis of Queens University (Canada) and David Richardson of the University of Hull (U.K.), reassess scholarly understanding of the Middle Passage. Their evidence confirms the general accuracy of Curtin's census, refines many of his calculations, and reduces his margins of error. In particular they show that deaths on Middle Passage voyages were much lower than Buxton and other abolitionists had estimated.

Despite a major research effort in the last few decades, less is known about the movement of African peoples to the New World than the much smaller movement of their European counterparts before the mid-nineteenth century. Given that the record keepers were Europeans who regarded Africans as outsiders, it is likely that we shall never have as much information on the personal lives of individual Africans making the Atlantic crossing as we do of Europeans. But on the identities of large groups entering the African stream as well as the size and demographic characteristics of these groups, the picture is much less discouraging. Indeed, in a few years it may well be the case that in these areas, and in the early modern period at least, we will actually know more about these aspects of African than of European transatlantic migration. As knowledge of the patterns of the trade is basic to evaluations of the cultural implications of long-distance movements of people, this is an exciting prospect. One of the developments that has made it possible is, of course, the computer revolution and the related, but ultimately more

From David Eltis and David Richardson, "The 'Numbers Game' and Routes to Slavery," *Slavery and Abolition* 18. 1997, pp. 1–3, 5–10. Reprinted by permission of Frank Cass Ltd.

important, explosion in archival research that has occurred since the late 1960s.

Historians are sometimes prone to exaggerate the significance of published works, but the largest single influence over the exploitation of the archives was arguably the publication in 1969 of Philip Curtin's *Census* of the Atlantic slave trade. It was a landmark in the historiography not just of the slave trade but in the larger fields of slavery and migration. Drawing almost exclusively on previously published work, Curtin provided the first detailed assessment of the overall volume of the transatlantic traffic in enslaved Africans between 1500 and 1867. His estimates of the trade—up to 11.8 million slaves embarked at the coast of Africa and 9.4 million arrivals in the Americas—was substantially lower than most of the figures previously assumed by historians, some of which were several times greater than those calculated by Curtin. Curtin's book provided, however, more than a reassessment of the overall dimensions of the Atlantic slave trade, valuable though that was. In the course of producing his census, he also generated data on temporal changes in the scale of the trade in slaves; on mortality levels of slaves in the Atlantic crossing or middle passage; on the numbers of slaves carried by different national carriers; and on shifts in the geographical distribution of slave departures from Africa and of slave arrivals in the Americas. In each of these areas, Curtin's findings represented a major advance on existing knowledge of the transatlantic slave trade.

The radical nature of Curtin's revision of the most frequently cited of the earlier estimates of the magnitude of the Atlantic slave trade provoked a lively and, at times, heated debate. Most discussion centred on the last two centuries of the trade, for which records are most abundant and when the movement of African slaves across the Atlantic was unquestionably at its height. Disagreements continue over estimates of the scale of slave shipments by some countries. Consequently, the "numbers game" relating to the volume of the Atlantic slave trade is likely to remain a significant historical industry for some time to come. The latest estimates tend, nevertheless, to corroborate Curtin's overall assessment of the trade, at least for the period from 1650 to 1870, though they also suggest that he probably overestimated slave shipments before 1700 and underestimated them in the nineteenth century. On the basis of the most recent surveys, it appears that some 10.1 million people left Africa for America in 1660–1867, most of them carried in British, Portuguese, and French ships. This is close to Curtin's assessment which suggested that between 1650 and 1870 some 10.5 million entered the transatlantic traffic, with some 8.9 million surviving the Atlantic crossing. Assuming that, at most, one million slaves were shipped from Africa before 1650, then the most recent evidence suggests that perhaps 11 million Africans were forced to leave their homeland for America between 1500 and 1870.

Further refinements of estimates of the magnitude of the Atlantic slave trade will doubtless occur. But an important by-product of these efforts to quantify the trade has been the discovery of new records in Europe and America relating to the shipping and sale of African slaves. Such records have generally been regarded as the most reliable sources for gauging the dimensions of the trade in slaves. The discovery and analysis of such records has, therefore, been a major feature of debates since 1969 over the volume of the slave trade. . . .

It is sometimes suggested that recent quantitative approaches tend to sanitize the slave trade and need to be balanced by placing a greater emphasis on the personal experiences of the slaves themselves. There are, of course, autobiographies of African slaves, such as that of Olaudah Equiano (or Gustavus Vassa). . . . Moreover, some historians have sought to draw individual and collective portraits of the lives of slaves, whether during the course of their enslavement or on American plantations. . . . We welcome such research. But we also believe that it is difficult to assess the significance or representativeness of personal narratives or collective biographies, however detailed, without an understanding of the overall movement of slaves of which these individuals' lives were a part. The reconstruction of slaving voyages and, even more importantly, the creation of a single, consolidated data base of voyages offers the best means available for charting the routes to slavery of Africans forced into exile from their homelands. In other words, voyage histories, when combined, represent a powerful tool for understanding the African diaspora and the contribution of Africans to the creation and development of the transatlantic world between 1500 and 1850.

Since 1992 several scholars have collaborated in seeking to build an integrated and consolidated data set of transatlantic slaving voyages. Hosted by the W.E.B. Du Bois Institute of Harvard University, the project has brought together a number of published and unpublished data sets and, through consultation of previously unused records, has also enhanced existing sets and created additional ones. . . . [W]ith the exception of some 571 voyages which were undertaken between 1595 and 1640, almost all the voyages included in the Du Bois Institute set were undertaken between the mid-seventeenth century and 1870. As yet, therefore, this data set contains little information about the Atlantic slave trade during its first century, but it does cover the years when the transatlantic traffic in slaves was at its peak. Overall, the set currently includes records of over 26,000 slaving voyages or probably more than two-thirds of those undertaken after 1650. This represents the largest data set for any area of transatlantic migration or trade currently available or, indeed, of any pre-nineteenth century migration anywhere. It is not overstating its significance, therefore, to suggest that, when more widely accessible, it will be relevant to the work of all scholars interested in the African diaspora and the African-American heritage. It will, moreover, help to illuminate the human experience of the victims of this tragic chapter in modern history. . . .

From the Du Bois Institute data, it appears that between 1662 and 1867 over four out of five slaves left Africa from just four regions—the Gold Coast, the Bights of Benin and Biafra, and West-Central Africa. The data also permit even more disaggregated analysis of departures by providing details of shipments by ports. This shows that, just as slave ship departures from Europe and the Americas were concentrated at relatively few ports, so large proportions of the slaves exported were shipped at a small number of outlets in Africa. Prominent among these were Cape Coast Castle and Anomabu on the Gold Coast; Whydah in the Bight of Benin; Bonny and Calabar in the Bight of Biafra; and Cabinda, Benguela, and Luanda in West-Central Africa. The history of those ports in this period was clearly dominated by slave trafficking. On the American side, arrivals of slaves were more dispersed geographically; nevertheless, some 40 per cent of slaves landed in Brazil, over 20 per cent in the British Caribbean, about 17 per cent in the French West Indies, and over 10 per cent in the Spanish islands. Overall, this preliminary analysis suggested that over 90 per cent of the slaves arriving in the Americas between 1662 and 1867 disembarked at places in the Caribbean islands and Brazil. Even though the United States had a substantial slave population by 1810, arrivals in mainland North America constituted probably no more than 7 per cent of the total. The main findings of this paper related, however, not to Africa and America separately, but rather to the intensity of the links between particular regions in the two continents.

Some attempt to trace connections between regions of departure and arrival of slaves was made by Curtin, but the Du Bois Institute data allow one to trace in detail the principal routes to New World slavery followed by Africans. . . . For instance, with the exception of Bahia, which largely drew on slaves from the Bight of Benin, slaves from West-Central Africa dominated arrivals in South America. In the West Indies, St Domingue also depended heavily on slaves from south of the equator, but elsewhere in the Caribbean slaves from West Africa dominated arrivals. Moreover, within the Caribbean, the proportions of slaves entering particular colonies or groups of colonies from individual subregions of West Africa were uneven. Thus, the Gold Coast seems to have supplied a disproportionate share of slaves arriving at Barbados, Surinam, and the Guyanas, while the Bight of Benin played a similar role in the case of the French islands outside St Domingue. In the other major Caribbean islands—Jamaica and the British Leeward Islands—the Bight of Biafra was easily the largest source of supply of slaves. Significantly, it appears that slaves from Senegambia and Sierra Leone represented a relatively small share of arrivals at the major American destinations. As the middle passage from these regions to the West Indies was shorter than that from the four regions to the south, this is striking and, together with the Bight of Benin's dominance of slave arrivals at Bahia, should caution one against assuming that geography and transport costs were of overwhelming importance in shaping the patterns of transatlantic slave routes. . . .

The Du Bois Institute data set not only allows us to begin to identify the principal transatlantic slave routes, but also offers closer investigation of the experiences of slaves in the Atlantic crossing or so-called "middle passage." This aspect of the slave trade has, quite rightly, consistently attracted attention since the late eighteenth century when the British Parliament first debated the appalling conditions endured by enslaved Africans in the Atlantic crossing. For many, the term middle passage has become synonymous with the cruelty and inhumanity of the traffic. Modern quantitative study of the middle passage was initiated by Curtin who relied heavily on data for eighteenth-century Nantes ships and figures generated by the British Foreign Office for 1817–43 in order to explore trends in shipboard mortality of slaves. Since Curtin's initial work, large amounts of new data have been unearthed, with the result that the Du Bois Institute data set now contains vastly more evidence on slave mortality than was available to Curtin. . . .

. . . [I]t appears that over the three and a half centuries of the transatlantic slave trade, perhaps 15 per cent (or over 1.5 million) of those who embarked at the African coast died during the Atlantic crossing. At the peak of the trade in 1760–1810 losses of slaves on the Atlantic voyage perhaps averaged 6,000–8,000 a year. Clearly, for a large number of those bound for sale in the Americas—the great majority, it should be noted, aged under twenty-five—the route to slavery ended either before leaving the African coast or in mid-ocean.

. . . Mortality rates on slave ships were highly unpredictable between one voyage and the next and added to the uncertainties surrounded to the trade. . . . [H]owever, . . . slave mortality rates tended to decline in the long run, . . . mortality varied by region of trade in Africa—ships from the Bight of Biafra having the worst record—and . . . in the late eighteenth century, the British appear to have been the most efficient in keeping slaves alive. The last finding may partly be ascribed to Parliamentary measures after 1788 to regulate slave-carrying and improve conditions on board ship. But the general trend in mortality seems to have reflected, in part at least, a more widespread capacity among carriers to shift the overall distribution of mortality rates by reducing the incidence of shipboard epidemics through technical and other changes.

PART

 Effects in
Africa

*With the help of the king . . . [we] assaulted the town . . . [and] took
250 persons.*

JOHN HAWKINS, 1568

*The truth is that a developing Africa went into slave trading and Euro-
pean commercial relations as into a gale-force wind, which shipwrecked
a few societies, set many others off course, and generally slowed down
the rate of advance.*

WALTER RODNEY

*The coastal exports of young adult slaves, twice as many men as women,
tended to transform the structure of the population and the organization
of society.*

PATRICK MANNING

*European trade with Africa can scarcely be seen as disruptive in itself,
for it did not oust any line of African production, nor did it thwart
development.*

JOHN THORNTON

John Hawkins

An Alliance to Raid
for Slaves

Because it is mentioned in two of the modern selections that follow, it is useful to begin with an early account of the slave trade by John Hawkins (1532–1595). Backed by powerful investors, this ambitious privateer from Plymouth, England, made three profitable slaving voyages to Guinea (as West Africa was then called) in the 1560s. This excerpt from his third voyage shows how trading and raiding were closely associated in the early English slave trade, but it also suggests how closely the European's success depended on finding an African ally who would cooperate with him—up to a point.

The ships departed from Plymouth, the second day of October, Anno 1567 and . . . arrived at Cape Verde, the eighteenth of November: where we landed 150 men, hoping to obtain some Negroes, where we got but few, and those with great hurt and damage to our men, which chiefly proceeded of their envenomed arrows: and although in the beginning they seemed to be but small hurts, yet there hardly escaped any that had blood drawn of them, but died in strange sort, with their mouths shut some ten days before they died, and after their wounds were whole; where I myself had one of the greatest wounds, yet thanks be to God, escaped. From thence we passed the time upon the coast of Guinea, unto Sierra Leone, till the twelfth of January, in which time we had not gotten together a hundred and fifty Negroes: yet notwithstanding the sickness of our men, and the late time of the year commanded us away; and thus having nothing wherewith to seek the coast of the West Indies, I was with the rest of the company in consultation to go to the coast of the Mine [i.e., the Gold Coast], hoping there to have obtained some gold for our wares, and thereby to have defrayed our charge. But even in that present instant, there came to us a Negro, sent from a king, oppressed by

From "The Third Troublesome Voyage . . . to the Parts of Guinea, and the West Indies, in the Yeeres 1567 and 1568 by M. John Hawkins," in Richard Hakluyt, *The Principal Navigations, Voyages, Traffiques and Discoveries of the English Nation* (New York, 1928) pp. 53–55. Spelling has been modernized.

other kings, his neighbors, desiring our aid, with [the] promise that as many Negroes as by these wars might be obtained, as well of his part as of ours, should be at our pleasure; whereupon we concluded to give aid, and sent 120 of our men, which the 15 of January, assaulted a town of the Negroes of our ally's adversaries, which had in it 8,000 inhabitants, being very strongly impaled and fenced after their manner, but it was so well defended, that our men prevailed not, but lost six men and forty hurt: so that our men sent forthwith to me for more help: whereupon considering the good success of this enterprise might highly further the commodity of our voyage, I went myself, and with the help of the king of our side, assaulted the town, both by land and sea, and very hardly with fire (their houses being covered with dry palm leaves) obtained the town, put the inhabitants to flight, where we took 250 persons, men, women, & children, and by our friend the king of our side, there were taken 600 prisoners, whereof we hoped to have our choice: but the Negro (in whose nation is seldom or never found truth) meant nothing less: for that night he removed his camp and prisoners, so that we were fain to content us with those few which we had gotten ourselves.

Walter Rodney

The Unequal Partnership Between Africans and Europeans

During the next three hundred years, the Atlantic slave trade changed in many ways. As the late West Indian historian Walter Rodney notes, Europeans obtained slaves by trading rather than raiding. But in this excerpt, published in 1972, Rodney also argues that the balance of power in the trading relationship soon shifted in favor of the European partners. The trade caused Africa to suffer population loss, deflected African energy away from productive activities, undercut African manufacturing with cheap manufactured goods, and tied Africans into an inferior relationship with a European capitalist economy that stifled their economic and technological progress. Although Rodney notes that many parts of Africa progressed during the era of the slave trade, he insists that these advances were despite the Atlantic trade, not because of it.

. . . Undoubtedly, with few exceptions such as Hawkins, European buyers purchased African captives on the coasts of Africa and the transaction between themselves and Africans was a form of trade. It is also true that very often a captive was sold and resold as he made his way from the interior to the port of embarkation—and that too was a form of trade. However, on the whole, the process by which captives were obtained on African soil was not trade at all. It was through warfare, trickery, banditry, and kidnaping. When one tries to measure the effect of European slave trading on the African continent, it is essential to realize that one is measuring the effect of social violence rather than trade in any normal sense of the word.

Many things remain uncertain about the slave trade and its consequences for Africa, but the general picture of destructiveness is clear, and that destructiveness can be shown to be the logical consequence of the manner of recruitment of captives in Africa. . . .

African economic activity was affected both directly and indirectly by population loss. For instance, when the inhabitants of a given area were reduced below a certain number in an environment where the tsetse fly was present, the remaining few had to abandon the area. In effect, enslavement was causing these people to lose their battle to tame and harness nature—a battle which is at the basis of development. Violence almost meant insecurity. The opportunity presented by European slave dealers became the major (though not the only) stimulus for a great deal of social violence between different African communities and within any given community. It took the form more of raiding and kidnaping than of regular warfare, and that fact increased the element of fear and uncertainty.

Both openly and by implication, all the European powers in the nineteenth century indicated their awareness of the fact that the activities connected with producing captives were inconsistent with other economic pursuits. That was the time when Britain in particular wanted Africans to collect palm produce and rubber and to grow agricultural crops for export in place of slaves; and it was clear that slave raiding was violently conflicting with that objective in Western, Eastern, and Central Africa. Long before that date, Europeans accepted that fact when their self-interest was involved. For example, in the seventeenth century, the Portuguese and Dutch actually discouraged slave trade on the Gold Coast, for they recognized that it would be incompatible with gold trade. However, by the end of that century, gold had been discovered in Brazil, and the importance of gold supplies from Africa was lessened. Within the total Atlantic pattern, African slaves became more important than gold, and Brazilian gold was offered for African captives at Whydah (Dahomey) and Accra. At that point, slaving began undermining the Gold Coast economy and destroying the gold trade. Slave raiding and kidnaping made it unsafe to mine and to travel with gold; and raiding for captives proved more profitable than gold mining. One European on the scene noted that "as one fortunate marauding makes a native rich in a day, they therefore exert themselves rather in war, robbery and plunder than in their old business of digging and collecting gold."

The above changeover from gold mining to slave raiding took place within a period of a few years between 1700 and 1710, when the Gold Coast came to supply about five thousand to six thousand captives per year. By the end of the eighteenth century, a much smaller number of captives were exported from the Gold Coast, but the damage had already been done. It is worth noting that Europeans sought out different parts of West and Central Africa at different times to play the role of major suppliers of slaves to the Americas. This meant that virtually every section of the long western coastline between the Senegal and Cunene rivers had at least a few years' experience of intensive trade in slaves—with all its consequences. Besides, in the history of eastern Nigeria, the Congo, northern Angola, and Dahomey, there were periods extending over decades when exports remained at an average of many thousands per year. Most of those areas were also relatively highly developed within the African context. They were leading forces inside Africa, whose energies would otherwise have gone towards their own self-improvement and the betterment of the continent as a whole.

The changeover to warlike activities and kidnapping must have affected all branches of economic activity, and agriculture in particular. Occasionally, in certain localities food production was increased to provide supplies for slave ships, but the overall consequences of slaving on agricultural activities in Western, Eastern, and Central Africa were negative. Labor was drawn off from agriculture and conditions became unsettled. Dahomey, which in the sixteenth century was known for exporting food to parts of what is now Togo, was suffering from famines in the nineteenth century. The present generation of Africans will readily recall that in the colonial period when able-bodied men left their homes as migrant laborers, that upset the farming routine in the home districts and often caused famines. Slave trading after all meant migration of labor in a manner one hundred times more brutal and disruptive.

To achieve economic development, one essential condition is to make the maximum use of the country's labor and natural resources. Usually, that demands peaceful conditions, but there have been times in history when social groups have grown stronger by raiding their neighbors for women, cattle, and goods, because they then used the "booty" from the raids for the benefit of their own community. Slaving in Africa did not even have that redeeming value. Captives were shipped outside instead of being utilized within any given African community for creating wealth from nature. It was only as an accidental by-product that in some areas Africans who recruited captives for Europeans realized that they were better off keeping some captives for themselves. In any case, slaving prevented the remaining population from effectively engaging in agriculture and industry, and it employed professional slave-hunters and warriors to destroy rather than build. Quite apart from the moral aspect and the immense suffering that it caused, the European slave trade was economically totally irrational from the viewpoint of African development. . . .

One tactic that is now being employed by certain European (including American) scholars is to say that the European slave trade was undoubtedly *a moral evil,* but it was *economically good* for Africa. Here attention will be drawn only very briefly to a few of those arguments to indicate how ridiculous they can be. One that receives much emphasis is that African rulers and other persons obtained European commodities in exchange for their captives, and this was how Africans gained "wealth." This suggestion fails to take into account the fact that several European imports were competing with and strangling African products; it fails to take into account the fact that none of the long list of European articles were of the type which entered into the productive process, but were rather items to be rapidly consumed or stowed away uselessly; and it incredibly overlooks the fact that the majority of the imports were of the worst quality even as consumer goods — cheap gin, cheap gunpowder, pots and kettles full of holes, beads, and other assorted rubbish.

Following from the above, it is suggested that certain African kingdoms grew strong economically and politically as a consequence of the trade with Europeans. The greatest of the West African kingdoms, such as Oyo, Benin, Dahomey, and Asante are cited as examples. Oyo and Benin were great long before making contact with Europeans, and while both Dahomey and Asante grew stronger during the period of the European slave trade, the roots of their achievements went back to much earlier years. Furthermore — and this is a major fallacy in the argument of the slave-trade apologists — the fact that a given African state grew politically more powerful at the same time as it engaged in selling captives to Europeans is not automatically to be attributed to the credit of the trade in slaves. A cholera epidemic may kill thousands in a country and yet the population increases. The increase obviously came about *in spite of* and not because of the cholera. This simple logic escapes those who speak about the European slave trade benefiting Africa. The destructive tendency of slave trading can be clearly established; and, wherever a state seemingly progressed in the epoch of slave trading, the conclusion is simply that it did so in spite of the adverse effects of a process that was more damaging than cholera. This is the picture that emerges from a detailed study of Dahomey, for instance, and in the final analysis although Dahomey did its best to expand politically and militarily while still tied to slave trade, that form of economic activity seriously undermined its economic base and left it much worse off.

A few of the arguments about the economic benefits of the European slave trade for Africa amount to nothing more than saying that exporting millions of captives was a way of avoiding starvation in Africa! To attempt to reply to that would be painful and time-wasting. But, perhaps a slightly more subtle version of the same argument requires a reply: namely, the argument that Africa gained because in the process of slave trading new food crops were acquired from the American continent and these became staples in Africa. The crops in question are maize and cassava, which became staples in Africa late in the nineteenth century and in the present century. But the spread of food crops is one of the most common phenomena in human history. . . .

All of the above points are taken from books and articles published recently, as the fruit of research in major British and American universities. They are probably not the commonest views even among European bourgeois scholars, but they are representative of a growing trend that seems likely to become the new accepted orthodoxy in metropolitan capitalist countries; and this significantly coincides with Europe's struggle against the further decolonization of Africa economically and mentally. In one sense, it is preferable to ignore such rubbish and isolate our youth from its insults; but unfortunately one of the aspects of current African underdevelopment is that the capitalist publishers and bourgeois scholars dominate the scene and help mold opinions the world over. It is for that reason that writing of the type which justifies the trade in slaves has to be exposed as racist bourgeois propaganda, having no connection with reality or logic. It is a question not merely of history but of present-day liberation struggle in Africa.

It has already been indicated that in the fifteenth century European technology was not totally superior to that of other parts of the world. There were certain features which were highly advantageous to Europe—such as shipping and (to a lesser extent) guns. Europeans trading to Africa had to make use of Asian and African consumer goods, showing that their system of production was not absolutely superior. It is particularly striking that in the early centuries of trade, Europeans relied heavily on Indian cloths for resale in Africa, and they also purchased cloths on several parts of the West African coast for resale elsewhere. Morocco, Mauritania, Senegambia, Ivory Coast, Benin, Yorubaland, and Loango were all exporters to other parts of Africa—through European middlemen. . . .

African demand for cloth was increasing rapidly in the fifteenth, sixteenth, and seventeenth centuries, so that there was a market for all cloth produced locally as well as room for imports from Europe and Asia. But, directed by an acquisitive capitalist class, European industry increased its capacity to produce on a large scale by harnessing the energy of wind, water, and coal. European cloth industry was able to copy fashionable Indian and African patterns, and eventually to replace them. Partly by establishing a stranglehold on the distribution of cloth around the shores of Africa, and partly by swamping African products by importing cloth in bulk, European traders eventually succeeded in putting an end to the expansion of African cloth manufacture.

. . . When European cloth became dominant on the African market, it meant that African producers were cut off from the increasing demand. The craft producers either abandoned their tasks in the face of cheap available European cloth, or they continued on the same small hand-worked instruments to create styles and pieces for localized markets. Therefore, there was what can be called "technological arrest" or stagnation, and in some instances actual regression, since people forgot even the simple techniques of their forefathers. The abandonment of traditional iron smelting in most parts of Africa is probably the most important instance of technological regression.

Development means a capacity for self-sustaining growth. It means that an economy must register advances which in turn will promote further progress. The loss of industry and skill in Africa was extremely small, if we measure it from the viewpoint of modern scientific achievements or even by standards of England in the late eighteenth century. However, it must be borne in mind that to be held back at one stage means that it is impossible to go on to a further stage. When a person was forced to leave school after only two years of primary school education, it is no reflection on him that he is academically and intellectually less developed than someone who had the opportunity to be schooled right through to university level. What Africa experienced in the early centuries of trade was precisely a loss of development *opportunity*, and this is of the greatest importance. . . .

The European slave trade was a direct block, in removing millions of youth and young adults who are the human agents from whom inventiveness springs. Those who remained in areas badly hit by slave capturing were preoccupied about their freedom rather than with improvements in production. Besides, even the busiest African in West, Central, or East Africa was concerned more with trade than with production, because of the nature of the contacts with Europe; and that situation was not conducive to the introduction of technological advances. The most dynamic groups over a great area of Africa became associated with foreign trade — notably, the Afro-Portuguese middlemen of Upper Guinea, the Akan market women, the Aro traders of Mozambique, and the Swahili and Wanyamwezi of East Africa. The trade which they carried on was in export items like captives and ivory which did not require the invention of machinery. Apart from that, they were agents for distributing European imports. . . .

Apart from inventiveness, we must also consider the borrowing of technology. When a society for whatever reason finds itself technologically trailing behind others, it catches up not so much by independent inventions but by borrowing. Indeed, very few of man's major scientific discoveries have been separately discovered in different places by different people. Once a principle or a tool is known, it spreads or diffuses to other peoples. Why then did European technology fail to make its way into Africa during the many centuries of contact between the two continents? The basic reason is that the very nature of Afro-European trade was highly unfavorable to the movement of positive ideas and techniques from the European capitalist system to the African pre-capitalist (communal, feudal, and prefeudal) system of production. . . . Placing the whole question in historical perspective allows us to see that capitalism has always discouraged technological evolution in Africa, and blocks Africa's access to its own technology. . . . [C]apitalism introduced into Africa only such limited aspects of its material culture as were essential to more efficient exploitation, but the general tendency has been for capitalism to underdevelop Africa in technology.

The European slave trade and overseas trade in general had what are known as "multiplier effects" on Europe's development in a very positive sense. This means that the benefits of foreign contacts extended to many areas of European life not directly connected with foreign trade, and the whole society was better equipped for its own internal development. The opposite was true of Africa not only in the crucial sphere of technology but also with regard to the size and purpose of each economy in Africa. Under the normal processes of evolution, an economy grows steadily larger so that after a while two neighboring economies merge into one. That was precisely how national economies were created in the states of Western Europe through the gradual combination of what were once separate provincial economies. Trade with Africa actually helped Europe to weld together more closely the different national economies, but in Africa there was disruption and disintegration at the local level. At the same time, each local economy ceased to be directed exclusively or even primarily towards the satisfaction of the wants of its inhabitants; and (whether or not the particular Africans recognized it) their economic effort served external interests and made them dependent on those external forces based in Western Europe. In this way, the African economy taken as a whole was diverted away from its previous line of development and became distorted.

Patrick Manning

Social and Demographic Transformations

Historian Patrick Manning of Northeastern University places his interpretation of the slave trade's impact in the context of schools of historical interpretation that go back more than two centuries. He contrasts older views of
African societies as static with modern historians' presumption of an "African
dynamism" and further distinguishes between those who see Africa's history
as controlled from within ("emergent Africa") and those who see it as exter-
nally dominated ("Afrique engagée"). He places Rodney in the latter school,
but he criticizes Rodney's view that Africa was simultaneously being stifled
by its relationship with capitalism while some parts of the continent were experiencing positive development despite the trade. In effect, Manning faults
Rodney for trying to have one foot in each camp. Manning then goes on to
support the interpretation of "Afrique engagée," stressing that the demographic and social effects of the slave trade were interconnected with the economic effects, a point that he subsequently developed in his book *Slavery and
African Life: Occidental, Oriental and African Slave Trades* (1990).

The old interpretations and the old disputes on Africa and the slave trade
have left their mark. The vision of eternal Africa allowed room for dis-
agreement about the impact of the slave trade, and these disagreements
have found their way into the current literature. The contrasting interpretations separated those who contended that the transatlantic commerce in slaves brought major changes to African societies from those
who denied that trade in slaves disturbed the African social order.
Archibald Dalzel, the eighteenth-century English slave trader and propa-
gandist, argued that African society remained unaffected, and he quoted

From Patrick Manning, "Contours of Slavery and Social Change in Africa," *American Historical Review* 88, no. 4, October 1983, pp. 836–839, 844–851, 853, 856–857. Copyright
© 1983. Reprinted by permission of the American Historical Association, and the author.

King Kpengla of Danhomè* in support of his position. David Livingstone, the mid-nineteenth-century explorer and missionary, argued forcefully that, to the contrary, slavery and the slave trade were devastating to African society. At the turn of the twentieth century Sir Harry Hamilton Johnston, an imperial man-on-the-spot and amateur scholar, attempted to synthesize these conflicting positions in an interpretation that is in some ways more optimistic than either: "Abominable as the slave trade has been in filling Tropical Africa with incessant warfare and rapine . . . , its ravages will soon be repaired by a few decades of peace and security during which this prolific, unextinguishable negro race will rapidly increase its numbers."

Both the similarities and the differences among these arguments are instructive. Dalzel and Johnston saw African societies as robust and able to withstand the pressures of the slave trade, while Livingstone viewed African societies as fragile and easily shattered. All three, however, shared the view of African societies as static. Although it had survived the slave trade intact, the "prolific, unextinguishable negro race," in Johnston's words, had not progressed—had not gained the ability "to start the children from a higher level than the parents." This vision of eternal Africa, emphasizing stagnation and resistance to change, took root and survived in the minds of observers largely because of the difficulty of knowing what changes had taken place. This difficulty, in turn, stemmed not only from the scarcity and dispersal of documentation on precolonial Africa but also from the blurring of perception brought about by cultural differences between African and European observers.

Contemporary Africanist historians have shown remarkable success in bridging the gaps within the documentary record and between cultures, not least because of the growing number of African contributors to the literature. Yet the rise of the Africanist tradition has not been sufficient to resolve the role of the slave trade in precolonial Africa. Instead, the earlier contending views—whether trade in slaves exerted great or small influence on African historical development—have aligned themselves with two interpretive tendencies that have grown up within the Africanist literature. For instance, Basil Davidson, writing in the early 1960s when many African countries were regaining their independence, argued, "Viewed as a factor in African history, the precolonial connection

---

*Also spelled "Dahomey." *Ed.*

with Europe—essentially, the slave trade—had powerfully degrading consequences for the structure of society." Some years later John D. Fage brought to the debate the revised figures on the magnitude of the slave trade; he concluded that the eighteenth-century loss of four million persons from West Africa did not reduce its population, and he later added that the region's social institutions similarly remained unaffected. Considering many of the same data but also taking underdevelopment into account, Walter Rodney reasoned that, on the contrary, the trade in slaves had brought great harm to African economic and political structures. A decade later Joseph C. Miller argued, with reference to West Central Africa, that a domestically generated cycle of drought, disease, and famine did more to limit population and provoke social change than did the impact of slave exports.

All of the participants in this recent discussion of the impact of the slave trade on Africa have assumed an African dynamism. The differences among them are in the relative emphases they have given to external forces of change. Can the external forces be safely minimized and treated as boundary conditions for a situation in which the major forces for change were domestic, as Fage and Miller have argued? Such an analytical approach may be termed the vision of "emergent Africa": as the historical reconstruction of African social change has become increasingly detailed, this approach has become widely influential in the thinking of Africanist historians. Or must external factors be drawn fully into the analysis of precolonial forces for change, as Davidson and Rodney have contended? This is the vision of "Afrique engagée," which focuses on such interactions as much as on domestic evolution. The choice between the two is determined by ascertaining which leads to the most detailed and yet elegant interpretation of the historical record.

John Fage's view of the role of the slave trade in precolonial Africa dominated the opinions of historians during the 1970s. For West Africa, Fage compared eighteenth-century slave exports that averaged forty thousand per year with a population he estimated at twenty-five million and a growth rate he estimated at 1.5 per thousand—or, some thirty-eight thousand—per year. Hence, "the effect of the export slave trade in the eighteenth century may have been more or less to check population growth," and its impact was in consequence minimal even at the height of slave exports. Fage continued, "The conclusion to which one is led, therefore, is that whereas in East and Central Africa the slave trade, sometimes conducted in the interior by raiding and warring strangers, could be extremely destructive of economic, political and social life, in West Africa it was part of a sustained process of economic and political development." West Africa's domestic processes of evolution were potent enough, in Fage's view, to absorb, neutralize, and, conceivably, even benefit from the effects of participation in slave exports. Although he admitted that the negative effects of slave trade might have been greater outside of West Africa, other scholars have claimed that, particularly for Central Africa, the population and social institutions successfully withstood the pressures of the slave trade. This is the vision of emergent Africa, as applied to the impact of the trade in slaves.

Basil Davidson and Walter Rodney, while basing their views on the assumption of an evolving, developing African society, nevertheless asserted that the slave trade had a significantly detrimental effect on African society. Theirs was a vision of a precolonial Afrique engagée and of a continent that suffered from the engagement. The details of their arguments, however, rely not so much on demographic reasoning (both assumed that the African population did not decline) as on the interruption of African institutional and social progress. "The years of trial," as Davidson called the precolonial era, "were years of isolation and paralysis wherever the trade with Europe, essentially a trade in slaves, could plant its sterilizing hand." Although Davidson, with his slaves-for-guns thesis, and Rodney, with his underdevelopment thesis, listed striking examples to support this view, neither was able to develop a sustained and detailed analysis. Moreover, their image of the meeting of European and African influences depicted not so much a true interaction of the two as the truncation of the latter by the former. Their interpretation thus veers back toward Harry Johnston's image of eternal Africa, except that Davidson and Rodney emphasized the negative, rather than the positive, contributions of European contact to African development.

With a reformulation of the argument, however, the vision of Afrique engagée has gained validity as the relevant framework for interpreting the role of the slave trade in precolonial African history. The limits of Fage's interpretation are centered in his aggregative approach: he did not give much attention to the breakdown of slave exports by sex or age or to the impact of changes in quantities and prices of slave exports over time. Disaggregation of the data, when combined with analysis based on demographic principles and price theory, leads to results that are different from, and in some cases contradictory to, those previously accepted. The interactions of the New World demand for slaves with domestic conditions in Africa brought about—long before the late nineteenth century Scramble for Africa—pervasive social change. Such social changes included the expansion and subsequent transformation of polygyny, the development of two different types of African slavery, the creation and subsequent impoverishment of a class of African merchants, and a final expansion of slavery in the decades before the Scramble. Although the most profound changes from the interaction of the slave trade and African conditions occurred along the western coast of Africa, almost all regions of Africa were touched by the influence of the export trade at one time or another. . . .

The Atlantic slave trade before 1650 rarely carried more than ten thousand slaves per year. Its aggregate impact o n the continent was, therefore, small, although the experiences of certain regions prefigured the sharp pressures that were subsequently felt on a broader scale. The Kongo kingdom, for instance, became the main source of slaves for the sugar plantations of São Thomé in the sixteenth century, and numerous sources confirm the corrosive effect of slave exports on Kongo political structure and on the spread of Christianity there. The Upper Guinea Coast supplied large numbers of slaves (predominantly male) as New World laborers in the early seventeenth century, and accounts of contemporary observers give strong support to the image of a predominantly female society left behind, in which women took over agricultural and fishing tasks to assure sufficient production. Although only these two regions, Senegambia, and perhaps the kingdom of Benin exported enough slaves in these early days to influence population size and composition, virtually every region on the western coast of Africa provided some slaves to European purchasers in the years before 1650. But slaves had not yet become Africa's dominant export: gold exports, especially from the Gold Coast, exceeded the value of African slave exports until the end of the seventeenth century.

A qualitative change in the slave trade took form at the turn of the eighteenth century; a four-fold increase in slave prices occurred within thirty years. From the late sixteenth century to the mid-eighteenth century, the quantity of slaves shipped across the Atlantic grew at an average rate of 2 percent per year. Driving this growing demand was the sugar plantation system, as Brazil came to be joined by Barbados, Jamaica, Martinique, and other colonies. By 1650 the New World had displaced the Middle East as the dominant destination of African slaves. During

the final years of price stability in the seventeenth century, African suppliers developed efficient methods for delivering more slaves with no increase in cost. But, by the opening of the eighteenth century, the limits
on the ability of Africans to provide cheap slaves had been reached, and
prices rose dramatically. The cost of obtaining slaves rose as prospective
captives learned to defend themselves better and as middlemen and toll
collectors interposed themselves into the process of delivery. For these
reasons as well as actual population decline, slaves became scarce relative to the level of demand. The price increases in this period led to the
establishment of something resembling a world market for slave labor,
in which New World demand and prices for slaves were so high that
both slave prices and the quantity of slaves moved were affected not
only along the western coast but in many regions of the African continent as well.

Two African regions bore the brunt of the expansion in exports at
the turn of the eighteenth century: the Bight of Benin and the Gold
Coast. Both of these regions experienced numerous wars among small
states near the coast, from which captives were sold to the Europeans.
For the Gold Coast, it meant the eclipse of gold as the main regional export for a time; for the Bight of Benin it brought entry into large-scale Atlantic trade. In both cases, the volume of slave exports rose within three
decades to a level that reduced the region's population, after which slave
exports declined slowly. Similar patterns of export increase to the limits
of population tolerance, with a subsequent slow decline in exports, can
be traced for other regions at other times. For Upper Guinea, the most
substantial export of slaves occurred between 1600 and 1630. For the
Senegambia, after a spurt of exports in the sixteenth century, exports rose
again to a peak in the late seventeenth century. For the Bight of Biafra,
slave exports shot up from the 1740s to the 1760s and remained at a high
level through the 1820s. The Loango coast experienced a sharp increase
in export volume in the years from 1720 to 1740 and another increase
to a still higher volume from 1780 to 1800. Angola also experienced two
great spurts in exports: one in the mid-seventeenth century, after which
slave exports declined, and one during the 1720s to 1740s, after which
exports remained at a high level into the nineteenth century.

Each of these sudden regional expansions in the slave trade
caused—and reflected—changes in the methods and the morality of obtaining slaves. War, judicial procedures, and kidnapping were the main
processes by which slaves were obtained—war predominated in most of

West Africa, kidnapping predominated in the Bight of Biafra, and judicial procedures played a leading role in Central Africa. For the Gold Coast, Ray Kea has documented changes in the technology and social organization of war that preceded the expansion of slave exports there. As war was transformed from the combat of elites, with minimal and defensive war aims, to combat based on musketry, on the *levée en masse*, and on objectives of territorial conquest, a seemingly endless stream of conflicts and captives was unleashed. A similar transformation accompanied the rise of slave exports from the Bight of Benin.

Were the wars provoked by the desire to sell slaves, or were the captives simply a by-product of wars fought for other reasons? Observers of the slave trade have debated the question inconclusively ever since the Atlantic trade began. Philip Curtin posed this choice with an eye to sustaining the vision of emergent Africa: he contrasted a political model and an economic model for enslavement in the Senegambia and concluded that the evidence best supported the political model. E. Phillip LeVeen offered the economist's response. The decision to export slaves captured according to the political model depended on the level of prices, and thus slave exporting, as opposed to capturing, fits the economic model. The test of the issue is the responsiveness of slave export quantities to price changes. Even for small and well-defined areas, the elasticity of slave supply fluctuated sharply with passage of time. Much of the apparent disorder, however, can be resolved by distinguishing periods when the system of supply was stable and positive price-responsiveness was clear (1730 to 1800 in the Bight of Benin) from periods when the ability of merchants to supply slaves was either improving sharply (1740 to 1780 in the Bight of Biafra) or declining (1690 to 1730 in the Bight of Benin). These three examples can be set within the vision of Afrique engagée. In the Bight of Benin in the eighteenth century, domestic and external forces were locked in an equilibrium of sorts; in the Bight of Biafra in the mid-eighteenth century, domestic conditions changed more rapidly than can be explained by the influence of external forces alone; and in the Bight of Benin from the late seventeenth through the early eighteenth century external influences were the main source of African sociodemographic change.

As the demand for slaves continued to grow, opportunities for restrictive and monopolistic practices arose. Richard Nelson Bean, who has collected the best data on prices, joined with Robert Paul Thomas to argue that the Atlantic slave market was competitive and did not allow for monopoly profits, since European shippers could escape price gouging in one African port by going to another. The contrary position is based on the argument that, since European shippers required a speedy turn-around and good relations with their African suppliers, they were tied to a single port. Even without monopoly profits, however, some African slave exporters may have collected high rates of profit through economic rent—that is, those merchants who were able to obtain slaves at unusually low cost still sold them at the prevailing market price. The African revenues from slave exports, which rose along with prices at the turn of the eighteenth century, were almost all turned into expenditures on imported goods: the value and volume of these imports thus increased dramatically at the same time that export prices rose.

The sudden increases in mercantile profit and in the volume of imported goods simultaneously began to restrict African population size. The technique of using New World inventories of slaves to project the ethnic origins of slave exports has established that, for the Bight of Benin, slaves came almost entirely from the Aja-speaking peoples in and around the kingdom of Danhomè, near the coast. The full demographic drain on the Bight of Benin was concentrated on this group, which experienced a loss estimated at over 3 percent of the population each year for over forty consecutive years. This loss was sufficient to reduce the Aja population substantially over the course of a century, both in absolute terms and in relation to the surrounding ethnic groups, notably the Yoruba. . . .

The coastal exports of young adult slaves, twice as many men as women, tended to transform the structure of the population and the organization of society. A surplus of women developed, so that polygyny was reinforced, and work done by women in some places replaced that done by men. African traditions of family structure and division of labor, no matter how deeply instilled, could not but bend before these demographic pressures. The tradition of female agricultural labor in the matrilineal belt of Zaire and Angola may have been strengthened as an accommodation to the shortage of men for production. Similarly, although the institution of polygyny preceded the slave trade, its extent was reinforced by the surplus of women. In addition, a surplus of women meant that men did not need to wait until their late twenties and thirties to marry their first and second wives. Indeed, the fear of enslavement may have encouraged men to marry at a young age. . . .

The demand for slaves affected African polities by causing them not only to participate in slave exports but also to attempt to end it. The kingdom of Benin successfully withdrew from supplying slaves early in the sixteenth century. The Oyo Empire, though by reputation long tied to the slave trade, probably contributed only minimally to the export of slaves from Africa until late in the eighteenth century. And Boubacar Barry has interpreted the political events of the late seventeenth century in the Waalo kingdom of Senegal as an abortive attempt to withdraw from the slave trade. It is for the kingdom of Danhomè that the issue of attempted withdrawal from the slave trade has caused the most controversy. There is a certain plausibility to the notion that, in an area that was ravaged by trade in slaves and that experienced depopulation along with internecine wars, one state should attempt to conquer the whole region to end such conflicts and prevent social collapse. The question remains whether King Agaja's wars of the 1770s were an attempt to do so. But Danhomè's invasion and subjugation by the distant yet powerful Oyo made any such expanded Aja state impossible, and from 1730 to 1830 Danhomè faced a ring of weakened but by no means vanquished enemies; the internecine wars provided the New World with an inordinately large proportion of its slave laborers.

The case of Asante, to the west, represents a slightly different resolution of the same problem. Asante rose in the late seventeenth century to challenge Denkyira, the Gold Coast's dominant power, and eventually succeeded in incorporating virtually all the Twi-speaking peoples. As a result, the export of the people of Asante declined after about 1730, and the large number of slaves exported from the Gold Coast in succeeding years came increasingly from the interior Voltaic peoples. In Oyo, only with the constitutional crisis and a series of factional disputes that began in the 1770s did that kingdom's export slave trade become significant, and the magnitude of slave exports grew with the decay of the state. Thus, although the slave trade certainly affected politics, the nature of the trade's impact varied sharply from polity to polity; sometimes, as in the case of Oyo, politics influenced the trade in slaves more than the trade influenced internal affairs.

The aggregate demographic impact of the slave trade on Africa reached a peak in the late eighteenth century, when slave exports averaged some one hundred thousand per year, and this high level of export continued into the early nineteenth century. During this period, the foci of enslavement tended to move from west to east and from coast to interior. For this period, then, it is most appropriate to assert that slave exports diminished the African population.

One method of assessing the population drain on individual ethnic groups entails, as mentioned above, making a New World inventory of slaves' ethnic origins. A second approach focuses on whole regions, assessing the ability of regional populations to reproduce themselves in the face of the population drain resulting from slave exports. Roger Anstey, David Northrup, and, most effectively, John Thornton have used this procedure to good effect. Thornton's results indicate a decline in the population of the whole Congo-Angola region during the eighteenth century, and his analysis further suggests that, during the height of the export trade, most of the regions of the West African coast could have withstood the pressure from the trade in slaves only with difficulty. A third approach, continental in scope, has been adopted by Joseph Inikori. His method focuses not so much on the actual reduction in population as on the difference between the actual population of Africa and the counterfactual population that might have existed in the absence of slave exports.

Yet another approach involves the estimation of the impact of the slave trade through computer simulation. In this case, a model African population is postulated, divided into raiding and raided groups, and assigned a series of demographic and slave-trade rates: fertility, mortality, age-sex composition of the captured population, division of the captives between domestic and exported slaves, and so forth. Preliminary projections of the model's results suggest that the slave trade caused losses that, if not devastating to the continent, were certainly severe. For the western coast, a region with an estimated population of twenty-five million in 1700, some six million slaves left in the course of the eighteenth century. The total number enslaved is projected at some twelve million, with four million retained in domestic slavery and over two million lost to death in the course of enslavement. Under these conditions, the African population in 1800 was substantially less than it would have been in the absence of the trade in slaves. For the northern savanna and Horn, whose exports rarely exceeded twenty thousand per year, losses in slave exports were felt more acutely than the numbers alone suggest, because of the predominance of women exported. As a result, the northern savanna and the Horn were probably unable to experience any increase in population during the seventeenth and eighteenth centuries.

The demographic drain of the slave trade interacted with Africa's periodic droughts and famines. As the experience of the nineteenth century suggests, the incidence of drought and famine served at once to increase and to decrease slave exports. The onset of bad times caused the destitute to sell themselves or their children into slavery; but the decline in population resulting from famine tended to reduce the number of slaves. Stephen Baier and Paul E. Lovejoy have documented the great drought of the northern savanna in the mid-eighteenth century, which caused hardship, migration, and economic decline. Climatic recovery in the following decades led to economic growth, which was reflected both in the increase in slave exports and in the rise of the Sokoto Caliphate. Jill Dias and Joseph C. Miller have documented a cycle of drought, famine, and epidemic in Angola that severely limited population growth. These Malthusian checks on population provide the primary evidence for revising downward Inikori's estimates of the counterfactual African population: Africa's population would surely have been substantially greater without the slave trade, but to know how much so requires a better knowledge of the effects of famine and disease than we now have. Miller may, however, have gone too far in arguing that the limits imposed by disease and drought were so great that these factors, rather than the slave trade, provided the fundamental limits on Angola's population.

The selective export of women from the coastal regions had its greatest impact in the late eighteenth century. The results of the simulation model suggests [*sic*] that, while the sex ratio among those populations that lost slaves remained roughly equal, the proportion of adult women to men rose substantially for the western coast as a whole: the estimated ratio of adult women to men rose to roughly six to five among the raiding populations. But in those areas with the heaviest participation in slave exporting, the disparity in the sex ratio became greater. John Thornton's analysis of the Portuguese censuses for Angola indicates that the ratio of adult women to men was as much as two to one. On the one hand, this sex ratio shows how African societies could attempt to cope with an enormous drain on the population with losing their ability to reproduce; the people of Angola virtually became a livestock herd to be harvested. On the other, one woman was exported for every two to three men, and the loss of the women's reproductive potential made it all the more difficult for the population to maintain

itself. The bulk of the agricultural labor fell on the women who remained in Angola, and the incidence of polygyny remained high. . . .

By the mid-nineteenth century, a dramatic reversal in the character of the Atlantic slave trade had taken place. Most New World areas
had dropped out of the slave trade, and slave imports were illegal in the
remaining areas of demand—Cuba and Brazil. As a result, although the
prices of slaves in the New World rose because of the scarcity of new imports, the export demand for slaves at any given price on the African
coast had fallen significantly, and the price of slaves in Africa fell almost
as significantly. The relatively scarce price data available for the early
nineteenth century are somewhat contradictory, so the precise timing of
the price decline remains to be confirmed. But it is clear that, sometime
between 1780 and 1850, the price of slaves on the African coast fell, in
real terms, by one-half. The mechanisms of slave supply remained in
place, however, so that a glut on the slave market became evident. This
nineteenth-century glut brought a pervasive change in the character of
African slavery: as slaves, particularly male slaves, came within the purchasing power of African buyers, the scope of African slavery expanded
greatly in the mid-nineteenth century, although the total number of
people captured may not have changed greatly.

As more women remained in Africa, the number of births dramatically increased; and, as more men stayed, the previous drain of the adult
male population ended, although the process of enslavement for the
African market still implied a significant mortality. These changes resulted in rapid population growth. In addition, the large number of
cheap male slaves now made the situation on the coast much more like
that in the savanna, where male slaves were used for agricultural labor.
Thus the coastal areas now developed slave plantations that produced
for palace populations, for the African market, and for export. The mid-
nineteenth-century growth in the export of palm oil, coffee, and peanuts
thus reflected not only the rise in European demand for these products
but also a significant decline in the cost of production because of the
fall in slave prices. . . .

Ethnographers of the early twentieth century, writing in the last
days of [African] slavery, described the institution as relatively benign,
emphasizing the legal and societal protections available to slaves as well
as their potential for upward mobility. These reports—written after slave

raiding and the trade in slaves had ceased and after slaveholders had lost the support of the state—stand in sharp contrast to the travelers' reports of the late nineteenth century, which tell of brutal raids, immense loss of life, and massive exploitation of slaves by masters. Each of these views of African slavery was appropriate to the precise time at which it was written. Both views, but particularly the former, have in turn been taken by subsequent scholars as appropriate characterizations of African slavery across the centuries.

The vision of emergent Africa, based on the assumed existence of continuous pressures for change within African societies, tends to suggest that both of these static views of servile institutions were invalid, without posing an alternative. The vision of Afrique engagée, by explicitly re-introducing external forces of causation into a framework that assumes an African dynamism not only confirms that suggestion but indicates the nature and timing of some important African social changes. In so doing, this historiographical approach must admit to a range in the type of interactions. In some cases, domestic forces dominated the interactions; the expansion and transformation of polygyny under the influence of the slave trade, for example, took place in the context of a previous African attachment to multiple marriage. In other cases, external forces dominated the interaction; both depopulation and the impact of imported goods, for instance, represent the domination of outside influences. And the precise combination of domestic and external forces provided the key impetus to certain changes, notably in the rise of Asante and Danhomè, the collapse of Kongo, and the mutual reinforcement of the slave trade, famine, and epidemic.

The return on this increased complexity in analytical framework is a clearer time-perspective on African society. African slavery, along with a range of associated institutions, underwent successive transformations in the seventeenth, eighteenth, and nineteenth centuries under the impact of changing economic, demographic, and political conditions. Suzanne Miers and Igor Kopytoff, in an essay that sits firmly within the emergent Africa tradition of analysis, have gone so far as to criticize the use of the term "slavery" in Africa on the grounds that it implies a greater uniformity in African institutions of servitude than is warranted. Their emphasis on the specificity, in sociological cross-section, of African systems of slavery is valid in principle if somewhat exaggerated in practice. To their sociological specificity must be added, however, the specificity of African societies in historical time-perspective, as they changed through the action of the diverse creative powers within them and the varying external pressures upon them. In the era of the slave trade, the external influences were so powerful as to set in motion comparable trends in social change in many parts of the African continent two centuries before the colonial conquest did in a vastly different fashion.

John Thornton

Africa's Effects on the Slave Trade

The most recent excerpt (this volume's second from John Thornton's book) accepts that Africa suffered serious demographic damage from the slave trade, but Thornton is less willing than Manning to blame external factors for Africa's social ills and is quite unwilling to accept Rodney's under-development thesis. Instead, Thornton argues that Africans participated in the slave trade willingly, with full understanding, and from a position of strength. He suggests that in many places a preexisting trade in slaves was simply diverted into the Atlantic.

The success of Africans in resisting the early European attempts at raiding their coasts meant that the interactions that would follow would be largely peaceful and commercial—for it would not be until 1579 that a major war would develop, in Angola, and even there it rapidly became an indecisive standstill. There would be no dramatic European conquests in Africa, and even the slaves who would flood the South Atlantic and sustain colonization in America would be purchased more often than captured. This state of affairs was already being put in place by [the Portuguese] expeditions in 1456–62 and would characterize relations between Europeans and Africans for centuries to come.

From John Thornton, *Africa and Africans in the Making of the Atlantic World, 1400–1800*, 2nd ed. Reprinted with the permission of Cambridge University Press.

African naval victories might not necessarily guarantee that the commerce that grew up in place of raiding was truly under African control or necessarily served their interests (or the interests of the wealthy and powerful in African society). Indeed, many scholars in recent years have most often seen the commerce of Atlantic Africa with Europeans as destructive and unequal, with Europeans reaping most of the long-range profits and Africans unable to benefit or being forced, through commercial weakness, into accepting trade that ultimately placed Africa in its current situation of dependency and underdevelopment.

Perhaps the most influential scholar to advocate such a position was Walter Rodney, whose work on Africa's Atlantic trade concluded that the commerce with Europe was a first, decisive step in the underdevelopment of Africa. As Rodney saw it, this was because Africa was at a lower level of economic development than Europe and was thus forced into a sort of "colonial" trade in which Africans gave up raw materials and human resources (in the form of slaves) in exchange for manufactured goods—a form of dependency that certainly characterizes modern African trade. . . .

An examination of African economic development by 1500 and the exact nature of the Atlantic trade, however, does not support this pessimistic position. Africans played a more active role in developing the commerce, and they did so on their own initiative. On the one hand, the Atlantic trade was not nearly as critical to the African economy as these scholars believed, and on the other hand, African manufacturing was more than capable of handling competition from preindustrial Europe.

In order to understand the role of the African economy in the Atlantic trade we need to examine two related issues, both of which are raised in the works of scholars who see Africans as junior and dependent trading partners. First is the assumption of African backwardness in manufacturing, based largely on the analogy with Africa's present lack of manufacturing capacity and its impact on modern African economies. Second is the assumption of commercial domination, in which Europeans somehow were able to control the market for African goods, either through monopoly or through commercial manipulation of some other sort. . . .

Europe exported a wide range of goods to Africa before 1650, of which we can recognize several categories. First and surely foremost in terms of volume was cloth—a whole world of textiles of dozens of types by the seventeenth century. Then there were metal goods, principally iron and copper, in raw (iron bars and copper manillas) and worked form (knives, swords, copper basins and bowls, etc.). Next there was currency, consisting of tons of cowry shells. This trade was especially important in Benin and the Slave Coast though shells were also imported into central Africa. Finally there is what we might describe as nonutilitarian items, such as jewelry (beads for the most part), mechanical toys and curiosities, and alcoholic beverages.

What is significant about all of these items is that none were "essential commodities." Africa had well-developed industries producing every single item on the list, and although not all of them were produced in every district, a substantial number of these items were imported into regions where there was clearly no pressing need, in a strictly functional sense, to import them.

It was, in short, not to meet African needs that the trade developed or even to make up for shortfalls in production or failures in quality of the African manufactures. Rather, Africa's trade with Europe was largely moved by prestige, fancy, changing taste, and a desire for variety—and such whimsical motivations were backed up by a relatively well developed productive economy and substantial purchasing power. The Atlantic trade of Africa was not simply motivated by the filling of basic needs, and the propensity to import on the part of Africans was not simply a measure of their need or inefficiency, but instead, it was a measure of the extent of their domestic market. . . .

In the end, then, the European trade with Africa can scarcely be seen as disruptive in itself, for it did not oust any line of African production, nor did it thwart development by providing items through trade that might have otherwise been manufactured in Africa, even if one differentiates, say, high-quality cloth from low or high-grade steel from low. There was no reason, therefore, that Africans should have wanted to stop the trade, or that their desire to continue it was based on necessity. . . .

It is fairly clear . . . that European merchants, whether acting under the direction of states or companies, were unable to monopolize the trade of Africa. It is just as clear that African states, although attempting the same sort of thing, were ultimately no more successful. No African state ever really dominated the trade of any part of the African coast. African sovereignty was just as fragmented as the theoretical sovereignty that Europeans tried to maintain over the trade.

However, the African states did help to balance whatever economies of scale individual European merchants or companies may have had. Thus, it might be argued that a well-capitalized European merchant could have taken economic advantage, at least in the short run, of intense competition between hundreds of African traders. The African states' role in commerce limited this effect, however, thus offsetting whatever advantages a shipper's scale of operations might have afforded.

State requirements put a great number of legal and technical obstacles between European merchants and African buyers, as well as making the state itself a regular participant in the trade. A Dutch commercial guide of about 1655, for example, records the gifts and taxes that had to be paid in a variety of countries along the "Slave Coast" area from the Volta to Cameroon. Those at Allada were perhaps the most complicated, although perhaps only because the writer of the guide (apparently resident in São Tomé) understood them best. There, the prospective buyer of slaves and cloth from Allada had to present a complex series of presents to dancers, food sellers, linguists, brokers, Allada nobles, and the king himself, both upon arrival and upon departure. That such a system was not unique to Allada is clearly shown in the variety of customs the guide describes at Benin, Calabar, the Niger delta, and the Gabon region. . . .

These negotiations, which were often time-consuming and which many Europeans visitors thought to complain of, were essentially a manifestation of the insistence on the part of authorities in African states that they benefit first and certainly from trade. They were often willing to provide return gifts, sometimes of substantial value, after customs were paid . . . as a way of making a special connection between themselves and the European with whom they were trading. But typically their desire was to ensure that they received first choice of the best goods and the best price, which perhaps constituted a second tax that went along with the gifts that made up the customs charges. . . .

But after African rulers had insisted on involving their sovereign rights to control trade or guarantee their profits, they were usually content to allow trade to take place freely once they had received their share. But very often even this trade was far from being the commercial free-for-all of a real market. This was because although African states allowed private trade, they played a major role in determining which Africans would be able to trade. The African bourgeoisie, like their counterparts in Europe, thrived largely because the state supported their position, and in many ways they used this patronage to their advantage.

If Africans were experienced traders and were not somehow dominated by European merchants due to European market control or some superiority in manufacturing or trading techniques, then we can say confidently that Africa's commercial relationship with Europe was not unlike international trade anywhere in the world of the period. But historians have balked at this conclusion because they believe that the slave trade, which was an important branch of Afro-European commerce from the beginning, should not be viewed as a simple commodity exchange. After all, slaves are also a source of labor, and at least to some extent, their removal from Africa represented a major loss to Africa. The sale of slaves must therefore have been harmful to Africa, and African decisions to sell must have been forced or involuntary for one or more reasons.

The idea of the slave trade as a harmful commerce is especially supported by the work of historical demographers. Most who have studied the question of the demographic consequences of the trade have reached broad agreement that the trade was demographically damaging from a fairly early period, especially when examined from a local or regional (as opposed to a continental) perspective. In addition to the net demographic drain, which began early in some areas (like Angola), the loss of adult males had potentially damaging impacts on sex ratios, dependency rates, and perhaps the sexual division of labor.

In addition to these demographic effects, historians interested in social and political history have followed Walter Rodney in arguing that the slave trade caused social disruption (such as increasing warfare and related military damage), adversely altered judicial systems, or increased inequality. Moreover, Rodney argued that the slave trade increased the numbers of slaves being held in Africa and intensified their exploitation, a position that Paul Lovejoy, its most recent advocate, calls the "transformation thesis." Because of this perception of a widespread negative impact, many scholars have argued that the slave trade, if not other forms of commerce, must have been forced on unwilling African participants, perhaps through the type of commercial inequities that we have already discussed or perhaps through some sort of military pressure. . . .

When Rodney presented his conclusions on the negative impact and hence special status of the slave trade as a branch of trade, it was quickly contested by J. D. Fage, and more recently, the transformation thesis has been attacked by David Eltis. As these scholars see it, slavery was widespread and indigenous in African society, as was, naturally enough, a commerce in slaves. Europeans simply tapped this existing market, and Africans responded to the increased demand over the centuries by providing more slaves. The demographic impact, although important, was local and difficult to disentangle from losses due to internal wars and slave trading on the domestic African market. In any case, the decision makers who allowed the trade to continue, whether merchants or political leaders, did not personally suffer the larger-scale losses and were able to maintain their operations. Consequently, one need not accept that they were forced into participation against their will or made decisions irrationally.

The evidence for the period before 1680 generally supports this second position. Slavery was widespread in Africa, and its growth and development were largely independent of the Atlantic trade, except that insofar as the Atlantic commerce stimulated internal commerce and development it also led to more widespread holding of slaves. The Atlantic slave trade was the outgrowth of this internal slavery. Its demographic impact, however, even in the early stages was significant, but the people adversely affected by this impact were not the ones making the decisions about participation. . . .

Thus, . . . the slave trade (and the Atlantic trade in general) should not be seen as an "impact" brought in from outside and functioning as some sort of autonomous factor in African history. Instead, it grew out of and was rationalized by the African societies who participated in it and had complete control over it until the slaves were loaded onto European ships for transfer to Atlantic societies.

The reason that slavery was widespread in Africa was not, as some have asserted, because Africa was an economically underdeveloped region in which forced labor had not yet been replaced by free labor. Instead, slavery was rooted in deep-seated legal and institutional structures of African societies, and it functioned quite differently from the way it functioned in European societies. . . .

Thus slaves could be found in all parts of Atlantic Africa, performing all sorts of duties. When Europeans came to Africa and offered to buy slaves, it is hardly surprising that they were almost immediately accepted. Not only were slaves found widely in Africa, but the area had a well-developed slave trade, as evidenced by the numbers of slaves in private hands. Anyone who had the wherewithal could obtain slaves from the domestic market, though sometimes it required royal or state permission, as in the Gold Coast. Europeans could tap this market just as any African could.

Moreover, the most likely owners of slaves—wealthy merchants and state officials or rulers—were exactly the people with whom European traders came into contact. Because merchants selling gold, ivory products, mats, copper bracelets, pepper, or any other trade commodity in Africa would also be interested in the buying and selling of slaves, European merchants could readily find sources. This was not so much because Africans were inveterate slave dealers, as it was because the legal basis for wealth in Africa lay in the idea of transferring ownership of people. This legal structure made slavery and slave marketing widespread and created secondary legal mechanisms for securing and regulating the sale of slaves, which Europeans could use as well as Africans.

The significance of African slavery in the development of the slave trade can be clearly seen in the remarkable speed with which the continent began exporting slaves. As soon as the Portuguese had reached the Senegal region and abandoned their early strategy of raiding for commerce, 700–1,000 slaves were exported per year, . . . reaching as many as 1,200–2,500 slaves per year by the end of the century. . . . The reason that such dramatic numbers were reached immediately may indicate nothing more . . . than that a preexisting engagement with foreign markets was transferred to Atlantic ones. Most of the early European slave trading with West Africa, even that with such relatively remote regions as Benin and the Niger delta, known in the sixteenth century as the "River of Slaves," was simply an internal trade diverted to the Atlantic. . . .

That existing internal use and commerce in slaves lay behind the export trade is even more strongly suggested by the trade of central Africa. Unlike the West African trade, which drew on an ancient slave trade with North Africa and might thus have already been affected by external contacts, the central African region had no such external links. Nevertheless, the king of Portugal regarded Kongo as sufficiently important a potential exporter of slaves that he granted settlers in São Tomé privileges to engage in the slave trade in 1493, just a few years after the development of official trade there. . . . Unfortunately we possess no early statistics for the volume of this trade, but . . . around 1507, in addition to some 2,000 slaves working on sugar plantations, the island held

5,000–6,000 slaves awaiting reexport. Presumably these slaves were recent imports who had probably arrived within the last year, and certainly half, but probably the majority, originated in central Africa. . . .

Slaves from central Africa were so numerous that they soon exceeded the capacity of São Tomé and the Mina trade to absorb them, and so they began the long journey to European markets. . . . Thus, at some point, probably within twenty years of first contact, central Africa was able to supply exports of slaves equal to the entire exports of West Africa. Clearly this sort of volume could not simply have been the occasional export of odd misfits. Nor have we any reason to believe that the Portuguese were able to either acquire the slaves themselves (except as clients of the Kongo kings) or force the Kongo to obtain the export slaves against their will. Instead, the growth of Kongo's trade had to draw on a well-developed system of slavery, slave marketing, and slave delivery that preexisted any European contact.

We must therefore conclude that the Atlantic slave trade and African participation in it had solid origins in African societies and legal systems. The institution of slavery was widespread in Africa and accepted in all the exporting regions, and the capture, purchase, transport, and sale of slaves was a regular feature of African society. This preexisting social arrangement was thus as much responsible as any external force for the development of the Atlantic slave trade.

PART

 V

Effects in Europe and the Americas

VARIETY OF OPINION

The triangular trade made an enormous contribution to Britain's industrial development. The profits from this trade fertilized the entire productive system of the country.

ERIC WILLIAMS

Williams's dramatic revaluation of the role of the slave trade and slavery . . . in the British industrial revolution . . . now has few defenders, even among those who argue for high profits.

SEYMOUR DRESCHER

After arriving in Louisiana, the Bambara maintained an organized language community, formed alliances with the Indian nations who were in revolt against the French, and conspired to take over the colony.

GWENDOLYN MIDLO HALL

133

> *[S]eeing the dominance of particular African . . . ethnicities in most American settings . . . is at variance with the central forces shaping the early modern Atlantic world.*
>
> PHILIP D. MORGAN

Eric Williams

Slavery, Industrialization, and Abolition

In his classic study *Capitalism and Slavery*, Eric Williams argues vigorously that the industrial revolution in Britain was closely linked to profits from the trade in African slavery. He includes in his calculations revenues from all parts of the "triangle trade" in the Atlantic—that is, from the trade of goods to Africa, from the Middle Passage, and from the sugar production in the Caribbean brought back to Europe. He further ties the British abolitionist effort to the rise of the new industrial class.

Britain was accumulating great wealth from the triangular trade. The increase of consumption goods called forth by that trade inevitably drew in its train the development of the productive power of the country. This industrial expansion required finance. What man in the first three-quarters of the eighteenth century was better able to afford the ready capital than a West Indian sugar planter or a Liverpool slave trader? . . . [A]bsentee planters purchased land in England, where they were able to use their wealth to finance the great developments associated with the Agricultural Revolution. . . . [T]he investment of profits from the triangular trade in British industry . . . supplied part of the huge outlay for the construction of the vast plants to meet the needs of the new productive process and the new markets. . . .

. . . The triangular trade made an enormous contribution to Britain's industrial development. The profits from this trade fertilized the entire productive system of the country. . . . But it must not be inferred that the triangular trade was solely and entirely responsible for the economic development. The growth of the internal market in England, the ploughing-in of the profits from industry to generate still further capital and achieve still greater expansion, played a large part. But this industrial development, stimulated by mercantilism, later outgrew mercantilism and destroyed it.

In 1783 the shape of things to come was clearly visible. The steam engine's potentialities were not an academic question. Sixty-six engines were in operation, two-thirds of these in mines and foundries. Improved methods of coal mining, combined with the influence of steam, resulted in a great expansion of the iron industry. Production increased four times between 1740 and 1788, the number of furnaces rose by one-half. The iron bridge and the iron railroad had appeared; the Carron Works had been founded; and Wilkinson was already famous as "the father of the iron trade." Cotton, the queen of the Industrial Revolution, responded readily to the new inventions, unhampered as it was by the traditions and guild restrictions which impeded its older rival, wool. Laissez faire became a practice in the new industry long before it penetrated the text books as orthodox economic theory. The spinning jenny, the water frame, the mule, revolutionized the industry, which, as a result, showed a continuous upward trend. Between 1700 and 1780 imports of raw cotton increased more than three times, exports of cotton goods fifteen times. The population of Manchester increased by nearly one-half between 1757 and 1773, the numbers engaged in the cotton industry quadrupled between 1750 and 1785. Not only heavy industry, cotton, too—the two industries that were to dominate the period 1783–1850—was gathering strength for the assault on the system of monopoly which had for so long been deemed essential to the existence and prosperity of both.

The entire economy of England was stimulated by this beneficent breath of increased production. The output of the Staffordshire potteries increased fivefold in value between 1725 and 1777. The tonnage of shipping leaving English ports more than doubled between 1700 and 1781.

English imports increased fourfold between 1715 and 1775, exports trebled between 1700 and 1771. English industry in 1783 was like Gulliver, tied down by the Lilliputian restrictions of mercantilism. . . .

In June, 1783, the Prime Minister, Lord North, complimented the Quaker opponents of the slave trade on their humanity, but regretted that its abolition was an impossibility, as the trade had become necessary to almost every nation in Europe. Slave traders and sugar planters rubbed their hands in glee. The West Indian colonies were still the darlings of the empire, the most precious jewels in the British diadem.

But the rumblings of the inevitable storm were audible for those who had ears to hear. The year of Yorktown was the year of Watt's second patent, that for the rotary motion, which converted the steam engine into a source of motive power and made industrial England, in Matthew Boulton's phrase, "steam-mill mad." Rodney's victory over the French, which saved the sugar colonies, coincided with Watt's utilization of the expansive power of steam to obtain the double stroke for his pistons. The peace treaty of 1783 was being signed while Henry Cort was working on his puddling process which revolutionized the iron industry. The stage was set for that gigantic development of British capitalism which upset the political structure of the country in 1832 and thereby made possible the attack on monopoly in general and West Indian monopoly in particular. . . .

The attack on the West Indians was more than an attack on slavery. It was an attack on monopoly. Their opponents were not only the humanitarians but the capitalists. The reason for the attack was not only that the West Indian economic system was vicious but that it was also so unprofitable that for this reason alone its destruction was inevitable. The agent for Jamaica complained in 1827 that "the cause of the colonies altogether, but more especially that part of it which touches upon property in slaves, is so unattractive to florid orators and so unpopular with the public, that we have and must have very little protection from Parliamentary speaking." Hibbert was only half right. If West Indian slavery was detestable, West Indian monopoly was unpopular, and the united odium of both was more than the colonies could bear.

The attack falls into three phases: the attack on the slave trade, the attack on slavery, the attack on the preferential sugar duties. The slave trade was abolished in 1807, slavery in 1833, the sugar preference in

1846. The three events are inseparable. The very vested interests which had been built up by the slave system now turned and destroyed that system. The humanitarians, in attacking the system in its weakest and most indefensible spot, spoke a language that the masses could understand. They could never have succeeded a hundred years before when every important capitalist interest was on the side of the colonial system. "It was an arduous hill to climb," sang Wordsworth in praise of Clarkson. The top would never have been reached but for the defection of the capitalists from the ranks of the slave-owners and slave traders. The West Indians, pampered and petted and spoiled for a century and a half, made the mistake of elevating into a law of nature what was actually only a law of mercantilism. They thought themselves indispensable and carried over to an age of anti-imperialism the lessons they had been taught in an age of commercial imperialism. When, to their surprise, the "invisible hand" of Adam Smith turned against them, they could turn only to the invisible hand of God. The rise and fall of mercantilism is the rise and fall of slavery. . . .

The strength of the British sugar islands before 1783 lay in the fact that as sugar producers they had few competitors. In so far as they could, they would permit none. They resisted the attempt to introduce the cultivation of sugar (and cotton) into Sierra Leone on the ground that it would be a precedent to "foreign nations, who have as yet no colonies anywhere," and might prove detrimental to those who possessed West Indian colonies; just as a century previously they had opposed the cultivation of indigo in Africa. Their chief competitors in the sugar trade were Brazil and the French islands, Cuba being hampered by the extreme exclusiveness of Spanish mercantilism. This situation was radically altered when Saint Domingue forged ahead in the years immediately following the secession of the mainland colonies. . . .

Whereas before, in the eighteenth century, every important vested interest in England was lined up on the side of monopoly and the colonial system; after 1783, one by one, every one of those interests came out against monopoly and the West Indian slave system. British exports to the world were in manufactured goods which could be paid for only in raw materials—the cotton of the United States, the cotton, coffee and sugar of Brazil, the sugar of Cuba, the sugar and cotton of India. The expansion of British exports depended on the capacity of Britain to absorb the raw material as payment. The British West Indian monopoly, prohibiting the importation of non-British-plantation sugar for home consumption, stood in the way. Every important vested interest—the cotton manufacturers, the shipowners, the sugar refiners; every important industrial and commercial town—London, Manchester, Liverpool, Birmingham, Sheffield, the West Riding of Yorkshire, joined in the attack on West Indian slavery and West Indian monopoly. The abolitionists, significantly, concentrated their attack on the industrial centers.

The West Indian planters in the eighteenth century were both exporters of raw cotton and importers of cotton manufactures. In both respects, as we have seen, they had become increasingly negligible. The steam engine and the cotton gin changed Manchester's indifference into downright hostility. As early as 1788 Wilberforce exulted at the fact that a liberal subscription towards abolition had been raised at Manchester, "deeply interested in the African trade." Manchester was unrepresented in the House of Commons before 1832, so its parliamentary denunciation of the West Indian system comes only after that date. . . .

As early as 1788 an abolition society was started in Birmingham and a liberal subscription collected for the cause. In this society the ironmasters were prominent. Three of the Lloyd family, with their banking interests as well, were on the committee. The dominant figure, however, was Samuel Garbett. Garbett was an outstanding figure of the Industrial Revolution, more reminiscent of the twentieth than the eighteenth century. In his breadth of vision, the scope of his activities, the multiplicity of his interests, he reminds us of Samuel Touchet. Like Touchet a partner in the spinning enterprise of Wyatt and Paul, Garbett was an associate of Roebuck's in the Carron Works, a shareholder with Boulton and Watt in the Albion Mills and in the copper mines of Cornwall. "There were indeed," writes Ashton, "few sides of the industrial and commercial life of his day that he did not touch." In addition his energy was thrown into the politics of industry rather than into the details of administration. He became the ironmaster's spokesman to the government. This was a dangerous man indeed to have as an opponent, for Garbett, in the larger sense, was Birmingham.

At a meeting of many respectable inhabitants of Birmingham on January 28, 1788, Samuel Garbett presiding, it was decided to send a petition to Parliament. The petition stated, *inter alia*, that, "as inhabitants of a manufacturing town and neighbourhood your petitioners have the commercial interests of this kingdom very deeply at heart; but cannot conceal their detestation of any commerce which always originates in violence, and too often terminates in cruelty." Gustavus Vasa, an African, visited Birmingham, and received a sympathetic welcome.

This was not to say that Birmingham was unanimous or single-minded on the issue of abolition. The manufacturers still interested in the slave trade held counter-meetings and sent counter-petitions to Parliament. But Samuel Garbett, the Lloyds and others of that caliber were, from the West Indian standpoint, on the wrong side of the fence. . . .

The capitalists had first encouraged West Indian slavery and then helped to destroy it. When British capitalism depended on the West Indies, they ignored slavery or defended it. When British capitalism found the West Indian monopoly a nuisance, they destroyed West Indian slavery as the first step in the destruction of West Indian monopoly. . . .

This study has deliberately subordinated the inhumanity of the slave system and the humanitarianism which destroyed that system. To disregard it completely, however, would be to commit a grave historical error and to ignore one of the greatest propaganda movements of all time. The humanitarians were the spearhead of the onslaught which destroyed the West Indian system and freed the Negro. But their importance has been seriously misunderstood and grossly exaggerated by men who have sacrificed scholarship to sentimentality and, like the scholastics of old, placed faith before reason and evidence. Professor Coupland, in an imaginary interview with Wilberforce, asks him: "What do you think, sir, is the primary significance of your work, the lesson of the abolition of the slave system?" The instant answer is: "It was God's work. It signifies the triumph of His will over human selfishness. It teaches that no obstacle of interest or prejudice is irremovable by faith and prayer."

This misunderstanding springs, in part, from a deliberate attempt by contemporaries to present a distorted view of the abolitionist movement. When the slave trade was abolished in 1807, the bill included a phrase to the effect that the trade was "contrary to the principles of justice, humanity and sound policy." Lord Hawkesbury objected; in his opinion the words "justice and humanity" reflected on the slave traders. He therefore moved an amendment excluding those words. In so doing he confined the necessity of abolition solely to expediency. The Lord Chancellor protested. The amendment would take away the only ground on which the other powers could be asked to co-operate in abolition. The Earl of

Lauderdale declared that the words omitted were the most essential in the bill. The omission would lend color to the suspicion in France that British abolition was dictated by the selfish motive that her colonies were well-stocked with Negroes. "How, in thus being supposed to make no sacrifice ourselves, could we call with any effect upon foreign powers to cooperate in the abolition?" The Lords voted for the original version.

The British humanitarians were a brilliant band. Clarkson personifies all the best in the humanitarianism of the age. One can appreciate even today his feelings when, in ruminating upon the subject of his prize-winning essay, he first awoke to the realization of the enormous injustice of slavery. Clarkson was an indefatigable worker, who conducted endless and dangerous researches into the conditions and consequences of the slave trade, a prolific pamphleteer whose history of the abolition movement is still a classic. His labors in the cause of justice to Africa were accomplished only at the cost of much personal discomfort, and imposed a severe strain on his scanty resources. In 1793 he wrote a letter to Josiah Wedgwood which contains some of the finest sentiments that motivated the humanitarians. He needed money and wished to sell two of his shares in the Sierra Leone Company, founded in 1791 to promote legitimate commerce with Africa. "But," he pointed out, "I should not chuse to permit anyone to become a purchaser, who would not be better pleased with the good resulting to Africa than from great commercial profits to himself; not that the latter may not be expected, but in case of a disappointment, I should wish his mind to be made easy by the assurance that he has been instrumental in introducing light and happiness into a country, where the mind was kept in darkness and the body nourished only for European chains." Too impetuous and enthusiastic for some of his colleagues, Clarkson was one of those friends of whom the Negro race has had unfortunately only too few.

Seymour Drescher

The Williams Thesis After Fifty Years

Historian Seymour Drescher testifies to the importance of Eric Williams in shaping the debates about the importance of the slave trade, but the University of Pittsburgh historian finds that five decades of research have undermined the specific arguments and facts the West Indian historian advanced in support of his thesis. Notable among these works was Drescher's 1977 study *Econocide: British Slavery in the Era of Abolition.*

Ten years ago I began an assessment of *Capitalism and Slavery* with my understanding of a classic: "If one criterion of a classic is its ability to reorient our most basic way of viewing an object or a concept, Eric Williams's study supremely passes that test." The passage of a fifth decade has provided abundant evidence of the pivotal status of *Capitalism and Slavery.* The original publisher reprinted the book in 1994 with a new Introduction by Colin A. Palmer. Hilary Beckles, Selwyn Carrington, William Darity and Thomas Holt, among others, have assessed Eric Williams's impact upon, and inspiration for, West Indian scholars. Most recently, Walter Minchinton has demonstrated the sustained discussion of the Williams/Drescher debate among historians of Caribbean slavery. During the past decade Barbara Solow edited the results of two international conferences inspired by Williams's scholarship. And, on the eve of the fiftieth anniversary of *Capitalism and Slavery,* Joseph Inikori delivered his Elsa Goveia Memorial Lecture on "Slavery and the Rise of Capitalism." . . .

A . . . central hypothesis of *Capitalism and Slavery* was Williams's dramatic revaluation of the role of the slave trade and slavery in the rise of British capitalism and especially in the British industrial revolution. Williams's assertion of extraordinary profits for the slave trade was one of

From "Capitalism and Slavery After Fifty Years," *Slavery and Abolition,* 18.3, December 1977, pp. 212–222. Reprinted by permission of Frank Cass Ltd.

his first empirical affirmations to come under attack. The slave trade's primacy in funding British growth now has few defenders, even among those who argue for high profits.

A more interesting question concerns the role of the British slave system as a whole in British metropolitan economic growth. There has been a double shift of historiographical emphasis in regard to the link between slavery and the rise of capitalism. The first relates to the rapid development of comparative analysis, well illustrated in Barbara Solow's second edited volume, *Slavery and the Rise of the Atlantic System* (1991). One of its important and conclusive findings seems to be that the further one proceeds outside the British orbit, the greater is the evidence against a generic linkage between New World slavery and the rise of European industrial capitalism.

Perhaps the most spectacular negative example is Portugal, which sponsored slaving, slavery and coerced labour systems for well over four centuries in areas as diverse as Asia, Europe, the Atlantic islands, Africa and Brazil. Whatever Portuguese slavery may have contributed to British industrial expansion, it did little for the Portuguese themselves. At the end of its long legal toleration of chattel slavery, Portugal, as Eric Hobsbawm noted, "was small, feeble, backward by any contemporary standard . . . and only the eye of faith could detect much in the way of economic development." Pieter Emmer, a Dutch historian of European expansion, has recently concluded that Dutch investment in overseas slavery may well have considerably retarded industrial development in the Netherlands.

Such a devaluation of the generative role of slavery only impacts on the Williams thesis insofar as one extends the model to the Northern European colonies, as he did in *From Columbus to Castro* (1970). Ironically, the greatest contribution of the slave trade to industrialization within a Continental European economy may have occurred only after, and because of, the abolition of the British slave trade in 1807. A recent study of Spanish economic development concludes that the slave trade to Cuba, accelerated by the cessation of British Caribbean imports, became crucial for the formation of industrial capital in Spain. The Spanish industrialists were to be among the last in a long line of economic interests hostile to closing down the Atlantic slave system. For Continental Europe as a whole, the slave empires would seem to justify Patrick O'Brien's judgement about the impact of the overseas world on metropolitan economic development—"the periphery was peripheral."

Nevertheless, one of those unforeseen shifts of historiographical focus points to a new and significant shift in the evaluation of slavery's role in capitalist development, one that encompasses the Atlantic world rather than Europe alone. In Barbara Solow's second collection, O'Brien and Engerman conclude that slavery accelerated the "Americanization" of British imperial trade in the eighteenth century: "the development of an Atlantic economy is impossible to imagine without slavery and the slave trade." In drawing attention to the centrality of slavery in the British imperial economy of the eighteenth century, Williams was surely a harbinger of what recently seems to have been ratified as a paradigmatic shift. The concept of "Atlanticization" differs from the argument in *Capitalism and Slavery*. Even as regards the British case, O'Brien and Engerman appear carefully to avoid saying that it is impossible to imagine European *industrialization* without slavery and the slave trade. They do not argue that slavery played a major role even in British industrialization. Engerman further elaborates his reservations in an article on the Atlantic economy in relation to those of Britain, America, Africa and elsewhere. He remains exceedingly skeptical about the specific timing and mechanisms of Williams's account of slavery's contribution to British industrialization. The "necessary magnitudes" strike him as too small to bear the causal weight Williams assigned to them, "considering Britain's lack of uniqueness in regard to its slave systems and its uniqueness in regard to industrial development."

Moreover, one must bear in mind another challenge to the traditional concept of British economic development. Economic historians have radically challenged the very notion of a British industrial "revolution" in the period that was crucial to Williams's thesis. Complaints by some historians of slavery that *Capitalism and Slavery* has been neglected or even suppressed by economic historians of British industrialization, overlook this tendency to view metropolitan growth as more drawn out than it has been portrayed in the conventional account. One historian of slavery has gone even further in this direction than the most radical of "gradualists" in British economic history. Joseph Inikori has recently suggested that Great Britain, far from emerging as the leading "capitalist" nation of the period 1780–1830, did not become either capitalist *or* industrial until well after the British had already completely abolished their slave system. For most historians of slavery, however, capitalism is still considered to have been characteristic of at least some Northern European societies (such as England and the Netherlands) as early as the seventeenth century.

144   Seymour Drescher

Although Williams did not specifically frame his account of early modern slavery in terms of the whole Atlantic economy, his story of eighteenth-century slavery is consistent with some recent efforts to analyse the impact of Atlanticization on British economic growth and policy. In place of Williams's own emphasis on the overall profits of the slave trade and the British-protected tropical slave economy, for example, historians have turned their attention to the role of overseas slavery in stimulating British capitalist networks and institutional developments, in providing a major growth sector for British overseas exports, and in constituting a market for British goods in periods of major political and military threat — brought to a climax by Napoleon's Continental Blockade.

The broadening consensus on slavery's decisive role in the creation of the Atlantic economic system has therefore continued to stimulate the more unresolved debate over slavery's precise contribution to British industrialization. In the most recent summary of that debate, Robin Blackburn reaffirms the conclusion that Britain's surge ahead of its Continental rivals during the half century or so before Waterloo occurred when, and because, the economic contribution of the British slave sector to British growth was at its peak. Correspondingly, the ending of the slave trade decelerated the "resource increment" of that sector to metropolitan growth. To that extent, Williams's strategy of linking slavery to shifting patterns of British overseas capitalism remains fruitful.

However, this new and more rigorous assertion of slavery's effects on the rise of British capitalism has effectively undermined the central chronology of *Capitalism and Slavery*'s second major economic thesis. Williams asserted that, following the American Revolution, the economic decline of [the] British Caribbean stimulated the destruction of British slavery by British industrial capitalists. Williams's thesis rested upon a dramatic reversal of the power between two major class actors: "old" planters and "new" capitalists. Williams's account therefore depended crucially upon the timing of British slavery's economic decline and the triumph of industrial free trade capitalism. This has produced a profound disjunction in the historiography of *Capitalism and Slavery*. Many of those who have recently argued in favour of a strong positive contribution of "rising slavery" to British economic development (*inter alia* O'Brien, Engerman, Solow, Crouzet, Inikori, Cuenca-Esteban and Blackburn) have explicitly or implicitly undermined Williams's "decline thesis." For all of these historians there was simply no late eighteenth-century reversal of the economic role of the slave Americas. They have all demonstrated the continuity of slavery's contribution to British trade at least into the early nineteenth century. As Robin Blackburn succinctly concludes, "[T]he slave systems of the late-eighteenth and early nineteenth century New World had far outstripped those of the earlier mercantilist epoch. Although New World slavery now confronted mortal antagonists, it had yet to reach its apogee." The implications of their collective economic finding is unavoidable: If the slave colonies made a significant contribution to British economic growth in the generations before 1783 they were as or more significant in the generation after 1783, the "take-off" period in the conventional Industrial Revolution. Although still vigorously disputed by one historian, the New World foundations of the decline thesis in Williams's own terms has thus been undermined. . . .

Another important component of the Williams decline thesis has undergone a similar major challenge, the metropolitan side of his original equation. Williams's principal metropolitan actor in slavery's destruction was a grand coalition of British industrialists, East India investors and free traders, coalescing in the wake of the American and industrial revolutions. It is now widely noted that Britain's "swing" towards both free trade and India did not seriously begin until more than four decades after peace with America, and a generation after abolitionists had their initial victories in parliament. Moreover, the pioneering industrial bourgeoisie was divided over abolitionist policies from the outset. The cotton interest of Manchester, the site of Britain's first mass abolitionist mobilization, was less united against the slave trade than almost every other occupational group in that city. Economic interests, even when they had specific conflicts with those invested in slavery, usually had no desire whatever to undermine the foundations of what they considered as a legal form of property and trade.

The industrial bourgeoisie as a collectivity is, therefore, no longer allotted more than a peripheral and often a negative role in the crucial turn against the British slave trade. Cain and Hopkins's recent major overview of British imperialism emphasizes the continued policy preponderance of the gentlemanly capitalism of landowner mercantile interests in the formulation of early nineteenth-century imperial policy and the insignificance of an industrialist interest in abolition in particular: "[T]he important point is that it [abolition] was not promoted by a rising industrial bourgeoisie seeking to reach the goals of liberty and free trade set for it by a later generations of Whig historians," among whom one may, in this regard, number Eric Williams.

In the absence of a capitalist economic bloc, some historians have invoked the emergence of an ideology rather than an interest. They posit a "mentality" of bourgeois industrial hostility to slavery in the late eighteenth century. The substitution of an intangible capitalist spirit or ideology for tangible capitalist interests, has actually tended to drive *Capitalism and Slavery* to the historiographic periphery. The outstanding recent example of this approach is *The Antislavery Debate: Capitalism and Abolitionism as a Problem in Historical Interpretation*, edited by Thomas Bender. . . .

If economic historians have slowly created a new framework for relating capitalism to slavery, social historians and social scientists have developed a corresponding challenge to Williams's assumptions about the transition to free labour. For Williams, as for most of his contemporaries, the story of abolition was primarily a history of elites. The major actors were "class" actors: slavers, planters, merchants, bankers, industrialists and politicians. The novelty of *Capitalism and Slavery* lay above all in the dominant causal role it accorded to what have come to be called "hegemonic" interests. In *Capitalism and Slavery*, slave resistance finally undermined the system, but only a generation after the metropolitan capitalists had turned against it. Slave resistance became historiographically significant only after a new generation of scholarship on culture, resistance and gender had transformed the social history of slavery. Thereafter, Williams's own bipolar model of slaves and capitalists was replaced by a complex mosaic of slaves as autonomous individual agents and social actors. Significantly, two Marxist-oriented historians who have stressed the key role of slaves in the ending of slavery turn to C.L.R. James's *Black Jacobins* for inspiration. Eugene Genovese and Robin Blackburn both view the Haitian (not the American or Industrial) Revolution as the turning point in the history of slavery. Thus, Blackburn's *Overthrow of Colonial Slavery* (1988) judged Williams['s] capitalist-driven model to be "mechanical and unsatisfactory," while Genovese's *From Rebellion to Revolution* simply relegated *Capitalism and Slavery* to the "other works" section of his bibliographical essay. . . .

Finally, the abolitionists. In its designation of the abolitionists as but one more elite (a "brilliant band"), *Capitalism and Slavery* remained entirely conventional. Williams not only confirmed abolitionism as a top down operation but sharply devalued its causal role. Even more belatedly than in the case of the slaves, the metropolitan masses have begun to find their place in the historiographies of both British slavery and of British metropolitan development. As recently as ten years ago, abolitionists had not been integrated into the history of the modern social movement. The abolitionist rank-and-file were decontextualized by "Whig" historiography into altruistic but passive respondents to an elite-led crusade. This perspective obtained whether those elites were portrayed, by the "imperial school," as altruistic agents of moral progress, or, by the anti-colonial school, as agents of capitalist industrialization.

Recently, and for the first time, the political power of popular anti-slavery is therefore being analysed as an independent variable, rather than subsumed as a chorus responding to elite propaganda. Even those who continue to focus on the role of elites in the implementation of British emancipation now sharply distinguish between popular and elite roles in the process. Most importantly, it is now widely recognized that popular abolitionism was a principal transformer of the changing attitude toward slavery from the 1780s.

The abolitionist breakthrough has, for the first time, become the object of separate analysis in historical monographs. The recognition of this popular dimension of anti-slavery is also changing scholarly views of the general relationship between religious and economic change in Britain. The most recent historian of popular Methodism concludes that

> the abolition of slavery in the British colonies was neither an economic necessity whose time had come nor a disinterested political gesture from an established political elite, but was, to a considerable extent, a victory for new religious and political forces unleashed both by evangelical enthusiasm and by the structural changes in British society in the period of the Industrial Revolution.

Historians are recognizing the implications of fifty years' futile prospecting for a grand coalition of economically-based antislavery elites and their ideologies. Scholars now routinely investigate the cumulative impact of changing patterns of demography, migration, organization, culture and communication; of political agitation, shared beliefs and social interaction on both sides of, and across, the Atlantic.

Is there an emergent perspective on *Capitalism and Slavery* after half a century? The debates of the past decade seem to have vindicated

Williams's insistence upon, if not his precise formulations of, the significance of slavery in the formation of the modern world economy. The narrow grounds of his own arguments have been discarded or deepened in ways that neither his earliest enthusiasts nor detractors could have anticipated. Historians who once treated the overseas tropics as conceptually and empirically marginal to the long march of European development have grown used to treating the world beyond the line as a significant variable in their causal networks. This is as true for the new Marxist as for the New Economic History. Even those who systematically discount the paramountcy of New World "primitive accumulation" in the economic transformation of the industrial world regard the concept as within the pale of causal plausibility.

On the other hand, there is widespread recognition that, however suggestive it remains, *Capitalism and Slavery* is also a work of its time. David Brion Davis appropriately identified Williams's approach as a variant of the "economistic" school, dating back to the Enlightenment. He endorsed a materialist philosophy of history, and a view of history as a progression of stages of society. Less consciously Williams also shared, with his more "idealist" historiographical predecessors, a sense of British global expansion as a world-historical master narrative. The Industrial and the American revolutions were the twin turning points in that narrative. Those turning points were denoted by a series of transformations: in economic organization, from agriculture to industry; in political economy, from mercantilism to free trade; and, above all, in social relations, from slave to free labour. These metamorphoses were the conceptual building blocks of *Capitalism and Slavery*.

Each one of these pivotal benchmarks has been reassessed over the past half century. The very idea of history as a series of discreet stages of interlocking economic, social, political and ideological orders has been eroded. We are now more acutely aware that New World slavery was, economically, superbly equipped to cross the great divide between the "first" and "second" British empires, between mercantilism and laissez-faire, between commercial and industrial capitalism, between the windmill and the steam engine, between the horsecart and the railroad. Capitalism was supremely agnostic and pluralistic in its ability to coexist, and to thrive, with a whole range of labour systems right through the abolitionist century after 1780: with slavery; with indentured servitude; with sharecropping; with penal labour; with seasonal contract labour and with day labour; with penally constrained or unconstrained free labour.

In the longer run, we can see more clearly than Williams's generation that the "rise of free labour" during [the] conventional age of industrialization was, in some respects, a myth. . . .

As with every attempt to make sense of human experience *Capitalism and Slavery* will in some respects seem increasingly dated. Indeed, any effort to turn *Capitalism and Slavery* into a sacred text, and to measure orthodoxies, apostasies and heresies by it, remains a risk for the future. Eric Williams was, after all, the founding father of a nation, and the intellectual voice of a region as well as a historian. The literary and the mass media may well enshrine his most striking formulations long after they no longer command the assent of professional historians, who spend their analytic lives uncovering new data and revising theories. In this regard, the appeal of *Capitalism and Slavery* may be enhanced by what one historian has called "history-as-rhetoric" rather than history-as-scholarship. Those inclined to proffer *Capitalism and Slavery* as worthy of scholarly inspiration would do well to remind their readers that Williams's book became a classic because it challenged the heirs of a complacent historiography to take note of neglected dimensions of the story. Fifty years later Williams's message of the need to *challenge* is as worth repeating as his challenging message.

Gwendolyn Midlo Hall

An African Nation in Colonial Louisiana

In her prize-winning study of black culture in colonial Louisiana, Gwendolyn Midlo Hall argues that the Bambara people of West Africa retained a close national identity under both French and Spanish rule. This Rutgers University professor's evidence of Bambara cultural unity

Reprinted by permission of Louisiana State University Press from *Africans in Colonial Louisiana: The Development of the Afro-Creole Culture in the Eighteenth Century* by Gwendolyn Midlo Hall. Copyright © 1992 by Louisiana State University Press.

inspired scholars to examine evidence of the survival of other African nations under slavery, even in parts of the Americas where she believed this was unlikely.

The most important kingdoms of Senegambia maintained a tight control over which peoples could be enslaved and sold to the Europeans. It seems that during the 1720s, neither the Fulbe nor the Mandinga sold their own people or allowed others to sell them. The Bambara (Bamana) enjoyed no such protection during the 1720s. Bambarana, the land of the Bambara, was located on the upper reaches of the Senegal River beyond Galam, near the Niger River. Evidently, no Frenchman had entered Bambara country during the 1720s. Labat called the Bambara kingdoms above Galam "Bambara Cana" and described the region as extremely fertile, heavily populated, and strong militarily, where all the Bambara were slaves of the king and the lords. Labat was no doubt referring to the kingdom of Mamari Kulubali, founder of the Bambara kingdom of Segu. He wrote: "That is just about all one can say for now. Perhaps in the future some employee of the Company will be found who is curious enough to make a voyage to that country and give us a description." . . .

Between 1727 and 1729, when almost all the slave-trade voyages organized by the Company of the Indies went to Louisiana, the trading post at Galam was sending about one thousand *captifs* down the Senegal River to St. Louis each year. Other Bambara slaves were coming from the French post near the mouth of the Gambia River. High mortality in the *captiveries* [onshore slave pens], aboard the ships, and after landing would indicate that the slaves embarked during this period came from some distance inland. It seems clear that Bambara slaves arrived in Louisiana in large numbers and they were truly Bambara. . . .

Captured and enslaved Bambara did not all go to the Atlantic. Some went to the desert or to interior markets, and some were retained locally. Many among the enslaved women were sold to the trans-Sahara trade to fill the harems of North Africa and the Middle East. While all slaves captured and owned by warriors could be sold, the king first claimed one-half to two-thirds of the booty captured in formal military campaigns and less formal cavalry raids. Only some of the king's slaves could be sold.

Many were instead incorporated into the elite guard and cavalry troops. Some of the king's slaves worked the state's fields near Segu.

Who were the Bambara brought to Louisiana? We know quite a bit about the Bambara during the early eighteenth century without relying entirely upon Eurocentric sources and/or projecting backward in time. The Bambara are a Mande people with a strong tradition of oral history. They trace their ancestry to the great thirteenth-century Mali empire in the region where the upper Niger River intersects Mali and Guinea. The modern Mande peoples are, besides the Bambara, the Mandinka, Maninka, Malinke, Mandinga, Manya, Dyula, Duranko, and Wangara. Their dispersal throughout the West African savannah, mainly because of the imperialistic campaigns of the ancient Mali empire, led to their developing mechanisms for retaining their cultural focus in spite of their geographical displacement. They all speak mutually intelligible dialects of Mandekan and share values defining kinship, politics, and economy. More than recognition of common ancestry, their system of beliefs united them into a "philosophy, ideology, or cosmology—which defines appropriate behavior for individual actors and allows in turn the interpretation of the behavior of others." . . .

The Bambara came to Louisiana equipped with a concept of sovereignty that was based upon control of people rather than of territory; with experience in creating new spiritual and legal communities; and with extensive experience in self-governing organizations. Bambara social organization had flexible strength, and it traveled well. Traditional Bambara societies did not consist of vast, centralized, hierarchical, despotic institutions. They did not resemble European kingdoms. . . .

Although Bambara social organization is rigidly hierarchical and a sense of equality is absent, it is segmented and its members enjoy a high level of participatory democracy. Individual Bambara have a strong sense of justice. They participate in organized groups from early childhood, divided according to age and gender. . . . Women have their own powerful hierarchical societies of which less is known because Bambara women are more traditional and closed-mouth than the men. Women's role in practice is more active and autonomous than their status under traditional law would indicate. A woman can inherit all the goods of the head of the family, even a chief, in the absence of a male heir. The Mali empire once had a Keïta woman at its head, daughter of Naré, fa Maghan. . . .

During the late 1720s, when large numbers of Bambara were loaded aboard slave ships destined for Louisiana, the Bambara heroic tradition, . . . validated above all in troubled times, asserted itself. They revolted at sea. After arriving in Louisiana, the Bambara maintained an organized language community, formed alliances with the Indian nations who were in revolt against the French, and conspired to take over the colony.

The Bambara, arriving in Louisiana in large numbers after 1726, first encountered Indians as their fellow slaves. . . . Many of the newly arrived Africans . . . were sent to Natchez. These African slaves played a prominent role in the devastating massacre of the French settlement at Natchez on November 28, 1729. At the time of the massacre, the settlement consisted of 200 French men, 82 French women, 150 French children, and 280 black slaves. Before beginning this massacre, the Natchez [Indians] assured themselves of the support of several blacks, including those of the White Earth concession and two of their *commandeurs* (slave foremen), who told the other blacks that they would be free if they supported the Natchez. Those slaves who refused to support the Natchez were threatened with being sold to the Chickasaw along with the French women and children. . . .

When the Natchez acknowledged their defeat at Red River in 1731, they raised a white flag and sent an Indian who spoke a little French to negotiate. The French informed the Natchez that before discussing anything else, they had to send them all the blacks who were in the fort, which they did at once. . . .

Africans who had lived among the Natchez and the Choctaw did in fact maintain ties with Indian nations wishing to drive out the French. Many of these slaves were Bambara belonging to the Company of the Indies, and upon their return, they plotted with the Natchez, the Chickasaw, the Illinois, the Arkansas, and part of the Miami to coordinate an uprising among African slaves in all the French settlements with attacks upon the French by these Indian nations. . . .

The uprising was scheduled to take place on June 24, 1731, but the conspirators were not yet ready, and it was put off until June 29. During this delay, the plan was uncovered by the French: All the whites from Pointe Coupee to Balize were to be massacred. All the Bambara had joined together to free themselves and take possession of the country by this revolt. The other blacks in the colony who were not of the Bambara nation were to serve them as slaves. It was reported that four hundred Bambara slaves were involved in this conspiracy. French officials did not wish to deepen the investigation because of the damages that would be caused to private individuals if they lost their slaves. . . .

Edward Brathwaite, writing about Jamaica, defined *creolization* as a sociocultural continuum radiating outward from the slave community and affecting the entire culture in varying degrees. This definition is relevant for the United States as well as for the Caribbean. It is especially significant for Louisiana, where the slave culture was early and thoroughly Africanized and the first generation of Creole slaves grew up in stable, nuclear families composed of African mothers and fathers and creole siblings. We have seen that almost all the black slaves either arrived directly from Africa between June, 1719, and January, 1731, or were the descendants of these first slaves. Two-thirds of these Africans came from Senegambia from a limited number of nations living in a relatively homogeneous culture area. The fragmentation of language and culture communities associated with the African slave trade and slavery in the Americas was limited among slaves in Louisiana. It appears that throughout the eighteenth century, under Spanish rule as well as French, Senegambia remained a more important source of slaves in Louisiana than did Central Africa. The Louisiana experience calls into question the common assumption that African slaves could not regroup themselves in language and social communities derived from the sending cultures. . . .

The pattern of introduction of black slaves into French Louisiana contrasts sharply with that of the English colonies that became part of the United States. The early contingent of slaves introduced into the Chesapeake and Carolina came from the British West Indies and constituted a relatively small minority. They were one or more generations removed from Africa and spoke English or a creolized version of English when they arrived. They spoke a more standard English than those who came after them, constituted a small minority, and interacted fairly freely with their masters, as well as with the English servants. . . .

. . . The Anglo-American society into which Africans were introduced, when they began to arrive in significant numbers, was much more stable than the society in French Louisiana. Thus, the culture of the United States was most heavily Africanized from Louisiana after 1803, when the slave plantation system spread west, when New Orleans was the major entrepôt for new slaves, and when the largest slave plantations of the antebellum South were established in the state. The massive post-Reconstruction migration of African-Americans up the Mississippi

Valley spread a partially anglicized Afro-Creole folk culture throughout the United States.

In early Louisiana, the uneven distribution of the newly arrived Africans facilitated their cultural autonomy. There were large concentrations of slaves in the hands of a few members of the military-bureaucratic elite that ruled the colony. Most of the white colonists owned either no slaves or very few. . . .

. . . This concentration of Africans, many of them from the same ethnic group, on relatively few estates facilitated the preservation and adaptation of African cultural patterns. It is, furthermore, clear that Africans could not be confined to their masters' estates and isolated from contact with other Africans belonging to the same language community. We have seen that four hundred Bambara slaves living throughout lower Louisiana allied themselves with Indians to overthrow the French regime and take control of the colony. Twelve years later, a group of slaves belonging to several different masters met to judge and sentence Corbin, the master of one of these slaves. Corbin had threatened to shoot his slave for running away; and his brother had indeed shot the slave with a gun loaded with a charge of salt. A group of slaves met and "a service was sung in the style and language of the *nègres.*" They evidently sentenced Corbin to death and eventually carried out his execution. A slave who belonged to Corbin's neighbor shot at Corbin and ran away. Remarkably, this slave thereafter returned to his master, and his master pardoned him. We can only conclude that the master was so dependent upon the slave that he had to take the risk. But the slave did not stay long. When his master sent him for provisions, he went into another neighbor's barn, took a horse, and ran away again. Two months after the "service" was held, Corbin went to hunt near his house, saying he would return shortly. He was never seen again, nor was his body found. Thereafter, a slave named Jeannot mutinied against and abused his master, threatening to set fire to his cabin and taunting him by saying he knew who killed Corbin.

African religious beliefs, including knowledge of herbs, poisons, and the creation of charms and amulets of support or power, came to Louisiana with the earliest contingents of slaves. All adult Bambara males knew how to make charms. There are examples of slaves accused of being poisoners during the 1720s. Bonnaud confirmed through a postmortem examination that his *commandeur* had been poisoned. Petit, another *nègre* of Bonnaud, was suspected of the crime because he had threatened several times to kill the *commandeur* through magical means, since the *commandeur* had flogged him under orders of their master. Since Petit Nègre "came from a tribe reputed to be adept at poisoning, it was feared that many more persons would become his victim," according to the Superior Council. The council concluded that while it "does not admit the existence of sorcerers, it does punish poisoners, and perhaps it is poisons which do all the damage attributed to sorcery."

This document from the Superior Council does not identify the tribe "reputed to be adept at poisoning," but if the tribe had been Bambara, the reputation would probably have been well deserved. . . .

The continued importance of Senegambian slaves in Louisiana [in the late 1700s] requires an explanation. Although Senegambia was an early source for the Atlantic slave trade, by the eighteenth century it played a relatively minor role. Nevertheless, because of timing, as well as preference among slave owners, slaves from Senegambia were brought to Louisiana in large numbers. As we have seen, two-thirds of the slaves brought to Louisiana under French rule came from Senegambia. There was a substantial, well-organized Bambara language community in early Louisiana. . . . The next surge in the slave trade in Senegambia took place as a result of the consolidation of another empire: that of Ngolo Jarra, a former slave soldier who founded a new dynasty and greatly expanded the Kingdom of Segu. This expansion in the export of slaves from Senegambia coincided with a resurgence in the African slave trade to Louisiana under Spanish rule. It is less clear whether the new African slaves listed on inventories in Spanish Louisiana as Bambara were all actually Bambara. By the late eighteenth century, *Bambara* had taken on a generic meaning and was widely applied to peoples coming through St. Louis from the interior of the continent. The vagueness of Bambara identity resulted from the incorporation of many different ethnic communities into the Bambara warrior group. On the other hand, the old Bambara, as well as the old colonists in Louisiana, must have been able to tell who was a Bambara and who was not.

Philip D. Morgan

African Cultural Dynamics in the Americas

In the view of Philip Morgan, historians like Gwendolyn Midlo Hall have gone too far in positing the persistence of conservative African cultures in the Americas. A professor at Johns Hopkins University, Morgan uses newly compiled slave trade statistics to argue that African slave communities were generally too diverse to recreate a single African culture. Instead, he finds evidence that Africans in the New World engaged in dynamic cultural borrowing and innovation.

. . . Prior to 1820 two to three times as many Africans as Europeans crossed the Atlantic to the New World. Much of the wealth of the Atlantic economy derived from slave-produced commodities in what was the world's first system of multinational production for a mass market. Slavery defined the structure of many Atlantic societies, underpinning not just their economies but their social, political, cultural and ideological systems. If slavery then must be situated squarely at the center of the Atlantic world, it also must be considered as a single sphere of inquiry, encompassing Europe, Africa and the Americas. Slavery must be viewed in its full Atlantic context. . . .

. . . John Thornton's lavishly praised *Africa and Africans in the Making of the Atlantic World* . . . argues, among other things, that randomization was not a function of the middle passage; rather, slave ships drew their entire cargo from only one or two African ports, and their catchment areas were homogeneous. Thus, "an entire ship might be filled, not just with people possessing the same culture, but with people who grew up together." Once in the Americas, most slaves "on any sizeable estate were probably from only a few national groupings." Therefore, Thornton

From Philip D. Morgan, "The Cultural Implications of the Atlantic Slave Trade: African Regional Origins, American Destinations and New World Developments," *Slavery and Abolition* 18.1. April 1977, pp. 122–126, 128–136, 139, 141–142. Reprinted by permission of Frank Cass Ltd.

continues, "most slaves would have no shortage of people from their own nation with whom to communicate." In Thornton's view, particular African national groups tended to dominate particular slave societies in the Americas; Africans in the New World often shared common languages and cultures that helped them survive in a hostile setting. In most parts of the Americas, it is now contended, slaves perceived themselves as part of communities that had distinct ethnic or national roots.

Thornton's book ostensibly ends in 1680, but he and others are willing to argue that ethnicity or nationality was central to slave life beyond the seventeenth century. In a general text designed by Thornton and others for the college student and informed reader, the concept of nation as an ethno-linguistic entity serves as the key social force driving the development of slave life well beyond 1680. One or two African nations in most New World settings, it is argued, dominated most slave societies. Gwendolyn Hall credits transplanted Bambara as the central players in Afro-American culture in Louisiana. "The Louisiana experience," she observes, "calls into question the common assumption that African slaves could not regroup themselves in language and social communities derived from the sending cultures." Mervyn Alleyne believes that "one African ethnic group (the Twi) provided political and cultural leadership" among Jamaican slaves; he also thinks that "entire functioning languages" and "entire religions," not just general cultural orientations or religious beliefs, were carried to Jamaica. Michael Mullin has argued that "ethnicity," which he sees as a euphemism for tribalism, was particularly important among Anglo-American slaves, especially in the West Indies. Thus, for Mullin, Coromantee was "the most conspicuous and important nationality in Anglo-America." In short, an orthodoxy seems to have emerged that sees slaves as forming identifiable communities based on their ethnic or national pasts. . . .

Exciting new material is beginning to emerge from an extraordinarily important project sponsored by the W.E.B. Du Bois Institute for Afro-American Research at Harvard University. With David Eltis, David Richardson and Stephen D. Behrendt at the helm, this project is compiling information on all known individual voyages drawn from the records of all the major European and American slaving powers. To date, records exist on almost 27,000 voyages, extending from the late sixteenth to the late nineteenth centuries. When complete, the project will have information on well over half of all the ships that made a transatlantic slave voyage. This project has already compiled the largest data set for the study of the long-distance movement of peoples before the twentieth century. As a result of this project, and the work on which it builds, we now know more about the forced migration of Africans than the voluntary migration of Europeans in the early modern era. . . .

As David Eltis and David Richardson* have argued, the key findings of their consolidated and comprehensive set of data concern neither Africa nor the Americas treated alone, but rather the connections between the continents. In short, Eltis and Richardson and Behrendt are engaged in true Atlantic history. They are able to view the intercontinental flow of people from both sending and receiving poles. From the vantage point of Africa, it is now possible to look outward from each coastal region and trace where the forced migrants went. Most African regions funneled a majority of their forced emigrants to one region in the Americas. . . . In some cases, there was a subsidiary stream: thus a quarter of the Gold Coast's slaves went to Surinam and the Guyanas; a quarter of the Windward Coast's slaves went to St. Domingue; and a fifth of West Central Africa's slaves went to the French Caribbean. Nevertheless, the regional African perspective on slave destinations reveals a distinct geographic concentration, or in a few cases two concentrations, in where the slaves went.

Equally striking patterns emerge when the transatlantic links are examined from the more usual perspective of the American regions of disembarkation. What stands out—and these observations are only a variation on the emphases of Eltis and Richardson—are two extremes. First, the two main regions of Brazil—Bahia and the South-Central area—drew heavily on a single region of Africa. In Bahia's case about nine in ten Africans came from the Bight of Benin; in South-Central Brazil about eight in ten came from West-Central Africa. Second, at the other extreme, true for much of the Caribbean and North America, is the absence of a dominant single African provenance zone. No region of Africa, for example, supplied more than about 30 per cent of arrivals to either Cuba, Barbados, Martinique, Guadeloupe, or the Danish islands. Between the two extremes were some major destinations that received about half of their arrivals from a particular African coastal region: St. Domingue from West-Central Africa, the British Leeward Islands from the Bight of Biafra, and the Guyanas and Surinam from the Gold Coast. In each of these American destination—from St.

---

*See "The Achievements of the 'Numbers Game'" in Part III of this book. *Ed.*

Domingue to Surinam—the other half of their African influx came from a number of regions. Brazil, then, was exceptional in drawing slaves heavily from one region, while most other parts of the Americas drew on a wider mix of African peoples, even if in some cases about half of slaves came from one region. . . .

In several ways the preliminary findings of the Atlantic slave trade project seem to lend support to the emerging paradigm propounded by Thornton and others. Eltis and Richardson emphasize that "the distribution of Africans in the New World was no more randomized than was its European counterpart." With the exception of Bahia and Minas Gerais, they conclude that "the African part in the re-peopling of South and Central America was as dominated by West-Central Africa, as was its European counterpart by Iberians." In the Caribbean, they continue, "West Africa was as dominant as was West-Central Africa in South America." Even where the mixture of African peoples was greatest, African regions tended to supply slaves in sequence, therefore minimizing the mixture at any one time. In short, they conclude, "the picture of a confusing mix of African cultures with all the attendant barriers to establishing African carryovers to the New World needs revising." Revisionism then is widespread. My question is simple: is it justified? Was the slave trade markedly less random than we once thought?

To answer these questions, three central issues must be explored. First, how homogenous or heterogenous was the Atlantic slave trade seen from the vantage points of African coastal regions and American destinations? Second, is it best to focus attention on ports, seeing Atlantic slaving vessels largely visiting one or at most two African ports and then delivering their forced migrants to one American port? Finally, and most importantly, what do we mean by ethnic and national identity in the early modern era and what implications has this for New World cultural development? These questions will be addressed from an Atlantic perspective, thinking not just of Africa or America separately; but rather viewing them as linked or interconnected continents. The Atlantic was a bridge as well as a barrier; the lands ringing this ocean were joined as well as sundered by the sea. . . .

Even within a single African coastal region, marked shifts often occurred in the peoples forcibly expelled. The complex competition for trade was as much among Africans as among Europeans. The supply of slaves to the Bight of Benin, for example, changed drastically from the eighteenth to the nineteenth centuries. Down to the late eighteenth century, when the Oyo were a principal supplier of slaves to the Slave Coast, peoples from the north and west of Oyo—Nupe, Borgu, Hausa, and various Ewe-speaking peoples—were readily available. In the nineteenth century, after the collapse of the Oyo empire, Yoruba-speaking peoples dominated the flow leaving Bight of Benin ports, while the emergence of the Sokoto Caliphate in the Central Sudan generated a growing secondary stream of Hausa slaves. By the early nineteenth century "there were at least two demographically distinct components of the trade at the Bight of Benin," notes Paul Lovejoy, "one that brought males from the distant interior to the coast and another that siphoned off slaves (men, women and children) from the coast itself." Thus it is somewhat misleading to say that Bahia received virtually all its slaves from the Bight of Benin, if by this is meant to imply some uniformity over time. The ethnicity of those leaving the Slave Coast and arriving in Bahia changes drastically over time.

The relationship of coastal ports to hinterlands grew more complicated over time, which again enhanced the increasing diversity of peoples shipped across the Atlantic. Over time, for example, the region known as West-Central Africa came to cover a wider range of coastline and drew on an increasingly expanding hinterland, extending hundreds of kilometres from the coast. At least three, sometimes four, distinct commercial networks drew slaves from the interior toward the Atlantic shores. The mix of peoples flowing from that region grew more, not less, heterogeneous. Different ports within a single coastal region might draw upon different and fluctuating streams of peoples. Thus, along the early nineteenth-century Bight of Biafra coast, Igbo-speakers dominated slaves shipped from Bonny, Ibibio-speakers comprised 40 per cent of slaves shipped from Old Calabar, and slaves from much further inland—Nupe, Kakanda, and Hausa, for example—formed between 5 and 25 per cent of the exported slaves from various Biafran ports.

If the lens focuses primarily on the American side of the Atlantic, the emphasis again ought to be on heterogeneity. This is so because, as Eltis and Richardson have noted, the "geographic concentration of arrivals in the Americas is much less than that of African departures." Even if attention is directed to the places that received most Africans— a band stretching from about Cuba in the north to Central Brazil in the south—such American destinations encompass a much wider span of landscapes, climates, and environments than the coastline of West and West-Central Africa. If attention broadens to all the places in the Americas that received Africans—from New York in the north to Buenos Aires in the south—then the geographical diversity is staggering. New World slavery knew no limits; it penetrated every economic activity, every type of settlement, every setting. American slaves lived in temperate highlands as well as in tropical lowlands, on large continental plains and on small mountainous islands, on farms as well as on plantations, in cities as well as in the countryside; they worked in fields and in shops, in manual and skilled occupations, in civilian and in military life, up trees and down mines, on land and at sea.

Even when the lens zooms to a single region or city, such as Rio de Janeiro centred in South-Central Brazil, which, as noted, drew heavily on West-Central Africa for its slaves, heterogeneity still seems the most accurate description of its African residents. This may seem a ridiculous proposition, for on the face of it Rio seems the perfect place to find homogeneity. At least two-thirds of Africans living in nineteenth-century Rio traced their homelands to West-Central Africa. As Mary Karasch puts it, the "Central Africanness" of the city's slaves is fundamental to an understanding of their culture. Yet Karasch stresses Rio's "extraordinary ethnic diversity." Slaves from West-Central Africa were from three distinct sub-regions. The first, Congo North, supplied "thousands of ethnic groups" to Rio, and in certain decades—the 1830s and 1840s, in particular—the ethnic mix from Cabinda, the central port of Congo North, was especially notable. Second, although slaves from Angola came from a more restricted area than the Congos, they still comprised numerous ethnic groups and at least two major linguistic groups: the Kimbundu-speaking populations of Luanda and its hinterland; and the Lunda-Tchokwe of eastern Angola. Finally, the third important port and sub-region was Benguela in southern Angola, whence came Ovimbundu and Ngangela peoples among others. So, the West-Central origins of most Rio slaves was in fact a congeries of peoples, languages and cultures. Further, important as Central Africa was to Rio's slaves, as many as a fifth to a quarter of the city's Africans could trace their heritage to East Africa. The so-called Mocambique nation became one of the largest in the city. Finally, although West Africa was the least important source of Rio's slaves, so-called Minas and Calabars were prominent in the city. Rio, then, was truly a babel of African peoples. . . .

In another sense, however, whether a ship landed at one or two or more African ports is somewhat beside the point; rather, the real issue is the complexity of networks deep within Africa that funnelled slaves into nodal points on the coast. Joseph Miller has written a brilliant study of just such networks for West-Central Africa. As he points out, the whole region consisted of over 1,000 kilometres of coastline and a slaving hinterland that by the early nineteenth century extended 2,500 kilometres inland. Overall, slaves were drawn from locales within a region of 2.5 million square kilometres, an area larger than the United States east of the Mississippi River. In most of the central market places in the interior of West-Central Africa, traders dispatched slaves in sizeable caravans that marched at best 150 kilometres a month. As the moving frontier zone of slaving violence advanced eastwards, a complex fan of trade routes, ever more extensive and convoluted, radiated out into the interior. The sequence of multiple sales that attended transfers of slaves between their place of seizure and the coast could divert the flow in almost any direction. As slaves plodded westward, many died and others were added, so that by the time they reached the coast the caravans were indeed a motley crew. The process was, in Miller's words, an "agonizing progress toward the coast that lasted months if not years." The actual port of embarkation was therefore just one link in a highly complex chain. No other slaving hinterland was [as] large as West-Central Africa's, but then again no other coastal region supplied as many slaves to [the] New World. . . .

Most slave ships probably had a single destination, but whether most slaves were sold and remained in the vicinity of their point of disembarkation seems somewhat more problematic. The whole question of Africans' subsequent movements within the Americas is complicated. Much more is known about the first place of landing than the Africans' final destinations. Just as the African port of embarkation is easier to document than the complex chain that led from interior to coast, so it is infinitely easier to record slaves landing at an American port than it is to trace their later movements.

At certain times, a lively re-export trade in slaves unquestionably arose in various American ports. The British sometimes landed slaves in their Caribbean islands before taking them to the North American mainland. After 1763, slaves were commonly re-exported from most British islands in the eastern Caribbean. Equally well known is that Jamaica was a major re-exporter of slaves. Over the course of the eighteenth and early nineteenth century, Jamaica imported over 800,000 Africans and transshipped about 200,000. A British slave trade of sorts persisted for a quarter of a century after abolition when over 20,000 . . . slaves were shipped from the older islands to the newer colonies, especially Trinidad and Demerara. Smaller European slave-trading nations engaged in much re-exporting. Many slaves imported by the Danes were transshipped. The

Dutch were well known for landing slaves at islands like Curaçao and afterwards reshipping them to the Spanish–American mainland ports. Some slaves were transshipped from Curaçao to other Dutch colonies in the Caribbean or Guiana. War or market conditions sometimes forced a ship to alter its course and make more than one landing. With the growth of the Dutch free trade, Johannes Postma notes, the restless search for the most profitable markets often led to more than one landing. Before the direct trade to Cuba developed in the nineteenth century, Cuban and other Spanish Caribbean planters regularly purchased slaves in the well-established markets of Jamaica and Dominica. A robust inter-island and island-mainland trade existed in slaves as in much else.

But the forced migration of Africans in the Americas was not just confined to transshipment; far more consequential were the long marches on American soil, sometimes in stages, far into the interior. In many ways, then, America may be conceived as a mirror image of Africa: ports on either side of the Atlantic were funnels for large slaving hinterlands that fanned out across the land. As Miller points out, "Even the ships headed to a single Brazilian captaincy must, finally, be understood as moving through no more than an intermediate stage in a complex redistribution to further destinations." Rio received more slaves than any other New World port because it supplied Minas Gerais, was a route of access to São Paulo, and constituted a smuggling station on the way to the estuary of the Plate. . . .

Movement both within Africa and the Americas complicates not just the notion of port to port correspondences but also the conception of homogenous peoples being swept up on one side of the ocean and set down *en masse* on the other. Because many African slaves came in tortuous and convoluted ways from the interior to the coast, whatever ethnic identity they originally had was undoubtedly in flux. Furthermore, it is often impossible from a late twentieth-century vantage point to reconstruct what, if anything, that ethnic identity might have been. Miller's description of the functioning of the Angolan slave trade — "individuals being kidnapped, sold, resold, and captured again in the course of repeatedly disrupted lifetimes" — leads him to conclude that their so-called ethnic origins probably meant "very little." In addition, when Philip Curtin assembled a number of different samples of contemporaneous opinion on the ethnic distribution of the eighteenth-century Senegambian slave trade, what is most impressive is that three-quarters of the exported slaves occupy the "non-ethnic" category.

Only about 17 per cent of the slave exports from Senegambia were Wolof, 5 per cent Fulbé, and 3 per cent Sereer. Most slaves seem to have come from east of the heads of navigation—by way of Gajaaga and the Gambia—and cannot be assigned to a specific ethnic group.

Even more fundamental, how aware were people of belonging to an imputed ethnic and cultural tradition? Whether the search is for a pan-African culture, broad regional cultures—as in Thornton's tripartite division of West and Central Africa into something akin to Caesar's Gaul—or more localized ethnic cultures, the same problem inheres: are we not in danger of adopting the hermeneutics of the observer? Do we not fall into the trap of denying the social and cultural worlds created by local actors, of seeing similarities where the actors were aware only of difference? Consider, for example, the eighteenth-century use of the term Yoruba. As Robin Law has pointed out, originally the name designated only the Oyo, being the term by which the Hausa of northern Nigeria referred to the Oyo kingdom. Before the nineteenth century, he continues, "the name Yoruba was not used to designate the larger group of which the Oyo form part. . . . It must, indeed, be doubtful whether the various 'Yoruba' groups were conscious of forming, on linguistic or other grounds, any sort of unity or community." Similarly, David Northrup, writing of pre-colonial South-Eastern Nigeria, observes that "the largest unit of identity for most inhabitants does not appear to have been the primary ethnic unit such as Igbo or Ibibio, but rather the smaller dialect or cultural group." Indeed, Igbo-speakers enslaved in the early nineteenth century had apparently never heard the name Igbo in their homelands. Or consider the farmers of the central highlands of West-Central Africa, many of whom were shipped to Brazil; they became known as the Ovimbundu because they shared similar linguistic traits, but, notes Miller, "none of them in the eighteenth century would have claimed much unity." Ethnicity, in so far as it existed, was clearly very localized in precolonial Africa.

In fact, a distinct danger exists in applying terms such as ethnic group and nation indiscriminately in African and African-American studies. Thornton adopts rather uncritically early modern European usages by talking of "countries" or "nations" and even of "national loyalty," which are not just imposed taxonomies but anachronistic ones. As Karen Fog Olwig notes of Danish West Indian slaves, they "did not seem to identify strongly with nations, so when asked the name of his nation, a slave often responded 'with the name of the place where he lived in Guinea.'" Similarly, while ethnicity can be used to stand for some kind of group (*ethnos*), it is often a residual term applied when too little is known about some group to be able to label it more precisely. The ethnic lexicon of New World planters and slave traders—and they must be distinguished—is often mysterious. As David Geggus has pointed out in the Francophone context, the labels "Mine" and "Caramenty" obviously derived from the ports of Elmina and Kormantin "situated close together on the Gold Coast, but the sex ratios and morbidity levels of these two sets of slaves suggest that they were drawn from quite different, perhaps distinct" locales. Many ethnic labels were affixed inaccurately. Primarily on the basis of scattered references to large numbers of Bambara in early Louisiana, Gwendolyn Hall argues that they served as a charter group, but, as Philip Curtin had earlier noted, Bambara was a catch-all term. Some early Louisiana slaves doubtless were Bambara, an ethnic group, generally non-Muslim, who comprised the dominant people of the new kingdoms of Segu and Kaarta in the eighteenth century. But the word also meant, in Senegambian French, any slave soldier serving in Senegal, and it could be taken as a very general designation for all Malinke-speaking peoples, or even of all people from east of the Senegal and Gambia rivers. Curtin authoritatively declares that, "The 'Bambara' slaves shipped west as a result of eighteenth-century warfare or political consolidation could be dissident people who were ethnically Bambara, or they could just as well be non-Bambara victims of Bambara raiders." The term was more geographical than cultural. . . .

The foundation of Louisiana's Afro-Creole culture, Gwendolyn Hall claims, rests on the numerical predominance of Senegambia slaves imported to the colony in the early decades of the eighteenth century. Bambara she maintains, "played a preponderant role" in the formation of the colony's slave culture. They "constituted a language community," mounted rebellions, were accused of a disproportionate number of crimes, and influenced other slaves with their magical beliefs, evident in the widespread resort to *zinzin*, an amulet, or *grisgris*, a harmful charm, both Mande terms. Aside from whether Bambaras were a true ethnic group, the alleged paramount influence of Mande on Louisiana culture needs to be questioned. First, in the early 1720s, as Peter Caron has emphasized, Africans from the Bight of Benin dominated the colony's African population. The contribution of enslaved Aja peoples from the Slave Coast, Caron observes, may have been especially significant given the large numbers of children born to Africans between 1721 and 1726. Further, Caron demonstrates that most slaves from Senegambia came from the coastal areas, not the Niger bend, which is the area of Bambara and Mande influence. In addition, even by the middle of the eighteenth century most Louisiana slaves lived on units of ten or fewer Africans, which inhibited the domination of one ethnic group. For all these reasons and others, such as the much more heterogeneous and larger influx of Africans when Louisiana became a Spanish colony — it seems sensible to emphasize the pluralistic quality of Afro-Creole culture. The Congo influence in folklore and magic, the Fon role in voodoo, the Yoruba origins of shotgun houses, and the many African religious traditions (from Islam to Congo-Christianity to non-universal variants) that infused Louisiana religion must all be recognized. . . .

Overall, Africans in the Americas had to adapt to survive. They had no time for debates about cultural purity or precise roots; they had no necessary continuing commitment to the societies from which they came. They were denied much of their previous social and cultural heritages: the personnel who maintained their homeland institutions, the complex social structures of their ancestral societies, their kings and courts, their guilds and cult-groups, their markets and armies. Even what they brought they ruthlessly jettisoned because it was no longer applicable or relevant to their new situations. No wonder, as Mintz puts it, when we think of the history of African-American slaves, "we are speaking of mangled pasts." For that reason, he continues, "It is not the precise historical origins of a word, a phrase, a musical instrument or a rhythm that matters, so much as the creative genius of the users, molding older cultural substances into new and unfamiliar patterns, without regard to purity or pedigree."

Whether the focus is on African regional origins, American destinations, or New World cultural developments, the emphasis should be on heterogeneity, on fluid boundaries, on precarious and permeable zones of interaction, on hybrid societies, on mosaics of borderlands where cultures jostled and converged in combinations and permutations of dizzying complexity. A key way in which the many and disparate parts of the Atlantic world were coming together — albeit at unequal speeds — was in the creation of ever more mixed, heterogeneous cultures. The homogenizing tendency of stressing cultural unity in Africa, of emphasizing the non-random character of the slave trade, and of seeing the dominance of particular African coastal regions or ethnicities in most American settings, is a variance with the central forces shaping the early modern Atlantic world. This tendency should be resisted.

PART

 **VI** Abolition

---

VARIETY OF OPINION

Equiano would appear to have been one of the abolition lobby's most persistent and convincing speakers.

ADRIAN HASTINGS

The white men . . . say the slave trade [is] bad. . . . [Why] did they think it good before?

OSEI BONSU, KING OF ASANTE

[If I] could do without slaves—it would be better for [me]; but . . . that [is] impossible.

EYO HONESTY II, KING OF CREEK TOWN, OLD CALABAR

Any general account which attributes the rise of the antislavery movement to considerations of economic necessity is open to serious objections.

HOWARD TEMPERLEY

*The resistance of the slaves uniquivocally contributed . . . to the fact that
the slave sysem was increasingly seen in Britain to be not only morally
wrong and economically inefficient, but also politically unwise.*

MICHAEL CRATON

Adrian Hastings

Abolitionists Black
and White

The movement to end the slave trade began in Europe, not in Africa, but,
as the following piece reminds us, Africans and African Americans played
important roles in that movement. British historian Adrian Hastings explains the roles blacks played in the campaign that turned the British from
being the Atlantic's biggest slave traders to being the slave trade's biggest opponents. Prominent among them was the former captive Olaudah Equiano,
whose account of the Middle Passage appears in Part III.

On 19 March 1783 a young Christian Igbo in his late thirties called on
Granville Sharp, the anti-slavery agitator, at his London home, to bring
to his attention a report of how 130 Africans had been thrown into the
sea off a slave-ship for the sake of the insurance money. The Igbo was
Olaudah Equiano, and Sharp in consequence began another of his
campaigns to bring the perpetrators to justice. He was not successful. It
was the first recorded appearance of Equiano upon the public stage.

Captured by African traders from his home village at the age of 10
and sold to British traders, he was carried across the Atlantic, first to Barbados and then to Virginia. Here a British captain took a liking to the
boy, bought him, and took him to England, renaming him Gustavus

From Adrian Hastings, *The Church in Africa: 1450–1950*, pp. 173–175, 179–180, 182–184.
Copyright © 1994 by Adrian Hastings. Reprinted by permission of Oxford University Press.

Vassa. He received some education, sailed in many ships, and acquired a good deal of experience of both the West Indies and North America. He was baptized while still a boy in 1759 and later had an experience of conviction of salvation by faith in Christ alone while on a ship in Cadiz harbour in 1774. His pocket Bible, he could write, "was my only companion and comfort." In 1779 he had applied to the Bishop of London to be ordained and sent as a missionary to Africa, but this petition was not accepted. In the following years he emerged as a leader of London Africans, a considerable little community, and active in the struggle against slavery. It was as such that he approached Sharp in the spring of 1783.

One of Equiano's friends, Ottobah Cugoano, a Fanti with the English name of John Stuart, published in 1787 a book entitled *Thoughts and Sentiments on the Evils of Slavery*. It included the fiercest of denunciations of "abominable, mean, beastly, cruel, bloody slavery carried on by the inhuman, barbarous Europeans against the poor unfortunate Black Africans," "an injury and robbery contrary to all law, civilization, reason, justice, equity and charity." Writing in a Protestant country, the author appropriately insisted that "Protestants, as they are called, are the most barbarous slave-holders, there are none can equal the Scottish floggers and negroe-drivers, and the barbarous Dutch cruelties." This book was rapidly translated into French and appeared in Paris the following year.

Equiano and Cugoano were at once the intellectuals and the campaigners within the new African diaspora. It is true that there is some evidence that Cugoano's book may be the product in part of hands other than his own. One of them, indeed, may have been Equiano's. Two years later Equiano published a further book of his own which, while still being very much a piece of anti-slavery literature, was more naturally enthralling in being first and foremost an account of his life and adventures, including a quite lengthy description of his African childhood. There is no reason to think that Equiano did not write it. He was clearly a man of remarkable intelligence, versatility, and forcefulness, and his mastery of English is shown by letters surviving in his own hand. *The Interesting Narrative of the Life of Olaudah Equiano, or Gustavus Vassa*, as he entitled it, was indeed a very interesting book and it is not surprising that it went into eight British editions in his lifetime and ten posthumously. But Equiano's considerable contribution to the anti-slavery battle was not confined to his books and discreet interventions with Granville Sharp. He was a campaigner all over Britain, for some years, travelling almost incessantly to speak and sell his book in the principal

Crowded slave deck, 1860. From an actual photograph of the bark *Wildfire*, captured and brought into Key West, Florida. (Schomberg Center for Research in Black Culture, The New York Public Library/Art Resource, NY)

towns of the United Kingdom. Thus in 1791 he spent eight and a half months in Ireland, selling 1,900 copies of his narrative and being particularly well received in Belfast. The thought of this Igbo carrying on his campaign for the hearts and minds of the citizens of Birmingham, Manchester, and Sheffield in the late eighteenth century in favour (as he put it in a petition of 1788 addressed to the Queen) of "millions of my fellow African countrymen, who groan under the lash of tyranny" is as impressive as the book itself. Two points may especially be noted. The first is that it was not ineffective. Equiano died before Parliament declared the trade illegal in 1807 but it only did so because opinion in the country against the trade had steadily hardened, and Equiano would appear to have been one of the abolition lobby's most persistent and convincing public speakers. It is odd that his name does not appear in most accounts of the movement. The second is that Equiano represented at its most articulate a new social reality: a black, Protestant, English-speaking world which had grown up in the course of the eighteenth century on both sides of the Atlantic in the wake of the slave trade. A dozen of its leaders, "Sons of Africa," including Equiano and Cugoano, addressed a special memorial of thanks to Granville Sharp in December 1787. They had all been given, and willingly employed, European names, but it is noticeable that both Equiano and Cugoano chose to stress their African names on the title-pages of their published works, and Cugoano remarked insistently that "Christianity does not require that we should be deprived of our own personal name or the name of our ancestors." They had no problem in using both. . . .

There were at this time far more African Protestants west of the Atlantic than east of it, but it was appropriate that Equiano and Cugoano, the most vocal among them, should be based in London. London, one may well say, was not only the capital of the empire in which most of them lived (including, until the 1780s, the North American colonies), it was just at this point becoming a sort of capital of Africa itself. . . . No European state possessed more forts along the African coast; no nation carried in its ships more African slaves across the Atlantic; nowhere else in the world was there such knowledge or such concern for Africa, a concern demonstrated by the formal establishment in 1787 of the Committee for the abolition of the slave trade. It was essentially a British, and a London-centred movement. . . .

From the late 1780s Protestant Christianity would impinge upon Africa in a new and far more dynamic way. Granville Sharp, the charming, determined, but slightly eccentric protagonist of African freedom in London, was persuaded that it would be a real step forward if some of the black people in London, many of whom were penniless and in trouble, could be resettled on the coast of Africa. The "Black Poor" of London could be transformed into a flourishing, free agricultural community, an example of the way things could be without the slave trade. There was, in Sharp's vision, to be no governor. They would rule themselves according to the ancient Anglo-Saxon principles of the Frankpledge, as understood in eighteenth-century England. The government agreed to ship them out, and a first settlement was made in this "Province of

Freedom" as Sharp liked to describe it, in 1787. The settlers were, for the most part, from among the dregs of London society with seventy white prostitutes thrown in, while the problems even a very well-managed enterprise was bound to encounter were huge. Unsurprisingly, it was not a success. Some of the settlers were quickly re-enslaved; some turned slavers; many died; quarrels with the local inhabitants mounted until in December 1789 a neighbouring ruler burnt the settlement down. Reinforcements, indeed a new start and a governor, were imperative if the whole exercise was not to be dramatically counter-productive: apparent proof of the inability of freed blacks to make good. A Sierra Leone Company was established and new settlers sought. At that point Sharp seems to have received a letter from Cugoano suggesting that there were plenty of suitable blacks in Canada, formerly British servicemen, who would like to go to Sierra Leone and might even pay their way: "They are consisting of Different Macanicks such as Carpenters, Smiths, Masons and farmers, this are the people that we have immediate use for in the Province of freedom." Cugoano had been visited by Thomas Peters, a millwright, formerly a slave in North Carolina, then a sergeant in the Guides and Pioneers, now settled in Nova Scotia. Sharp met Peters, the director of the Company accepted the plan, and the Treasury agreed to cover the expenses of shipping. Thomas Clarkson, a leading abolitionist and a director of the Company, had a younger brother John, a navy lieutenant, who was willing to superintend the operation and did so very well. Fifteen ships were chartered to carry 1,100 emigrants from Halifax to Sierra Leone. In January 1792 they sailed; six weeks later they arrived in Freetown and the real history of Sierra Leone began. . . .

In 1807, however, a far more important development took place, the passing by the British Parliament of the bill for the abolition of the slave-trade, just twenty years after the Abolition Committee was first constituted in London and Cugoano's *Thoughts and Sentiments on the Evil of Slavery* had been published there. It was, despite the delay (in large part due to the counter-effect of the French Revolution and the war), an impressive achievement, going as it did against the undoubted economic interests of Britain and a powerful interested lobby of planters and merchants. It legally placed the interests of public morality above profit and market forces. It was in no way at the time a necessary achievement. It was managed by the combination of an efficient "moderate" leadership, at once religious and political, with a nation-wide public opinion produced by a great deal of campaigning. The sustained parliamentary spokesmanship of the morally impeccable Tory Wilberforce, personal friend for so many years of the Prime Minister, was invaluable, though the true architects of abolition were Granville Sharp and Thomas Clarkson, not Wilberforce. A cause which in the early 1780s still seemed eccentric was rendered respectable by the underlying support of the two greatest parliamentarians of the age—Pitt and Fox—and by its coherence with the best in contemporary thought, philosophical and religious. It would certainly not have been carried through without very powerful religious convictions at work which, starting from the Quakers, took hold of an exceptionally able group of upper-class Anglican Evangelicals, but it was by no means an inevitable consequence of the Evangelical Movement, and indeed its movers, Sharp and Clarkson, were far from typical Evangelicals. In America Evangelicalism brought no comparable conclusion. In Holland and France religion remained little affected by such concerns. Only in England did things take this course at the start of the nineteenth century, and it seems hard to deny that it was due to the persevering commitment to the abolitionist cause of a quite small group of men whose separate abilities and positions were knitted together to form a lobby of exceptional effectiveness.

Its effects upon Sierra Leone were to be momentous. The Act of Parliament sanctioned the stationing off the West African coast of ships of the Royal Navy charged with the interception of slavers. It was agreed that the cargo should be landed at Freetown, thus giving the tiny colony a new *raison d'être*. It badly needed one. The Sierra Leone Company's original aim of establishing a thriving settlement on the shores of Africa which would demonstrate by the success of legitimate commerce the economic pointlessness of the trade in slaves had wholly failed. The Company had never made any profits and its resources were exhausted. The British government had needed to subsidize it increasingly heavily just to keep Sierra Leone going at all. The unanticipated circumstances of a long war with France had destroyed any chance of realizing the original commercial aim, but there was, and long remained, only one really profitable trade on the West African coast and that was the slave trade, though a worthwhile timber trade was beginning to develop at this time. Inhabitants of Freetown, black as well as white, often abandoned the town, whose economy was negligible, to set up elsewhere along the coast as profit-making slavers.

From 1 January 1808 Sierra Leone became a Crown Colony, the authority of the Company being taken over by Parliament. It had a mere

2,000 inhabitants, the survivors and offspring of various groups of settlers brought there from Britain, Canada, or the West Indies. Reformers and parliamentarians in England had thought little about the consequences of intercepting slave ships or what to do with their liberated cargo. They will not have imagined how many they soon would be. Certainly the blockade was far from fully effective; indeed the majority of slavers—in southern waters the vast majority—evaded capture, and the total number of slaves reaching the Americas in the first half of the nineteenth century was not so much less than the total number in the second half of the eighteenth. Not until the middle of the century was the trade effectively crippled, and only in 1864 was the last load of a captured ship landed in Freetown. Nevertheless, if many still got through, many were captured, and Sierra Leone was transformed as a result. By 1814 there were 10,000 "recaptives," Liberated Africans, in the colony, more than three-fifths of the total population. With the ending of the Napoleonic War the trade increased and recaptives reaching Sierra Leone could number 3,000 a year. The original idea that they be apprenticed to existing citizens or enlisted in the army could never work with many of the people arriving, women above all, but the numbers were anyway far too great. Subsidized for years by the British government, most inevitably settled, officially or unofficially, in villages beyond the town.

Osei Bonsu and Eyo Honesty II

African Opponents of Abolition

British moves to end the slave trade were not immediately welcomed by those Africans who had profited from selling slaves. In 1820, Osei Bonsu, king of the powerful Asante empire behind the Gold Coast, expressed puzzlement to British representative Joseph Dupuis at why Britain had suddenly ceased purchasing slaves, and also justified a king's role in selling

From Joseph Dupuis, *Journal of a Residence in Asantee* (London, 1824), pp. 162–164; from Hope Masterton Waddell, *Twenty-Nine Years in the West Indies and Central Africa* (London, 1863), p. 429.

slaves. Thirty years later, King Eyo Honesty II, the most powerful man in the trading communities known to Europeans as Old Calabar, voiced similar views to a Scottish missionary. Fully aware of the horrors of the strong preying on the weak, Eyo argued that the continuation of slavery was unavoidable.

A. Views of Osei Bonsu, 1820

"Now," said the king, after a pause, "I have another palaver, and you must help me to talk it. A long time ago the great king [of England] liked plenty of trade, more than now; then many ships came, and they bought ivory, gold, and slaves; but now he will not let the ships come as before, and the people buy gold and ivory only. This is what I have in my head, so now tell me truly, like a friend, why does the king do so?" "His majesty's question," I replied, "was connected with a great palaver, which my instructions did not authorise me to discuss. I had nothing to say regarding the slave trade." "I know that too," retorted the king; "because, if my master liked that trade, you would have told me so before. I only want to hear what you think as a friend: this is not like the other palavers." I was confessedly at a loss for an argument that might pass as a satisfactory reason, and the sequel proved that my doubts were not groundless. The king did not deem it plausible, that this obnoxious traffic should have been abolished from motives of humanity alone; neither would he admit that it lessened the number either of domestic or foreign wars.

Taking up one of my observations, he remarked, "the white men who go to council with your master, and pray to the great God for him, do not understand my country, or they would not say the slave trade was bad. But if they think it bad now, why did they think it good before. Is not your law an old law, the same as the Crammo [Muslim] law? Do you not both serve the same God, only you have different fashions and customs? Crammos are strong people in fetische, and they say the law is good, because the great God made the book; so they buy slaves, and teach them good things, which they knew not before. This makes every body love the Crammos, and they go every where up and down, and the people give them food when they want it. Then these men come all the way from the great water [the river Niger], and from Manding, and Dagomba, and Killinga; they stop and trade for slaves, and then go home. If the great king would like to restore this trade, it would be good for the white men and for me too, because Ashantee is a country for war, and the people are strong; so if you talk that palaver for me properly, in the white country, if you go there, I will give you plenty of gold, and I will make you richer than all the white men."

I urged the impossibility of the king's request, promising, however, to record his sentiments faithfully. "Well then," said the king,

> you must put down in my master's book all I shall say, and then he will look to it, now he is my friend. And when he sees what is true, he will surely restore that trade. I cannot make war to catch slaves in the bush, like a thief. My ancestors never did so. But if I fight a king, and kill him when he is insolent, then certainly I must have his gold, and his slaves, and the people are mine too. Do not the white kings act like this? Because I hear the old men say, that before I conquered Fantee and killed the Braffoes and the kings, that white men came in great ships, and fought and killed many people; and then they took the gold and slaves to the white country: and sometimes they fought together. That is all the same as these black countries. The great God and the fetische made war for strong men every where, because then they can pay plenty of gold and proper sacrifice. When I fought Gaman, I did not make war for slaves, but because Dinkera (the king) sent me an arrogant message and killed my people, and refused to pay me gold as his father did. Then my fetische made me strong like my ancestors, and I killed Dinkera, and took his gold, and brought more than 20,000 slaves to Coomassy. Some of these people being bad men, I washed my stool in their blood for the fetische. But then some were good people, and these I sold or gave to my captains; many, moreover, died, because this country does not grow too much corn like Sarem, and what can I do? Unless I kill or sell them, they will grow strong and kill my people. Now you must tell my master that these slaves can work for him, and if he wants 10,000 he can have them. And if he wants fine handsome girls and women to give his captains, I can send him great numbers.

B. Views of Eyo Honesty II, 1850

The king maintained the utmost composure, paid respectful attention while we spoke, and then answered calmly in his own defence. He wished that he could do without slaves—it would be better for him; but, as the country stood, that was impossible. He did not employ men to steal slaves for him; nor would he knowingly buy those which were stolen. He bought them in the market, at market price, without being able to know how they were procured; and would let no man steal them from him. He admitted that they were obtained in various objectionable ways, and even expatiated on the subject. They came from different countries, and were sold for different reasons—some as prisoners of war, some for debt, some for breaking their country's laws, and some by great men, who hated them. The king of a town sells whom he dislikes or fears; his wives and children are sold in turn by his successor. A man inveigles his brother's children to his house, and sells them. The brother says nothing, but watches his opportunity, and sells the children of the other. He admitted that they were kidnapped also; but said that they came from different far countries, of which he knew nothing, and in which they had no other trade. Calabar people did not steal, but only bought, slaves. He concluded by saying, that he had so many, that his new people, if he did not protect them with a strong hand, would be constantly sold away again by the old ones, and reported to him as dead.

Howard Temperley

The Idea of Progress

In the excerpt from *Capitalism and Slavery* in Part V, Eric Williams argued that major economic changes lay behind Britain's sudden turning against the slave trade, although he acknowledged the importance of abolitionists, black and white. Howard Temperley assesses the merits of Williams's thesis and the opposing humanitarian explanation of British abolitionism. The University of East Anglia (U.K.) historian suggests that neither thesis—nor any blending of them—is satisfactory. Instead, he argues, British and American abolitionists gained confidence that moral progress was possible from the sustained economic growth without slavery in their countries.

From Howard Temperley, "The Ideology of Antislavery," in *The Abolition of the Atlantic Slave Trade*, ed. David Eltis and James Walvin (1981), pp. 21–30. Reprinted by permission of the University of Wisconsin Press.

The problem is easily stated: What was it, in the late eighteenth and early nineteenth centuries, that made men turn against an institution which, in one form or another, had existed since time immemorial? Why was slavery attacked *then?* Why not in the seventeenth century, or the sixteenth? Why, indeed, was it attacked at all?

Traditionally, the answers given to this question have taken two forms.

One is to describe how ideas, initially expressed by a handful of thinkers, were taken up, elaborated, added to, and ultimately incorporated into the beliefs of the population at large. This was essentially the approach of Thomas Clarkson, whose *History of Abolition* (1808) is notable both as the first attempt to provide a comprehensive account of the origins of the antislavery movement and as a model for later writers. In a foldout map which appears at the end of the introductory section of his work he shows how, beginning far back in the sixteenth century as tiny springs and rivulets, each marked with the name of some prominent thinker or statesman, the waters converge to become rivers, eventually "swelling the torrent which swept away the slave-trade." As Clarkson saw it, the victory of the abolitionists represented the triumph of right thinking over error, of the forces of light over the forces of darkness. It had been a long struggle, extending over centuries, but in the end truth had prevailed.

AM I NOT A SISTER ?

(Left) "Am I Not a Man and a Brother?" *Rhode Island Almanac, 1834.* (Right) "Am I Not a Sister?" From the cover of *The Liberty Almanac for 1851,* published by the American and Foreign Anti-Slavery Society. (Both courtesy Library Company of Philadelphia)

Until a generation ago few historians felt disposed to dissent from this view. Although less overtly Manichean in their approach, they were prepared to accept Clarkson's analysis, at least to the extent that they saw the ideas which eventually came together and energized the antislavery crusade as having originated in the distant past, in most cases with identifiable individuals or groups. Few later commentators would have chosen, as Clarkson did, to include Pope Leo X or Queen Elizabeth in their list of precursors, nor would they have cared to invoke, as Clarkson also did, the hand of Providence as a guiding force; but at bottom the processes they described were much the same. This, for example, is the approach adopted in the early chapters of Frank Klingberg's *The Anti-Slavery Movement in England* (1926), and in one form or another it informs the work of most early twentieth century writers and many later writers, a notable recent example being David Brion Davis's *The Problem of Slavery in Western Culture* (1966).

The principle [*sic*] challenge to this view has come from those historians who have seen the abolition of the slave trade and slavery as having been the result, not of moral, but of economic pressures. The classic statement of this case was Eric Williams's *Capitalism and Slavery* (1944). Williams, it is true, did not entirely discount the influence of moral teaching, to the extent that he saw the abolitionists as a "spearhead." They spoke "a language the masses could understand" and thereby "were successful in raising anti-slavery sentiments almost to the status of a religion in England." In this sense they helped the process along. But at bottom it was the forces of economic rather than moral change that mattered. It was "mercantilism" that created the slave system and "mature capitalism" that destroyed it. He states his case forcefully: "The attack falls into three phases: the attack on the slave trade, the attack on slavery, the attack on the preferential sugar duties. The slave trade was abolished in 1807, slavery in 1833, the sugar preference in 1846. These three events are inseparable."

Leaving aside for the moment the question of whether the evidence will actually support this view, we may simply note that what we have here are two fundamentally contradictory explanations as to why abolition occurred at the time it did. In the one case it is seen as the product of a long process of intellectual inquiry. The antislavery argument that was presented to Parliament and the British public in the 1780s and 1790s was not, and given its complexity could not conceivably have been, the achievement of one group or even of one generation.

Inevitably it was the work of many hands extending back over many generations. In the same way, the economic explanation is also dependent on the notion of gradual maturation which initially fostered slavery but ultimately created a conjunction of interests which destroyed it. In each case abolition is seen as the result of an extended chain of events which by the late eighteenth and early nineteenth centuries had created a situation in which the slave trade, and later slavery itself, could no longer be regarded as acceptable.

Comparing these two explanations, it may be noted that in one respect at least the economic view scores over what, for want of a better term, we may call the intellectual diffusionist account in that it is more firmly rooted in what are commonly regarded as the major developments of the period. Much of the plausibility of Williams's account, indeed, derives from the fact that Britain, the first nation to industrialize, also took the lead in the campaigns to abolish the slave trade and slavery. This is a development which the intellectual diffusionist account virtually ignores. Moreover, there is something patently unsatisfactory about any explanation of a historical event, particularly a historical event as important as the abolition of the slave trade and slavery, which is based on developments in the realm of ideas and which fails, at least in any detailed way, to relate those ideas to the actual lives of people of the period. Most ideas, as we know, have long pedigrees. Often, too, they are capable of acquiring a momentum of their own and can develop, almost regardless of changes in the material world, according to an inner logic of their own. But equally plainly ideas are shaped by circumstance, and the longer the time span the greater the likelihood of this happening. Thus in accounting for the attack on slavery we need to know not simply when ideas originated and who first formulated them, but what is was at a certain point in time that made man choose, out of all the ideas available, those particular ideas, and furthermore to act on them. To assume, as the abolitionists frequently did, that their ideas were right and that virtue requires no explanation is inadequate, since plainly not everyone agreed with them. We still need to be shown why what seemed right to the abolitionists—and, more to the point, to an increasingly large proportion of their contemporaries—had not seemed right to their predecessors.

Yet, if the intellectual diffusionist account has its pitfalls, so also does the economic explanation, the principal one being that it is exceedingly difficult to show that the overthrow of either the slave trade or slavery would actually have influenced the material interests of those who pressed for it, except, in some cases, adversely. So far as the attack on the British slave trade is concerned, as Seymour Drescher has recently argued in *Econocide: British Slavery in the Era of Abolition* (1977), the whole theory of West Indian decline upon which Williams bases his thesis is without foundation. West Indian decline was the result, rather than the cause, of abolition. Much the same may be said of the abolition of slavery itself, which further accelerated the decline process. As I attempted to show in an appendix to *British Antislavery, 1833–1870* (1972), the attack on West Indian slavery could not have been an attack on monopoly, since before 1833 a large proportion of the West Indian sugar crop was sold on the world market, which determined the price. Rather, it was the abolition of slavery, which reduced production below that necessary to supply British needs, that created a monopoly, thus driving up prices and creating a demand for an end to differential tariffs. Nor is it easy to fall back on the alternative argument, often used in such cases, and say that what mattered were not economic realities but how men perceived them, since in each instance the results that ensued were widely predicted. Plausible though it might appear at first sight, and attractive though it might remain in theory, the truth is that the economic explanation fails to take account of the fact that slavery was itself very much a capitalist institution, that in general it offered a good return on investment, that it provided a plentiful supply of cheap raw materials, and that the usual effect of emancipation was to drive up the price of the products upon which the burgeoning industries of Europe and America depended.

But if neither the economic nor the intellectual diffusionist accounts provide a satisfactory explanation, what alternatives are there? One obvious tactic, of course, is to try to link the two together. The problem here is that simple mixing does nothing to improve the quality of the initial ingredients. If both are defective, the same will inevitable be true of the final mixture. In the present instance, however, there is a special difficulty in that the two accounts are based not only on different but largely on diametrically opposing views of human nature. The intellectual diffusionists, in their explanation, place a high premium on disinterested benevolence and on the instinctive desire of those who were not themselves victims of, or indeed in any way implicated in, the practice of slaveholding to alleviate the sufferings of others. Williams, for his part, does not entirely discount this element. The abolitionists were "a brilliant band" and they, or at all events some of them, were genuine idealists. Nevertheless, their role has been "seriously misunderstood and grossly exaggerated," for what really destroyed the slave system was not altruism but greed, self-interest, and the lust for power—in other words, the same motives which had built it up in the first place. So unless we suppose, as Williams does, that there were two quite separate groups involved, it is hard to see how the two views can be reconciled. That there *were* two groups is a theoretical possibility, but this is a view which, on the basis of the available evidence, it has so far proved impossible to substantiate, and in any case it is hard to see where the profit motive lay.

One possible way of getting out of this impasse, however, is to look again at the conceptual framework which historians have used. And here we may begin by noting that there is something essentially artificial about the way in which altruism and self-interest have been juxtaposed, as if they were the only motives from which the participants acted. Williams is plainly guilty of this, but so also are the traditionalists in their emphasis on those elements of right thinking and self-dedication which led W. E. H. Lecky in his *History of European Morals* (1884) to describe the crusade against slavery as "among the three or four perfectly virtuous pages comprised in the history of nations." Large numbers of people, and certainly groups as large and variegated as those responsible for the overthrow of the slave trade and slavery, which of course included not only the abolitionists but all those who voted against these practices in Parliament and Congress, together with those who supported them in their efforts, are simply not moved, or at least not entirely moved, by abstract benevolence. Nor, for that matter, is economics, Adam Smith notwithstanding, merely the pursuit of individual self-interest. Adam Smith himself, significantly enough, disapproved of slavery for reasons which turn out on examination to have nothing to do with its immediate cost-effectiveness. Thus even in his system, and no less strikingly in those of his successors, economics in this broader sense is seen as being concerned not merely, or even primarily, with how best to pursue short-term individual gains, but with the way in which societies actually do, or in theory should, order their affairs. Viewed in this way economics and benevolence no longer appear as opposing principles. As the Victorians in particular were well aware, the two could not only be reconciled but were often mutually supportive. Thus, whether we look at economic thought or at the possible range of motives which led large numbers of individuals, the great majority of whom were not abolitionists in the narrow sense, to turn against the slave trade and slavery, we find ourselves dealing with large-scale, and in many respects overlapping, systems of belief which are far too complex to be categorized in terms of either self-interest or benevolence.

To call these systems ideologies is, perhaps, to invite misunderstanding, although it is not clear what other word will suffice. Certainly it is not intended here to postulate a rigid set of assumptions which everyone opposed to slavery shared. Perhaps the word could be used in that sense with regard to some antislavery groups which expected a strict orthodoxy of belief on the part of their members, although even then there are distinctions that would need to be recognized. But if we take ideology to mean an assortment of beliefs and values shared by the members of a society and used by them to explain and guide social action, no such rigidity need be assumed. Such an ideology would be expected to change along with the society that produced it, and whose aspirations and beliefs it reflected. Nor should we expect that it would be logically consistent. Much of the impulse for change would come, in fact, from attempts to reconcile internal contradiction. Not surprisingly, many within the society would claim that their beliefs were not simply personal, or for that matter social, but represented universal truths. But whether they did or not is a question which might appropriately be left to philosophers or theologians; for present purposes they should be regarded as social products.

So how might such a concept be used to explain the development of the antislavery movement? One way to begin is to examine the character of the two societies, Britain and the northern United States, which found themselves in the forefront of the struggle. And here we may start by noting that both had experienced remarkable rates of economic growth in the course of the eighteenth century. Probably nowhere else in the world was the relative increase in wealth and population more striking than in the thirteen colonies. This, as we all know, was one of the factors which persuaded the British government to attempt to tighten its hold on the colonists, and so helped to precipitate the break with the mother country. Yet Britain's own rate of growth during these years, although less marked in relative terms, was also impressive, whether we compare it with what had happened in previous centuries or with the experiences of her political rivals. This was, as economic historians continually remind us, a period of crucial importance for the Western world. Instead of the rhythmic expansion and contraction of populations and their products which had taken place over the previous millennium, the gains of the eighteenth century represented the departure point from which began the sustained growth that has characterized the modern world. Britain and her ex-colonies were in the forefront of this development. Materially speaking, they had reason to feel proud of their achievement.

A second characteristic that Britain and the northern states (as opposed to the South) shared was the fact that they had achieved this prosperity without direct recourse to slave labor, at least on any significant scale. To be sure, there was slavery in Britain right up to the end of the eighteenth century (the Somerset decision notwithstanding), and it lingered on in the northern states even longer. As late as 1820 there were still eighteen thousand slaves in the northeastern United States, and at the time of the first census in 1790 the figure was more than double that; but compared with the situation south of the Mason-Dixon line this represented a relatively modest stake in the institution. It must also be remembered that both Britain and the northern states had profited, and were continuing to profit on an ever-increasing scale, from the employment of slaves elsewhere. Nevertheless, the fact remains that, so far as their domestic arrangements were concerned, both were committed to an essentially free-labor system.

These points are too obvious to dwell on. Yet they are worth emphasizing if only because they help to explain why men in these two societies were so ready to accept ideas of progress, and in particular ideas of progress which linked individual freedom to material prosperity. The two, needless to say, are not necessarily connected. More often than not they have been seen as opposing principles, the assumption being that the pursuit of the one must necessarily entail the sacrifice of the other. Implicit in the whole idea of government is the belief that individual freedom must be given up to secure the benefits of an ordered society, among which must be included a measure of material satisfaction. How much freedom needs to be sacrificed is a matter of opinion, but history is not wanting in examples of societies welcoming tyrants because the alternatives of anarchy and lawlessness were regarded as even less acceptable. So the commonly expressed eighteenth century view that freedom and prosperity were not only reconcilable but mutually supportive, and that the more you had of the one the more you could expect of the other, is something that needs explaining. The explanation, I suggest, is to be found not in the ideas of the philosophers, still less in theories about the general progress of the human mind, but in the immediate lives of people of the period.

This, then, is one way of relating material and intellectual developments, and one that throws a good deal of light on the thinking of such figures as Adam Smith and the exponents of the secular antislavery argument generally. For what is striking about the secular case against slavery is the *assumption* that slavery was an economic anachronism. Smith's own attitudes are particularly revealing, because of all eighteenth century commentators he was probably the one best qualified to argue the case against it on strictly economic grounds. Yet, as already noted, the case he actually presents is not based on economics at all, at least not in any cost-accounting sense, but on the general proposition that greater freedom would lead to greater prosperity. Like other eighteenth century thinkers he expresses himself in terms of universal principles, but at bottom it is a historical argument, derived from his own beliefs about the nature of the historical process. Whatever the objective truths of Smith's arguments, the fact remains that they are very much the product of one kind of society, and indeed of one particular class within that society.

An obvious objection to this argument is that, while it may very well be true that Adam Smith rejected slavery for the reasons suggested, it is by no means clear that other people did. Very few, after all, were Smithians. The point that is being made here, however, is not that Smith was important for his teachings (although Clarkson was happy to cite him) so much as for what he reflected about the continuing processes that characterized the age in which he lived. Of course, not even Smith himself realized that the Western world was entering a new economic era. Nevertheless, it is evident that substantial increases in trade and improvements in agriculture had begun to be made long before Smith's time and so were readily observable by his contemporaries. Furthermore, if what is at issue here is the origin of the Western idea of progress, it should be borne in mind that this owed at least as much to developments in the field of knowledge as to material changes. Certainly by the end of the seventeenth century men not only knew more than their predecessors but knew that they knew more.

Yet even if we grant that these developments go some way toward explaining the secular case against slavery, it by no means follows that they motivated the early leaders of the antislavery movement, most of whom, if we may judge by the arguments they used, believed that they were acting out of religious principles. This is a tricky problem because by and large these principles stem directly from the Christian tradition. But if, instead of following the Clarkson method of attempting to trace them back to their origins, we ask simply what it was that brought them to the fore at this particular point in time, we can perhaps make a start by observing that what was fundamental to the whole attack on slavery was the belief that it was removable. Politics, we are continually reminded, is the art of the practical, but so also are ethics practical in the sense that what is irremovable may be deplorable, inconvenient, or embarrassing, but can scarcely be unethical. Ethics, in other words, implies optionality. Moralists may be more stringent in their views than politicians, but in this respect at least the underlying considerations are the same.

In a sense, of course, slavery always was removable to the extent that institutions men establish they can, given an adequate stimulus, usually get around to disestablishing. But until the eighteenth century that stimulus was generally lacking, with the result that slavery was accepted with that fatalism which men commonly reserve for aspects of nature which, whether they are to be celebrated or deplored, have to be borne. To argue against slavery was to argue against the facts of life. Before slavery could become a political issue—or even, in the proper sense, a moral issue—what needed to be shown was that the world could get along without it. And what better demonstration could there be than the development, within the heartland of Western civilization, of societies which not only did without slavery but which did very well without it, and which furthermore appeared to owe their quite remarkable dynamism to the acceptance of principles which represented the direct negation of the assumptions upon which slavery was founded.

This was not, of course, a development particularly likely to impress the inhabitants of those societies which relied directly on slave labor. They knew perfectly well how much they owed to their slaves, not only in a strictly economic sense, but for the maintenance of their whole way of life. They also knew that they were contributing in no small way to the prosperity of the free-labor societies by providing them with cheap raw materials and foodstuffs. And, by virtue of their position,

they were well placed to judge the revolutionary nature of the abolitionists' demands—what a rapid shift from slave to free labor would
mean in terms of political and social power. Often what they said in this
regard was a great deal more realistic than anything said by their opponents. Yet the fact remains that as societies they were overshadowed
by cultures whose values, deriving from a quite different set of historical
experiences, were in the process of changing in ways that made the justification of slavery, even on hardheaded economic grounds, increasingly difficult.

What I am suggesting, in other words, is that the attack on slavery
can be seen as an attempt by a dominant metropolitan ideology to impose its values on the societies of the economic periphery. And what I
am also suggesting is that this attack was the product of a widening ideological gap occasioned by the extraordinary success, not least in material terms, of those societies which practiced a free-labor system, among
which Britain and the northern United States were outstanding examples. For if we suppose that the manner in which societies gain their
existence helps to form the ideas of their members as to how people in
general should live, we must also, I think, concede that there were very
powerful reasons why men in these two societies (and one could add
France as a third) should have come to regard slavery as not only im-
moral but anachronistic.

This, of course, is a very different thing from saying that the promo-
tion of their own economic interest *required* the abolition of slavery, because in most cases it did not. Nor is it necessary to argue that relative to
the slaveholding societies the free-labor societies were becoming more
powerful, although sometimes this was so. It was much easier for Britain
to attack slavery after the departure of the American colonies. But by the
same token it became correspondingly more perilous for the Americans
themselves to do anything about it, and in the event little was done to
remove the institution until war made action possible. Thus any general
account which attributes the rise of the antislavery movement to considerations of economic necessity is open to serious objections.

Michael Craton

Slave Revolts and the End of Slavery

Well before the first successes of the abolitionists, slavery (and the slave trade) had already been abolished in the largest plantation colony of the West Indies, France's Saint Domingue (modern Haiti), by a massive slave rebellion. Profesor Michael Craton of the University of Waterloo (Canada) picks up on this point, explaining how slave revolts in British Caribbean colonies affected the pace of emancipation. His conclusion supports yet another thesis offered by Eric Williams.

I believe it to be axiomatic that all slaves wanted their freedom—that is, freedom to make a life of their own—and that all slaves resisted slavery in the ways best open to them, actually rebelling, if rarely, when they could or had to. In rebelling, they seized the weapons that were to hand and used the aid of whatever allies they could find. . . .

Between [1816] and [1834], not only did the emancipation movement come to fruition, but there was also a crescendo of slave unrest in the British West Indies, with highlights in three of the largest ever slave rebellions, in Barbados in April 1816, in Demerara in August and September 1823 and in Jamaica between December 1831 and February 1832. What this paper aims to do is to examine each of these major outbreaks, briefly describing the sequence of events, the causes alleged at the time and what I take to be the truer causes, and the outcome, both in the colonies and, even more important, in the metropole. It will try to establish the relative parts the principal actors played in the drama of British slave emancipation, which was enacted barely a year after the suppression of the Jamaican rebellion; the avowed Emancipationists, the British legislators, the West Indian planters, the missionaries and,

From *Out of Slavery: Abolition and After*, edited by Jack Hayward, 1985, pp. 110–122, 123–126. Reprinted by permission of Frank Cass Ltd.

above all, the British West Indian slaves themselves. My main purpose is to test the conclusions by Eric Williams, in 1944, that "the alternatives were clear: emancipation from above or emancipation from below," and of Richard Hart, in 1980, that British West Indian blacks were "slaves who abolished slavery."

The Barbados revolt began with trilling suddenness on Easter Sunday night, 14 April 1816, at a time when the slaves were free from work and had ample opportunities to organise under the cover of the permitted festivities. What made the outbreak all the more shocking to the planters was that there had never been an actual slave rebellion in Barbados, and not even a plot had been uncovered to ruffle their complacency for 115 years. Indeed, so convinced were the Barbadian planters of their physical and psychological control over their slaves that they were certain that a rebellion could only have been generated by outside forces, namely the English Emancipationists, and fomented by local agents other than slaves, specifically a cabal of disaffected free coloureds under the leadership of one Joseph Pitt Washington Franklin, "a person of loose morals and abandoned habits, but superior to those with whom he intimately associated."

Some 20,000 slaves were involved, from more than seventy-five estates, and within a few hours they had taken control of the whole southeastern quarter of the island. They fired the cane-trash houses as beacons and drove most of the Whites into Town, but did not commit widespread destruction or kill any of the hundreds of Whites virtually at their mercy. Having reached within sight of Bridgetown, they set up defensive positions, hoping and expecting the regime to negotiate.

They were soon disabused. Martial law was declared by the Acting Governor and the military commandant, Colonel Codd, was placed at the head of a punitive column. This consisted of regular troops, including the black First West India Regiment, and the much less disciplined and more vindictive white parochial militiamen. Codd encouraged the killing of all slaves who resisted and authorised the burning of houses and destruction of gardens, but still had to report that "Under the irritation of the Moment and exasperated at the atrocity of the Insurgents, some of the Militia of the Parishes in Insurrection were induced to use their Arms rather too indiscriminately in pursuit of the Fugitives." Whereas one white civilian and one black soldier were killed, at least fifty slaves died in the fighting and seventy more were summarily executed in the field. Another 300 were carried to Bridgetown for more leisurely trial, of whom 144 were in due course put to death and 132 deported.

Once the revolt was suppressed, the regime was at pains to exculpate itself. Whites asserted that slaves never gave bad treatment as a cause of revolt, and masters were eager to demonstrate, against their metropolitan critics, that Barbadian slaves were well fed, clothed and housed, were not cruelly punished, received good medical treatment and had opportunities to grow their own provisions and raise livestock, even to sell their surpluses. The official Assembly Report, not published until 1818, echoed the statement made by Colonel Codd as early as 25 April 1816:

> *The general opinion which has persuaded the minds of these misguided people since the proposed Introduction of the Registry Bill [is] that their Emancipation was decreed by the British Parliament. And the idea seems to have been conveyed by mischievous persons, and the indiscreet conversation of Individuals.*

However, such a spontaneous rebellion could not have occurred without widespread disaffection, organisation and leadership among the slaves themselves, and concerted, if unrealistic, aims. The [instigator] seems to have been a remarkable woman called Nanny Grigg, a literate domestic from Simmons's estate. Nanny had been telling her fellow slaves during 1815 that they were to be freed on New Year's Day. She claimed to have read this in the newspapers and said that her master and the other planters were "very uneasy" about it. Accordingly, she urged strike action, telling the other slaves "that they were all damned fools to work, for that she would not, as freedom they were sure to get." When the New Year came and went without emancipation, Nanny's advice became more militant. "About a fortnight after New-year's Day," reported another slave, "she said the negroes were to be freed on Easter-Monday, and the only way to get it was to fight for it, otherwise they would not get it; and the way they were to do, was to set fire, as that was the way they did in Saint Domingo."

Yet Nanny Grigg was no more than a firebrand. The real leaders and organisers of the slaves were tightly-knit groups, cells, of elite creole slaves led by rangers—that is, slave drivers, chosen by the Whites for apparent reliability, with much more freedom of movement than most of their fellows. Chief of all these was Bussa, the ranger of Bailey's estate, after whom the revolt has always been popularly known. What motivated Bussa and his lieutenants, it seems, was a hatred of slavery made intolerable by even worse than average conditions, coupled with a misguided sense that because the plantocracy now had enemies in England the time was opportune to rise up and dictate the terms under which the Blacks would continue to work on the sugar plantations.

What makes Bussa's revolt all the more poignant is the evidence that the rebels felt that they had the right to negotiate because they, even more than the Whites, were now true Barbadians. As Colonel Codd put it, "they maintained to me that the island belonged to them, and not to white Men." . . .

The chief miscalculations of the Barbadian rebels lay in underestimating the power of the local regime, in vainly presuming that the imperial troops would not be used against them (particularly the black West India Regiment), and in overestimating the support they might get from metropolitan liberals. In fact, even those in the metropolis who blamed the white Barbadians for bringing the rebellion on themselves by complacency and loose talk—calling slave registration but the thin end of a wedge leading to slave emancipation, and talking of imperial dictation over a Registry Act as tyranny worthy of rebellion in the style of the Americans in 1776—were horrified by the slave uprising. Not a single white person anywhere, it seems, reckoned the deaths of 264 rebel slaves as overkill.

[Abolitionist William] Wilberforce's own role was critical. Although he had supported the Corn Law in 1815 ostensibly in return for government support of the Slave Registry Bill, he was already wavering over the Bill before news of Bussa's revolt reached London at the end of May 1816. The news, though, seems to have convinced him that the Emancipationists had best "rest on their oars" for the moment. He did not oppose the address to the Prince Regent deploring the insurrection, and on 19 June made a speech so defensive and self-exculpatory that he came close to a rift with his brother-in-law, James Stephen. Clearly, Wilberforce was terrified by the thought that he might be held responsible for the Barbados slave revolt, and he may well have been influenced by none other than Monk Lewis himself, with whom he dined between Lewis's arrival in England on 5 June and his speech in the House on 19 June. Wilberforce's diary merely records that he and Lewis met "to talk over Jamaica," and discussed Lewis's plans "to secure the happiness of his slaves after his death," but it is inconceivable that

Lewis did not tell Wilberforce of the St. Elizabeth plot less than three months before, including the fact that the plotters had so memorably invoked Wilberforce's name. The idea of popular insurrection was anathema to Wilberforce, in England even more so than in the West Indies. In the period 1817–19, indeed, he spent almost as much effort in supporting the government's repressive measures at home, as he did on the West Indian cause.

Just as Bussa's revolt came in conjunction with the dissensions over the Slave Registry Bill, so the Demerara rebellion of August 1823 followed close on the heels of the next great wave of Emancipationist activity: T. F. Buxton's assumption of the leadership from the ailing William Wilberforce, the founding of the new Anti-Slavery Society in January 1823, Buxton's unsuccessful motion for gradual emancipation and Canning's canny substitution of an ameliorationist policy in May, and the Colonial Secretary, Lord Bathurst's first amelioration circular, which reached Georgetown on 7 July 1823. As happened in Barbados, the Guiana plantocracy angrily complained of imperial interference and dragged its feet over the implementation of the Bathurst circular. What further provoked the planters was that in British Guiana, unlike Barbados in 1816, nonconformist missionaries were already active and rapidly gaining converts, the most effective being the Rev. John Smith of the London Missionary Society, pastor of Bethel chapel on Le Resouvenir estate. . . .

Despite the planters' disclaimers, the Demerara slaves had even more cause to rebel than the Barbados slaves in 1816. Sugar monoculture had intensified and the slaves were worked harder and punished cruelly, callously shifted around with family ties ignored. Quamina, for example, on the day that Peggy, his wife of thirty years, lay dying, was refused leave to return to his house before sundown, when he found Peggy dead. For Christian slaves, the refusal of the planters to grant more than Sunday free from estate labour was particularly irksome, since it led to a conflict between the will to worship in chapel and the need to work provision grounds and go to market.

Christianity undoubtedly provided solace for many slaves, but less encouragement for rebellion. The missionaries, including Smith, were scrupulous in following their instructions to spurn political issues and counsel hard work and obedience. Bethel chapel was undoubtedly an important meeting place for slaves from the entire East Coast of

Demerara, but subversive discussions occurred outside rather than inside the building. Likewise, Quamina, though a revered figure, seems to have been drawn into the rebellion rather than leading it, carrying no arms and being absent from the fighting. A far more dangerous type of rebel was his son, Jack Gladstone, a backslider in chapel but an ardent and wily agitator who was later to give evidence against Parson Smith and got off with deportation to St. Lucia.

As far as the Whites were concerned, the revolt broke out with shocking suddenness on Monday 18 August. Nearly all the 30,000 slaves on the sixty estates over a thirty-mile stretch east of Georgetown were involved. Again, by a concerted policy, there was little property damage, and the Whites held captive were merely placed in the slave punishment stocks. Governor Murray, himself a planter, on the first morning confronted a party of rebels and asked them what they wanted. "Our rights," he was told. When Murray told them of the forthcoming Bathurst reforms, the rebels replied, in Murray's account, that "these things . . . were no comfort to them. God had made them of the same flesh and blood as the whites, that they were tired of being Slaves to them, that their good King had sent Orders that they should be free and they would not work any more." Murray then said that he would only negotiate once the rebels laid down their arms, at which the crowd grew ugly. Murray thereupon turned tail, galloped into Georgetown and ordered a general mobilisation.

The slaves were no match for the forces of the regime under Colonel Leahy, which, contrary to the slaves' wishful expectation, included well-drilled regulars, black and white, and Amerindians, as well as the local white militia. The only serious clash was at Bachelor's Adventure plantation, halfway down the coast, on 20 August, where 2000 slaves met with Leahy's 300 redcoats. "Some of the insurgents called out that they wanted lands and three days in the week for themselves, besides Sunday, and that they would not give up their arms till they were satisfied," wrote a militia rifleman. "They then said that they wanted their freedom," went another account, "that the King had sent it out—and that they *would* be free." Leahy did give the rebels three chances to lay down their arms, but when their leaders announced that "the negroes were determined to have nothing more or less than their freedom," and one prominent rebel waved a cutlass and dared the troops "to come on," Leahy gave the order to fire. The first volley scattered the rebels and in the ensuing orgy of hunting and shooting, particularly enjoyed by the militia, between 100 and 150 rebels were killed or wounded, at the cost of two wounded soldiers. The rest of the campaign was simply mopping up.

Besides the slaves killed in resistance, Leahy himself admitted that some sixty were shot out of hand, while an equal number were more ceremonially executed after military trials, a total of 250 slaves killed in all, compared with three Whites killed and a handful wounded. Quamina was hunted down and shot by Amerindians on 16 September, his body being hung in chains close to Bethel chapel, where it was left for months. Parson Smith was arrested and charged with complicity and incitement, tried under martial law, found guilty and condemned to death—with a recommendation for mercy—on 19 November. Suffering from galloping consumption, he died in his prison cell on 6 February 1824, a week before King George IV signed a reprieve with an order for deportation.

When the news of the Demerara revolt reached England in early October, it was a great disappointment for the Emancipationists but provided fresh ammunition for the pro-slavery lobby. Both sides were initially convinced that it was the timing of the Bathurst circular which had triggered the revolt, and even Zachary Macaulay went so far in attempting to reassure Buxton and Wilberforce as to maintain that the insurrection was "the work of Canning, Bathurst and Co. and not of your firm." Canning and the government duly reneged on their promise to impose the amelioration measures, except in Trinidad, and when Buxton opposed this in Parliament he felt himself to be "the most unpopular man in the House."

No one dared to defend in public the actions of the slaves. However, as the details of Smith's trial reached England, along with the news of the concurrent wrecking of Shrewsbury's Methodist chapel in Barbados and the Jamaican planters' over-reaction to a threatened revolt in Hanover parish, a more effective line of attack presented itself to the Emancipationists. Clearly, the West Indian Whites could be held chiefly to blame; not just for agitating the slaves by their repressions, resistance to reform and loose talk of secession, but, even more, for their lawless godlessness in attacking the Christian church and its adherents. Lord Brougham, in a four-hour attack on the colonial plantocracies on 1 June 1824, virtually, in Charles Buxton's phrase "changed the current of public opinion." John Smith, rather than any of the 250 dead rebels, was styled "the Demerara Martyr"; not just because of what was described as his Christ-like forbearance and fate, but because his teaching had actually prevented the slaves from greater excesses. In perhaps the most telling passage of his marathon speech, Brougham quoted the Rev. W. S. Austin, the Anglican rector of Georgetown who had been deported for daring to defend Smith at his trial, that "he shuddered to write that the planters were seeking the life of the man whose teaching had saved theirs." A fortnight later, in his last ever speech before Parliament, Wilberforce castigated the government for believing that such a body as the Guianese planters would ever reform itself, and helped wrest the minor concession that the Bathurst measures would be imposed on Demerara and St. Lucia as well as Trinidad.

The period between 1824 and 1832 saw a steadily widening gulf between the metropolis—Colonial Office, public and even Parliament—on the one hand, and the colonial plantocracies on the other. The Emancipationists, gaining confidence, made the crucial transition from gradualism to immediatism in May 1830, while, for their part, the colonial slaves increasingly took advantage of developing conditions. Slave unrest was wide-spread, almost endemic. Even in a non-plantation colony like the Bahamas, where the slaves were healthier, less hard worked and less supervised than elsewhere, dissatisfactions with slavery fed on rumours of imperial change. For example, the largest holding of Bahamian slaves, Lord Rolle's in Exuma Island, fearing a transfer to Trinidad and loss of their lifestyle, rose up early in 1830. A group of forty-four led by one Pompey, seized their master's boat and sailed to Nassau to lay their case before a governor, Carmichael Smyth, who enjoyed an exaggerated reputation for favouring slaves over their masters—being flogged for their rebellion but at least ensuring that they would not be moved from their island home.

Fittingly, though, it was in Jamaica—the richest and most populous plantation colony, with the harshest regime and most turbulent history of slave resistance—that the climactic and largest ever British slave revolt erupted around Christmas 1831. Jamaica was also the colony in which Christianity had most firmly taken root, a development that the planters regarded as chancy at best, highly dangerous at worst. Cautious proselytising by the established church or by the more "respectable" and regime-supporting sects—such as Moravians or Methodists—might usefully socialise the slaves. Yet the most ardent converts were the followers of "Native Baptist" preachers, who had originally come to Jamaica with the Loyalists in the 1780s, more than twenty-five years before the first white Baptist missionaries arrived in the colony. Obviously, the "brown Anabaptist priest" mentioned by Monk Lewis in 1816 was such a person. Another was Sam Sharpe, the pre-eminent leader of the 1831 rebellion, though he, like most of his kind, had more or less been subsumed into a white missionary's chapel as a deacon.

So many black deacons and their followers were to be involved in the Christmas rebellion that it was popularly known as the Baptist War — a fact that was initially a great embarrassment and only retrospectively useful to the white ministers who, like John Smith in 1823, were largely ignorant of what went on beyond their notice or understanding. From an extreme point of view, the preferred kind of "native" Christianity was quasi-millenarian, and thus politically explosive. Evidence garnered after the rebellion described "the rebel churchgoers' emphasis on membership and leadership, their fervent secret meetings, their use of dream, trance and oaths, their almost cabalistic reverence for the Holy Bible, [and] their choice of biblical texts stressing redemption, regeneration and apocalypse." Undoubtedly there was intrinsic tinder in the Native Baptist style, but a careful examination of the actions and aims of Sam Sharpe and his coterie of leaders suggests a close affinity to those of the vanguard led by Bussa in Barbados — who were, of course, not Christians — and that which included Jack Gladstone, Sandy and Telemachus in Demerara. The slaves' more or less authorised Sunday activities and the chapels provided cover for oganisation and planning, chapel services contributed to rebel rhetoric and contact with missionaries even provided a sense that the slaves were linked with sympathetic allies overseas. But Christianity was not essential to the slaves' resistance.

Consider the best evidence of Sam Sharpe's activities in the latter part of 1831. Though he was a slave and based in Montego Bay, Sharpe was practically free to roam far inland on the pretext of preaching. A favourite meeting place was the home of a senior slave called Johnson (later to die at the head of an armed body of slaves some have called the Black Regiment), on Retrieve estate, a dozen miles up the Great River valley. One condemned rebel called Hylton later described how the charismatic Sharpe

> *referred to the manifold evils and injustices of slavery: asserted the natural equality of man with regard to freedom . . . that because the King had made them free, or resolved upon it, the whites . . . were holding secret*

*meetings with the doors shut close . . . and had determined . . . to kill all
the black men, and save all the women and children and keep them in
slavery; and if the black men did not stand up for themselves, and take
their freedom, the whites would put them at the muzzles of their guns and
shoot them like pigeons.*

The slaves, said Sharpe, should be ready to fight, but merely
threaten force while engaging in strike action, binding "themselves by
oath not to work after Christmas as slaves, but to assert their claim to
freedom, and to be faithful to each other." A rebel slave called Rose
testified that Sharpe asked him to take the oath. "I said Yes. The oath
was if we should agree to sit down & I said Yes & so did every body in
the house say Yes. Must not trouble anybody or raise any rebellion." Another rebel called Barrett testified that, "Sharpe said that we must sit
down. We are free. Must not work again unless we got half pay. He took
a Bible out of his pocket. Made me swear that I would not work again
until we got half pay."

The Whites had some premonition of the drift of events as early as
15 December but largely ignored the signs, so that the uprising that
began with the refusal of thousands of slaves to go back to work after the
Christmas holiday ended on Tuesday 27 December, and the firing of
Kensington estate high above Montego Bay that night, was a stunning
shock. Almost immediately, the revolt spread over an area of 750 square
miles centred on the Great River valley, involving more than 200 estates
and perhaps 60,000 salves. The Whites, including a militia regiment defeated at a skirmish at Montpelier on 29 December, were driven into
the coastal towns, and the rebels controlled the western interior of the
island for nearly three weeks. Their hopes of bringing the regime to
terms, with the imperial government as mediator and the imperial
troops standing aside, turned out (as in 1816 and 1823) to be a cruel
delusion. The Governor, Lord Belmore, promptly declared martial law,
the military commander, General Sir Willoughby Cotton, acted with
ruthless efficiency, while the white militia exacted savage retribution for
their earlier setback.

This time, however, the regime's response was undoubtedly overkill.
Though the planters later claimed damages of over a million pounds (including the valuation of the slaves and the crops they had lost), no one
computed the damage to the slaves whose huts and provision grounds
were burned. Some 200 slaves were killed in the fighting (for less than

a dozen killed by them), while no less than 340 were executed, including more than a hundred after civil trials once martial law was lifted on 5 February 1832. Beyond this, the local Whites, largely under the aegis of an Anglican organisation called the Colonial Church Union, carried out a veritable pogrom against the nonconformist missionaries and their congregations, burning down virtually every chapel in Western Jamaica. Sam Sharpe himself was one of the last to die, being hanged in Montego Bay on 23 May 1832; his last statement being, in the words of an admiring Methodist missionary, "I would rather die on yonder gallows than live in slavery."

Had Sam Sharpe known what had already happened in England, and what was about to happen, he might have died happier. When the first news of the Jamaican rebellion reached England in mid-February, it found the country in the throes of the complex political ferment that accompanied the reform of Parliament itself. . . .

. . . [T]he very day after Sam Sharpe's execution in distant Jamaica, [T. F.] Buxton made his crucial speech in the Commons pressing for the appointment of a select committee, not just a committee of inquiry like that of the Lords, but one that would "consider and report upon the Measures which it may be expedient to adopt for the purpose of effecting the Extinction of Slavery throughout the British Dominions, at the earliest period compatible with the safety of all Classes in the Colonies." Buxton's motion was defeated, by 136 to 90, but a committee was appointed, although with a mandate far short of discussing the means of emancipation. And the evidence that the committee heard over the next six months, in conjunction with the rising wave of anti-slavery agitation throughout the country, made it inevitable that the Whig government would be bound to pass an Emancipation Act within eighteen months. Key actors in this phase were the refugee missionaries, especially William Knibb (who, on hearing as his ship came up the Channel that the Reform Bill had passed, is alleged to have said, "Thank God! Now I will have slavery down!"); though another important witness was the same Rev. W. S. Austin who had been deported from Demerara eight years before.

Even the English public, it seems, was far more easily stirred up by the evidence of the persecution of white missionaries than by the slaughter of slave rebels—and in this sense the missionaries, as in 1823, stole the martyrs' crown. But the missionaries would not have had a case to make without the actions of the slaves, whether the rebels were their parishioners or not. As far as Parliament was concerned, however, neither slaughtered slaves nor missionaries tarred and feathered were as effective as the general threat posed to the imperial economy—to the empire itself—by the virtual civil war between the slaves and their masters. The question for Parliament was essentially a political one; it was a matter of morality only in the sense that, in a liberal world, empire can only be maintained if its morality is justified. What Buxton was able to show in his great speech of 24 May, was that the actions of the slaves and the planters' counter attack showed up both slavery's immorality and its political impracticality. "Was it certain," asked Buxton,

> *that the colonies would remain to the country if we were resolved to retain slavery? . . . How was the government prepared to act, in case of a general insurrection of the negroes? . . . a war against people struggling for their rights would be the falsest position in which it was possible for England to be placed. And did the noble Lords think that the people* out of doors *would be content to see their resources exhausted for the purpose of resisting the inalienable rights of mankind?*

In perhaps his most brilliant and telling passage, Buxton then quoted Thomas Jefferson, a statesman by then universally respected but one of the most tortured of slavery's defenders. "A [slave] revolution is among possible events; the Almighty has no attributes which would side with us in [such a] struggle."

In sum, then, slave resistance and emancipationism were clearly intertwined in British slavery's final phase. News of slave resistance was disseminated more quickly, more widely and more thoroughly than ever before, while more and more slaves heard, if not always accurately, about Emancipationist activity in Britain. Moreover, slave resistance rose to a climax, in Jamaica, at the very point that the process was set in motion which led to the passing of the Emancipation Act on 31 July 1833. It remains to be decided, though, to what degree slave resistance and emancipationism, respectively, actually caused or speeded each other.

At the most obvious level, the Emancipation Act of 1833 was simply the political culmination of a widespread movement or campaign in the metropole. In conjunction with the general movement towards liberal reform, the small nucleus of convinced Emancipationists were able to carry the country towards a conviction that colonial slavery must be abolished. Through the interweaving of events—some of them, such as the victory of the Whigs and the passage of the Great Reform Bill, almost fortuitous—this popular conviction became translated into legislative fiat. This interpretation naturally plays down—if not actually denies—the effect of the actions of the slaves themselves in swaying first the British populace and then a sufficient majority in Parliament.

In an immediate sense, all the slave protests were certainly failures, and the slave rebellions of 1816 and 1823 actually set back the Emancipationist cause. Yet the slave resistance, not only rising to a crescendo but increasingly well publicised, gradually drove home the realisation both of the falsity of the assertion that the slaves were contented and of the plantocracy's claim to enjoy effective control. More than this, the increasingly paranoid behaviour of the colonial Whites both outraged and dismayed all levels of metropolitan opinion. . . .

At least some of the slave leaders . . . saw the political problems in its full dimensions. To achieve the aim of freedom, they realised, the slaves needed not only solidarity among themselves, but the strengthening of links with metropolitan allies against their immediate oppressors. Christianity was, at the least, a universalising medium, with the white missionaries as messengers and mediators; mediators not so much with God, or even that other Big Massa, the English king, but with the larger congregation of fellow Christians among the British populace. And, in the event, what was most impressive of all to this larger constituency (though the proslavery forces did their utmost to mask it) was that the rebel slaves, though resolute in their aims, were initially more pacific in their means than the plantocratic regimes which they confronted, only resorting to force . . . when met by actual force.

Thus, the resistance of the slaves unequivocally contributed—if not only in direct and obvious ways—to the fact that the slave system was increasingly seen in Britain to be not only morally wrong and economically inefficient, but also politically unwise. So, in assessing the contribution of the slaves themselves to the achievement of emancipation in 1833, one can conclude that while Richard Hart's 1980 claim that British West Indian blacks were "slaves who abolished slavery" is rather overstated, the earlier contention of Eric Williams that "the alternatives were clear: emancipation from above or emancipation from below" is much more than simply plausible.

Suggestions for Further Reading

For a comprehensive bibliography of the slave trade and slavery, see Joseph C. Miller, *Slavery and Slaving in World History: A Bibliography, 1900–1991* (1993), and the updates he publishes annually in the journal *Slavery and Abolition*.

General surveys of the Atlantic slave trade include Herbert S. Klein, *The Atlantic Slave Trade* (1999); Hugh Thomas, *The Slave Trade: The Story of the Atlantic Slave Trade, 1440–1870* (1997); Philip D. Curtin, *The Rise and Fall of the Plantation Complex: Essays in Atlantic History* (1990); Edward Reynolds, *Stand the Storm: A History of the Atlantic Slave Trade* (1985); James A. Rawley, *The Transatlantic Slave Trade* (1981); and Basil Davidson, *The African Slave Trade* (rev. ed., 1980). The early Atlantic slave trade is examined by David Eltis, *The Rise of African Slavery in the Americas* (2000), and John Thornton, *Africa and Africans in the Making of the Atlantic World, 1400–1800* (1998).

Collections of primary sources include Elizabeth Donnan, ed., *Documents Illustrative of the History of the Slave Trade to America,* 4 vols. (1930–1935), especially the first two volumes, which are not confined to the United States. Michael Craton, James Walvin, and David Wright, eds., *Slavery, Abolition and Emancipation: Black Slaves and the British Empire* (1976), has a strong focus on the Caribbean. On the African side, see Philip D. Curtin, ed., *Africa Remembered: Narratives by West Africans from the Era of the Slave Trade* (1967). Vincent Carretta has edited and annotated Olaudah Equiano, *The Interesting Narrative and Other Writings* (1995).

General collections of studies include the January 2001 issue of the *William and Mary Quarterly,* devoted to "New Perspectives on the Transatlantic Slave Trade," edited by David Eltis and Philip Morgan; David Eltis and David Richardson, eds., *Routes to Slavery: Direction, Ethnicity and Morality in the Transatlantic Slave Trade* (1997); Patrick Manning, ed., *Slave Trades, 1500–1800: Globalization of Forced Labour* (1996); Joseph E. Inikori and Stanley L. Engerman, eds., *The Atlantic Slave Trade: Effects on Economies, Societies, and Peoples in Africa, the Americas, and Europe* (1992); Barbara L. Solow, ed., *Slavery and the Rise of the Atlantic System* (1991); Barbara Solow and Stanley L. Engerman, eds., *British Capitalism and Caribbean Slavery: The Legacy of Eric Williams* (1987); and Paul E. Lovejoy, ed., *Africans in Bondage: Studies in Slavery and the Slave Trade* (1986).

Some national histories of the slave trade and its abolition are Johannes M. Postma, *The Dutch in the Atlantic Slave Trade 1600–1815* (1990); Jay Coughtry, *The Notorious Triangle: Rhode Island and the African Slave Trade, 1700–1807* (1981); Colin A. Palmer, *The British Slave Trade to Spanish America, 1700–1739* (1981); David R. Murray, *Odious Commerce: Britain, Spain and the Abolition of the Cuban Slave Trade* (1980); Robert Louis Stein, *The French Slave Trade in the Eighteenth Century: An Old Regime Business* (1979); and Leslie Bethell, *The Abolition of the Brazilian Slave Trade: Britain, Brazil and the Slave Trade Question, 1807–1869* (1970).

Overviews of the slave trade in Africa are presented by Patrick Manning, *Slavery and African Life: Occidental, Oriental, and African Slave Trades* (1990), and Paul E. Lovejoy, *Transformation in Slavery: A History of Slavery in Africa* (1983).

Studies of different parts of Africa during the era of the slave trade include Robin C. C. Law, *The Slave Coast of West Africa 1550–1750: The impact of the Atlantic Slave Trade on an African Society* (1991); Joseph C. Miller, *Way of Death: Merchant Capitalism and the Angolan Slave Trade, 1730–1830* (1988); Richard L. Roberts, *Warriors, Merchants, and Slaves: The State and the Economy in the Middle Niger Valley, 1700–1914* (1987); Patrick Manning, *Slavery, Colonialism and Economic Growth in Dahomey, 1640–1960* (1982); Robert W. Harms, *River of Wealth, River of Sorrow: The Central Zaire Basin in the Era of the Slave and Ivory Trade, 1500–1891* (1981); David Northrup, *Trade Without Rulers: Pre-Colonial Economic Development in South-Eastern Nigeria* (1978); Ivor Wilks, *Asante in the Nineteenth Century* (1976); Edward A. Alpers, *Ivory and Slaves in East Central Africa: Changing Patterns of International Trade to the Later 19th Century* (1975); Philip D. Curtin, *Economic Change in Precolonial Africa: Senegambia in the Era of the Slave Trade* (1975); A. J. H. Latham, *Old Calabar, 1600–1891: The Impact of the International Economy upon a Traditional Society* (1973); Phyllis M. Martin, *The External Trade of the Loango Coast* (1972); Kwame Daaku, *Trade and Politics on the Gold Coast, 1600–1720* (1970); Walter Rodney, *A History of the Upper Guinea Coast, 1545–1800* (1970); and I. A. Akinjogbin, *Dahomey and Its Neighbours, 1708–1818* (1967).

Important studies of African cultural survival and change in the Americas are Jane Landers, *Black Society in Spanish Florida* (1999);

Philip D. Morgan, *Slave Counterpoint: Black Culture in the Eighteenth-Century Chesapeake and Lowcountry* (1998); Ira Berlin, *Many Thousands Gone: The First Two Centuries of Slavery in North America* (1988); Michael A. Gomez, *Exchanging Our Country Marks: The Transformation of African Identities in the Colonial and Antebellum South* (1998); Michael Mullin, *Africa in America: Slave Acculturation and Resistance in the American South and the British Caribbean, 1736–1831* (1994); and Sidney W. Mintz and Richard Price, *The Birth of African Culture: An Anthropological Perspective* (1992).

The end of the slave trade is discussed in Seymour Drescher, *From Slavery to Freedom: Comparative Studies in the Rise and Fall of Atlantic Slavery* (1999); Thomas Bender, ed., *The Antislavery Debate: Capitalism and Abolitionism as a Problem in Historical Interpretation* (1992); Seymour Drescher, *Capitalism and Antislavery: British Mobilization in Comparative Perspective* (1987); David Eltis, *Economic Growth and the Ending of the Transatlantic Slave Trade* (1987); David Eltis and James Walvin, eds., *The Abolition of the Atlantic Slave Trade: Origins and Effects in Europe, Africa, and the Americas* (1981); Seymour Drescher, *Econocide: British Slavery in the Era of Abolition* (1977); and Roger Anstey, *The Atlantic Slave Trade and British Abolition, 1760–1810* (1975).

For the role of slave revolts in ending slavery, see Michael Craton, *Testing the Chains: Resistance to Slavery in the British West Indies* (1982), and C. L. R. James, *Black Jacobins: Toussaint L'Ouverture and the San Domingo Revolution* (2d ed., 1963).